MW01014457

Higher Education for Women
in Postwar America, 1945–1965

Higher Education for Women in Postwar America, 1945–1965

LINDA EISENMANN

The Johns Hopkins University Press
Baltimore

Johns Hopkins Paperback edition, 2007
2 4 6 8 9 7 5 3 1

The Johns Hopkins University Press
2715 North Charles Street
Baltimore, Maryland 21218-4363
www.press.jhu.edu

The Library of Congress has catalogued the hardcover edition of
this book as follows:
Eisenmann, Linda, 1952–
Higher education for women in postwar America, 1945–1965 /
Linda Eisenmann.
p.   cm.
Includes bibliographical references and index.
ISBN 0-8018-8261-3 (hardcover : alk. paper)
1. Women—Education (Higher)—United States—History—
20th century. I. Title.
LC1756.E57 2006
378.1′9822′097309045—dc22
2005009017

ISBN 13: 978-0-8018-8745-1
ISBN 10: 0-8018-8745-3

A catalog record for this book is available from the British Library.

Contents

Acknowledgments

This book began as a smaller effort to understand the context for the thirty-fifth anniversary of the Bunting Institute, predecessor of the Radcliffe Institute. In the 1990s, as assistant director of this research center for women scholars and artists, I wondered how a program started in 1960 had managed to remain salient across periods of enormous change. What had made Radcliffe's president Mary Bunting so prescient about how to foster women's careers?

As I investigated postwar academe, I discovered other programs started in 1960 that continued to serve women over time. The history of these efforts and their founders and clientele revealed the narrow expectations that post–World War II educators had for women's use of higher education. What fostered such constricted visions for women? Was it the impact of the 1950s "feminine mystique," so clearly described by Betty Friedan? Had the arrival on campuses of thousands of male World War II veterans prompted women to abandon higher education? Examining the literature on postwar higher education provided little information about women; although they appeared in large numbers, women seemed incidental to the main educational concerns. The literature on postwar women was growing but gave little specific attention to education. Thus, my initial effort to understand collegiate programs for women became a deeper examination of postwar ideology as well as the era's unique advocacy for women's concerns.

In the course of my investigation, I accrued many debts. For initial support, I thank Florence Ladd, former director of the Bunting Institute, as well as the Institute fellows and staff who offered helpful critiques. Through the Radcliffe College intern program, Sarah Burley and Amelia Kaplan offered able and creative research assistance. At the University of Minnesota, historian Donald Opitz generously shared his work on the development of the Women's Center and his ideas about the postwar era. At Sarah Lawrence College, director Alice Olson and archivist Patricia Owen graciously offered time, material, and access. The

University of Michigan Center for the Education of Women provided an invaluable residential fellowship that allowed access to original materials as well as an audience of supportive scholars. Michigan director Carol Hollenshead, librarian Jeanne Miller, and center founder Jean Campbell were immeasurably helpful.

All such projects owe debts to the librarians and archivists who, besides locating materials, offer ideas that enhance a scholar's work. I thank Cecelia Wisdom of the National Association of University Women, Lois Hendrickson at the University of Minnesota, Nancy MacKechnie at Vassar College, and Jane Knowles at Radcliffe College's Schlesinger Library. Sarah Hutcheon of the Schlesinger Library offered extraordinary interest and support.

I thank the University of Massachusetts Boston for sabbatical and travel support as well as a faculty research grant, and the Harvard Graduate School of Education for a visiting fellowship. John Collins of Harvard's Monroe Gutman Library provided ongoing research support and office space at a crucial point in the project. Likewise, Tom Eisenmann, Jill Greenthal, Michael Stella, and Allen Jarasitis found space when quiet working spots were needed. Carole Roberts and Fran Dittrich of John Carroll University supplied able clerical support. Daniel Ostrach provided superb editorial assistance.

Many colleagues have helped improve my writing and thinking. I extend appreciation for careful critiques by Patricia Albjerg Graham, Ronald Butchart, Nancy Diamond, Sevan Terzian, David Tyack, Andrea Walton, and especially Bruce Leslie, who read the entire manuscript twice. Colleagues in Harvard's longstanding Study Group on the History of Education provided a constructive audience. Johns Hopkins University Press editor Jacqueline Wehmueller and the Press's anonymous reviewer improved the book through careful attention. Philo Hutcheson, Jana Nidiffer, and most especially John Thelin and Barbara Beatty contributed enormously to my conceptualization of the project. Special thanks go to Patricia Graham, who provided my foundation in the history of education, and to Bernard Harleston, trusted colleague and mentor. Thanks to Dan and Matthew for cheerful help and boundless encouragement. Finally, both this project and my life are strengthened by the unwavering support of Steve Ostrach.

Higher Education for Women
in Postwar America, 1945–1965

Introduction

Writing from retirement in 1979, Esther Raushenbush, past president of Sarah Lawrence College and founder of a premier early 1960s program for helping older women return to college, reflected on women's higher education in the early years after World War II: "There was an explosion of interest, attention, and research about women in the 1950s—their role in society, their education, their personal dissatisfactions resulting from the difficulty in fitting new needs which education had created into old social patterns. The research of those years was directed toward helping women make adjustments; little concern was ever expressed about the responsibility of society to change those social patterns."[1]

Raushenbush's comments illustrate two important points about the history of women in the early postwar years. First, it seems surprising that a period often considered nonprogressive for women did, in fact, "explode" with research on their needs. Second is her acknowledgment that women were encouraged to adjust themselves to arrangements already in place rather than to question or change the social structure. Raushenbush's concern that postwar women's advocates rarely pushed for social change reveals the effect on her, as well as on many observers, of a post-1965 feminist perspective. Having become accustomed to the activism and demands that the women's liberation movement instigated later, in the 1960s and 1970s, commentators viewed the approaches and advocacy of an earlier generation as oddly quiet and even acquiescent.

Yet the work of women's advocates between 1945 and 1965, following women's energetic responses to World War II and preceding their later feminism, should be understood from the perspective of that era. The turn to social analysis and collective action that marked the post-1960s feminist movement and colored later views of female activism was largely absent in the thinking of early postwar women. In their minds, feminism was an identification to be avoided. Three decades removed from the suffrage movement, the term *feminism* connoted the unseemly activities of a previous suffragist generation; in a postwar milieu focused on women's domesticity, such activism was distasteful. In addition, many prominent women, including educators, had succeeded by following mainstream expectations, and they were disinclined to advise younger colleagues to do otherwise. Moreover, by the 1950s feminism was often linked to communism in the same way that homosexuality and civil rights activism had been tainted. Collegiate administrators, particularly, would wish to avoid such associations.

Activism was by no means absent in the postwar period. Rather, advocacy on behalf of women appeared as a series of individualized recommendations, attuned to each woman's personal calculus as she balanced difficult decisions about education, family, and career. Less reliant on social analyses and collective answers, advocates sought to adapt themselves and their recommendations to extant expectations. In Raushenbush's words, they tried to adjust themselves rather than to change society. This book explores the adaptive activism of postwar advocates for women, particularly regarding higher education, examining the nature of advocacy and its relationship to the expectations of the postwar era.

Yet as the discussion reveals, the story speaks primarily to white middle- and upper-class women who could pursue higher education and make choices about balancing their lives. The majority of African American women were still restricted in employment opportunities and less able to afford college than white women. Even those who chose higher education did so with stronger vocational goals than their white counterparts. Thus, white educational reformers seldom included African American women in their thinking; only later in the 1960s did the idea of individual choice extend widely to black women.

THE CONTOURS OF WOMEN'S POSTWAR LIVES

Postwar life presented vast uncertainties, and neither educators, policymakers, nor ordinary women agreed about the best approaches to making complicated decisions. American women received a variety of messages about their roles in postwar society, many revolving around families and communities as means to reestablish normalcy after the disruptions of war.

Militarily, politically, economically, technologically, and culturally, the United States was changing at a rapid pace. The nation found new, and less secure, relationships to old allies. As the Korean War developed, and other global areas became insecure, military issues gained a fresh immediacy. A new fear of communism, both at home and abroad, challenged liberalism. In 1952, the nation turned to a former military leader to guide it through peacetime change. The country faced the absorption of millions of returning veterans without a clear understanding of how their needs would affect the job market. To ensure economic stability, women who had held industrial and other jobs during wartime were often asked to step aside to ease men's labor force reentry. Scientific advances changed life at an exponential pace. Americans relocated from farms to cities to suburbs, envisioning suburban security as a new ideal. Both the civil rights movement and a sensitivity to globalism built slow support as means of redressing racial and economic inequities.

Because the war had brought so much uncertainty to American life, restabilizing the domestic front became a priority. Encouraging women to recommit themselves to home and family, easing women out of a labor force that needed space for men, and providing women with a new patriotic focus as domestic defenders of national security allowed Americans to feel safe in their homes. Thus, a domestic ideology combining women's patriotic duties with economic benefits and cultural preferences asserted itself in the postwar years.

Although women were encouraged to embrace domesticity, they remained in the workforce and pursued higher education in growing numbers. Contrary to assumptions about a drop in women's labor market participation after the war, adult women filled the workforce in increasing numbers with each decade. Many of these workers were older women no longer occupied with raising families. Economist Claudia Goldin suggests that the substitution of married women for single female workers at a steady increase of about 10 percent per decade represents the biggest shift in the recent American labor market since 1900.[2] Some of these changes were compounded by economic need; poorer women without the luxury to choose between domestic and economic expectations continued to work out of necessity.

Women's movement into higher education demonstrates a similar long-term upward trend. Throughout the twentieth century women increasingly turned to higher education as career preparation or to expand their choices. By 1920 they constituted 47 percent of all college students, the percentage dropping to 40 in 1940. During the war, women students and faculty often sustained institutions that suffered dramatic drops in male populations; in 1944, women constituted half of the college population. Women's contributions to campus life during a time of depleted human resources matched the effort they made to the wartime labor force. Yet the postwar influx of G.I. Bill veterans, combined with the power of the domestic ideology, caused the proportions of women in college and graduate school to decline to barely one-third. Even so, although the *proportion* of women students decreased with the influx of men, the actual *numbers* of women collegians grew steadily, with the single exceptions of 1950 and 1951.[3] Exploring these shifts in college populations and their effects on women students and faculty helps illuminate the era's advocacy for women.

HISTORICAL INTERPRETATIONS OF THE POSTWAR PERIOD

Until recently, military and political analyses dominated interpretations of the early postwar period. Women's roles received considerably less attention, perhaps influenced by popular images like the "Father Knows Best" television family with its sedate, white, middle-class, suburban household, where an at-home mother dutifully managed home and family, in full support of her husband's preeminent economic role.[4] But as scholars have gained distance on the early postwar era, they have reexamined women's history after the war in a larger context. William Chafe and Eugenia Kaledin have analyzed women's efforts in the arts, the labor force, and politics.[5] Others have emphasized the significance of domestic expectations that women could restabilize the nation by defending the home front.[6] As interpretations have developed beyond the stereotypes of Eisenhower-era indifference, historians have identified places where women's activism bridged earlier and subsequent generations. Postwar activism, operating within particular ideological expectations for women's patriotic and domestic contributions, often looked different from either earlier or later efforts.

Recognizing such differences, scholars are finding threads of advocacy for women in movements for labor unionism, civil rights, peace, feminism, and gay rights.[7] Dorothy Sue Cobble, Nancy Gabin, and Susan Hartmann have demonstrated that women's postwar labor activism shifted from the large, male-dominated unions to the "pink-collar" fields where women predominated. There they advocated for family-friendly policies and equal pay.[8] The peace movement gave women another outlet for activism as Harriet Alonso, Susan Dion, and Amy Swerdlow have shown.[9] The Women's International League for Peace and Freedom, for instance, continued an earlier tradition of maternalist politics even during the McCarthy era. The feminist movement, although neither popular nor prominent in the early postwar years, stayed alive through the efforts of the National Women's Party.[10] A nascent gay and lesbian movement suggested changes in women's behavior, as Allen Berube, John D'Emilio, and Donna Penn have explored.[11] The civil rights movement created a complicated relationship between black women and feminism;[12] it also trained white women for activism.[13]

Scholars have begun to explore the meaning of women's labor market activity after the war, observing racial, class, and marital differences.[14] In such studies, many researchers note the increase of female collegiate participation throughout the postwar period. However, although most acknowledge its apparent importance, few scholars have yet examined either the contours of women's higher education after the war or its relationship to labor force activity and domestic expectations.[15] This book attempts to connect women's experience in higher education to the larger societal expectations that influenced their postwar behavior.

GOALS OF THE BOOK

In examining women's postwar higher education, this book undertakes two interpretive challenges and one revisionist task. The first interpretive question asks why, with their numbers on campus increasing, women were nevertheless viewed as "incidental students" by postwar educational planners and policymakers. Although they constituted approximately one-third of college students throughout the period, campus policies, practices, and prominence increasingly developed without consideration of women's needs.[16] The second interpretive task is to understand the nature of postwar advocacy for women. Operating within a set of societal expectations and with a strong reluctance to identify as feminists, women's advocates relied on the notion of individual choice rather than on collective action to guide both their own activities and their recommendations for college students. Viewing the complicated set of decisions facing postwar females, leaders valued personal choice and individualized decision making over structural or cultural analysis that might have suggested discrimination and might have required politicized collective approaches.

The book's revisionist task is to identify those efforts on behalf of women as activism particular to the postwar era. Quieter, less demanding, and more accommodating than women's advocates before 1920 and after 1965, postwar activists nonetheless supported research on women, focused attention on their issues and needs, disseminated findings about new scholarship and good practice, and supported networks of like-minded advocates. At the same time, they faced internal charges of racism and external challenges to their professional advancement, each producing a particular activist response.

This book uses an institutional lens to examine women's participation in higher education. Although individual women appear as actors and activists, the institutional perspective allows a longer-term, more synthetic, and comparative view of collegiate developments. The institutional approach allows the tracing of threads across women's postwar activities, including short-lived educational commissions and projects that provide benchmarks for thinking about women's issues; professional associations that produced research, generated advocacy, and sustained challenges over time; and educational movements that rose in response to particular situations, sometimes fading as those issues changed.

The two chapters of Part One explore the first interpretive issue, showing how societal expectations for women affected their use of higher education. Chapter 1 sets the widest context, looking at four "ideologies" that influenced American women's postwar choices. It argues that four sets of expectations—patriotic, economic, cultural, and psychological—developed around postwar women's conduct. Each of these addressed a particular concern that had grown in American life but simultaneously concealed within it ways in which women were already challenging those norms. Chapter 2 examines women's use of higher education, exploring how the ideologies confounded students' approach to their schooling and educators' plans for their curricula. In suggesting that women became increasingly incidental on campuses while their numbers actually grew, the chapter explores three explanations: first, women lost out in the aftermath of the G.I. Bill; second, they remained ancillary in the fast-growing research universities, even as that sector established its preeminence; and third, problematic curriculum design emphasized preparation for domesticity as the best collegiate plan for women, regardless of their actual futures.

Parts Two and Three also use institutions to address the second interpretive challenge: understanding the nature of postwar activism for women. Part Two examines advocacy across organizations dedicated to research, practice, and policy on behalf of women. Its first chapter examines research efforts by the Commission on the Education of Women supported by the American Council on Education from 1953 to 1962. Throughout a difficult ten-year existence— continually marked by a battle to secure funding—the commission was one of only a few groups fostering research on women's education. The research base built by the commission emphasized women's individualized responses to their decisions about educational and domestic opportunities.

Chapter 4 examines higher education practice in two organizations with similar goals but different scope: the large-scale American Association of University Women (AAUW), open to a wide range of college graduates, and the smaller National Association of Deans of Women (NADW), a professional organization for collegiate administrators. Although AAUW had more money, members, and lobbying power than NADW, both groups disseminated information about women's education, fostered professional opportunities, and sustained networks of education professionals. The organizations also faced two challenges that complicated their approach to activism: internal charges of racial discrimination, which resulted in a federal lawsuit against AAUW; and an external professional challenge, as women deans found themselves demoted and diminished in postwar collegiate reorganizations.

Chapter 5 treats issues of policy in John F. Kennedy's President's Commission on the Status of Women, established in 1961. More short-lived than the ACE Commission or the two professional associations, the President's Commission (1961–63) explored women's lives and offered recommendations for enhancing their wider contributions to postwar society. This commission, with its broad agenda, had the greatest opportunity to influence advocacy and activism for women; however, confounded by issues of race and class, the commission, in its public report, backed away from the group's initial inclination to see education as a lever for wider social change.

Part Three focuses the lens more narrowly, examining the growth of women's continuing education programs in the early 1960s as an example of postwar advocacy. Designed specifically for women, these programs built on earlier adult education efforts but with a deeper awareness that women resuming collegiate training after long breaks brought unusual needs to campuses generally uninterested in their return. Continuing education exemplified the individualized focus of women's postwar advocacy. These programs, developed across the country, declined to set expectations for either women's completion of degrees or their movement into the job market. Their concentration on women's personal fulfillment symbolized a powerful preference for individual decision making. At the same time, activist efforts by these continuing education pioneers to address women's issues and assert their place in higher education created a base for the late 1960s feminist movement.

By concentrating on higher education commissions, associations, and campus-based programs, this study highlights the work of scholars, educational practitioners, and reformers rather than individual students. However, the institutional focus also spotlights the value of the networking that occurred as advocates worked across organizations on behalf of women. In an era that treated women's educational concerns so incidentally, opportunities for professionals to work together constituted a significant base for advocacy.

This work accentuates the middle-class, and even upper-middle-class, aspects

of postwar educational advocacy for women. Although higher education expanded its reach after the 1940s, collegiate clientele remained generally middle-class
throughout the postwar period. Community colleges, which in a later era served
more women, working-class, and minority students, were only beginning to gain
prominence.[17] Furthermore, the educational advocates of the period under consideration here prospered within the existing contours of higher education; thus,
their interests tended toward the types of institutions and students they knew
best. The continuing education movement, in particular, targeted white, married,
suburban mothers. Only over time did its advocates recognize the limited focus
of their efforts, acknowledging wider needs in the 1960s and 1970s.[18]

The interplay of ideology, advocacy, and activism unites this exploration of wom-
en's postwar collegiate education. Contradictory patriotic, economic, cultural,
and psychological ideologies for women's behavior affected their choices of curriculum, career, and family. Educational leaders proved similarly confounded by
the variety of postwar choices, disagreeing widely over the best sort of curriculum
to prepare women for their futures. The confluence of the ideologies also affected
how leaders approached advocacy. With so many choices and contradictory expectations about women, educators felt that only the individual woman could make
a calculus for planning her future. Such thinking influenced postwar activism
as well. Having succeeded in a milieu that valued adjustment more than radical
change, many female educators and professionals worked for what Raushenbush
called "respectful" reform.[19] Although their approach seemed tame compared to
the louder, more insistent demands appearing on campuses barely a decade later,
these early advocates believed they had used the best and potentially the most
effective approach to change.

By revising our definition of activism and acknowledging women's efforts
within the postwar context, this book reinterprets an era often denigrated for its
lack of attention to women. The educational commissions, professional organizations, and continuing education programs of the early postwar era differed from
later, more radical efforts, but nonetheless they created a base for the innovative
women's research institutes, women's studies programs, and women's resource
centers that transformed collegiate campuses only a decade or so later. The work
of advocates who paved the way for these developments merits examination on
its own terms. Doing so is a primary goal of this book.

PART ONE

Ideologies

CHAPTER ONE

Postwar Gender Expectations
and Realities

In 1964 Kathryn Greeley had three children (ages 7, 9, and 10), a physician-husband teaching pharmacology at a southern university, a master's degree in social work, and a résumé that included a few years' work with the YWCA, a half-year in France as a social worker, and a host of volunteer positions with local community and interracial groups. She described herself as feeling "safe at home with family and community work, [and] the right husband and a home and children that I really enjoy." She noted how her life resembled that of her parents: she was a professor's wife with a steady family income and a pleasant lifestyle. Her friends repeatedly reminded her how lucky she was.[1]

Although Greeley felt satisfied at home, she acknowledged that this might change as her children grew older. She suspected she might eventually join the many women who "get restless after their children go off to school and seem to need something to fill their lives," further noting that "jobs make me feel alive and important." Greeley explained that the best plan was the one she suggested to her own daughters: "If possible, don't meet the right man to marry until you have packed in plenty of school, and travel, and men, and jobs, and living." She recommended finding "some interesting career," observing that nursing and teaching offered real advantages for married women because they could work part-time as circumstances dictated. And science was the best choice of all because "there will be so many men in that field." For Greeley, the key to a woman's happiness was meeting the right man at the right time because it provided the ultimate flexibility for a modern female life.[2]

Kathryn Greeley was one of 311 female graduates from advanced studies at

Columbia University who, in 1966, answered a questionnaire about how their lives had progressed in the fifteen years following graduate study. Although better-educated than many of their contemporaries, Greeley and others in this study had shifted away from careers in favor of home responsibilities. While recognizing the appeal of the labor force, the women generally felt content concentrating on family and community.

Greeley and women like her became pivotal to rebalancing American life after the war's disruptions of the economy, international affairs, and family relations. Women—who had responded so patriotically during the war—became key to postwar readjustment. They could ease the economic strain of returning veterans by giving up jobs they had held during the war. They could affirm the American way of life against a communist threat by supporting their local communities. And they could reassert normal domestic relations by starting families, building homes, and enjoying a prosperous life.[3] In short, women were important players on the Cold War scene.

However, enormous changes had occurred during the war in the economy, in education, and in gender relationships, provoking a dissonance between cultural norms for women and their behavior at home and in the workplace. Images from the late 1940s and 1950s lauded a white, middle-class, suburban ideal, where an at-home mother like Kathryn Greeley managed home and family in full support of her husband's preeminent economic role.[4] But such images rarely reflected reality in an increasingly urbanized and industrialized nation, where people's awareness of racial and class diversity had sharpened during the war and women's ability to stay home with children was often possible only for the upper-middle class.

From the national need to reestablish familiar domestic and economic relations, a set of four ideologies emerged, shaping expectations for women's behavior in terms of *patriotic* duty, *economic* participation, *cultural* role, and *psychological* needs. Each of these ideologies addressed a particular concern in American life while also revealing ways in which postwar women were challenging or ignoring those norms, sometimes by choice, and often by necessity.

The ideologies cast a particularly strong influence on middle-class women, leaving them with difficult decisions about how to spend their time, energy, and work force involvement. For women of lesser means—including many women of color—there was less choice about whether to work or stay home. Only those with middle-class incomes and opportunities could approach the choices freely.

The predominance of home-oriented ideals disguised the fact that women increasingly worked and attended school throughout the postwar era.[5] Both numbers and percentages represented consistent upward trends from the beginning of the twentieth century, as women's work moved from the home to the paid labor force, and as more women chose to attend college. However, different women faced different opportunities. For socioeconomically disadvantaged women with little education, working outside the home was a necessity; yet even these women felt the pull of domestic ideals. Middle-class women found greater opportunities to attend college and use their education in a wider set of career choices. But at the same time, they faced decisions about balancing education, career, and home life.

THE PATRIOTIC IDEOLOGY

In September 1951, as the United States faced war in Korea, the American Council on Education (ACE) sponsored a conference on "Women in the Defense Decade."[6] Attended by more than 900 educators, government officials, and community representatives, the conference directed attention to women's most important role in the early postwar era: patriotic citizenship. The conferees' discussions revealed the uncertainty surrounding women's civic role: Should they remain at home, supporting America by defending its hearths, or should women respond to growing manpower concerns by undertaking training and employment in underserved areas? Both solutions were framed in a patriotic rhetoric that encouraged individuals to make personal decisions based on the country's needs.

Fresh from the demands of World War II, Americans were comfortable asking citizens to shift their interests to meet national needs. During the war, women had filled manufacturing, educational, clerical, and other roles left vacant by departing soldiers. With war's end, many women left their positions, some by choice and others by coercion. Just a decade earlier, a comparable challenge had been put to American women in the Great Depression. A good citizen, especially in a reserve labor pool, responded to national concerns.

The Korean conflict refocused questions about women's role in the labor force and the home. After World War II America seemed to have stepped back from the edge of chaos, but without a full sense of security. Atomic weapons had brought sustained fear into Americans' lives, reinforced by the growing Cold War. Relations with the Soviet Union had shifted from an uncomfortable alliance to confrontation by the late-1940s. The world's geopolitical future looked uncertain, with changes in China, Cuba, India, and, increasingly, in Africa raising the stakes for America's military and diplomatic efforts. The economy too posed concerns, although eventually inflation was tamed and a postwar depression avoided.[7] Women's part in this postwar world generally focused on their domestic contributions, despite their recent participation in the wartime workforce.[8]

Many have asked why the 1950s produced such a sharp turn toward the domestic ideal for women.[9] Perhaps a call for domesticity "naturally" results from the disruptions of war and depression. However, the specific and deep uncertainties raised by the Cold War prompted Americans to envision home and family as a haven from a world at risk. Economically, the nation worried about absorbing returning veterans, as well as about sustaining a level of productivity to meet domestic demands. Militarily, America faced immediate concerns in Korea and longer-term worries in other unstable areas of the world. Technologically, life was changing at an exponential pace. Politically, liberalism was challenged by a new fear of communism, both abroad and at home. Culturally, Americans were moving more, relocating geographically from farms to cities to suburbs. With so much uncertainty, the family provided a "psychological fortress."[10] Tranquility and control not possible on a larger scale could be achieved privately, household by household. In fact, civilian defense planners referred to women as "deterrence soldiers" in the domestic Cold War, highlighting the individual household as the center of defense efforts that spread concentrically to city, state, and nation.[11]

Conferees at "Women in the Defense Decade" revealed how lessons from women's wartime involvement translated into preparations for the coming decade: "The primary effort of women in a defense period, after supplying from their numbers the ones needed in the armed services, should be directed toward protection of the human relations in the home," noting that "the primary hope for security lies in the safeguarding of childhood."[12] Prominent guests clarified women's defense-related roles. Congresswoman Frances Bolton of Ohio called homemakers the first line of defense against economic inflation. Oliver C. Carmichael, president of the Carnegie Foundation for the Advancement of Teaching, emphasized how, whether at home or work, women have always "put the house in order, rearranged the furniture, and restored equilibrium when men have left affairs in disarray and confusion." Althea Hottel, dean of women at the University of Pennsylvania (and later, chair of ACE's Commission on the Education of Women), asked American women to pursue a crusade against communism by educating their children about the superiority of American life.[13]

Comparisons of American and Soviet lifestyles appeared frequently in contemporary Cold War analyses. The most prominent case, where women's domestic gains became an actual measure of economic and political success, occurred in the so-called "kitchen debate" between Vice President Richard Nixon and Soviet Premier Nikita Khrushchev at the 1959 American National Exhibition in Moscow. Beginning with comparisons of arms and armaments, Nixon and Khrushchev shifted to arguing over which nation had superior and widely available consumer goods. Nixon maintained that the ready availability of the products displayed in the exhibition's model home proved the superiority of a capitalist system. He argued that the home's labor-saving features allowed American women to avoid drudgery and sustain an affluent, attractive family life. Khrushchev countered that such an easy life prevented American women from matching the economic contribution of Soviet mothers, ridiculing the American goal of supporting full-time housewives.[14] But Nixon measured women's patriotic contribution in terms of their consumerism. Given the prominence of middle-class ideals, American women demonstrated success *because* they could afford to be home.

Nixon's argument emphasized women's patriotism through the domestic sphere, but others encouraged patriotism outside the home. American women had developed a long tradition of using traditionally feminine roles to support public causes and influence public life. In the early 1900s, for instance, women tackled social reform under the guise of "municipal housekeeping."[15] The 1950s reflected this approach, as women affected the larger environment through contributions to domestically oriented issues.

Two ways in which women exercised such influence were voting and local volunteerism. Showcasing American women's political involvement became a particularly common way to deprecate Soviet life. American magazines stressed the difference between Soviet women, valued for their labor, and American women, practicing political decision making. Senator Margaret Chase Smith wrote that American women could reverse a "socialist, dictatorial trend" through strengthening their political commitments. Margaret Hickey, past president of the National Federation of Business and Professional Women's Clubs, urged women to "make politics your business. Voting, office holding, raising your voice for new and better laws are just as important to your home and your family as the evening meal or spring housecleaning."[16]

Others pushed women toward activism, while still supporting their domestic role. Journalist Dorothy Thompson called for mothers to band together around disarmament. The Women's International League for Peace and Freedom (WILPF), extant since World War I, created radio ads appealing specifically to women as defenders of their families, noting that "a bomb doesn't care in the least whether you are wearing a soldier's uniform or a housewife's apron." WILPF also pushed women to recognize their strengths as a voting bloc, noting that "if women were to use their influence unitedly on any issue—and especially on the issues of Peace and Freedom—they could change the direction of their own nations' policies and the world's thinking."[17]

But even as women's patriotism was encouraged as defense of the home, they received a second, not entirely consistent message: they were needed to relieve manpower shortages, especially in scientific and technical areas. The Korean War highlighted American concerns over technological manpower, prompting calls to consider women as scientific workers. In 1950 and 1951, brief public discussion occurred over including women in the military draft. Although ultimately exempted, women were increasingly catalogued as potential sources of "womanpower."

Analysts popularized the potential of women's technological contributions. In the April 1951 *Bulletin of Atomic Scientists*, Eugene Rabinowitch editorialized about "scientific womanpower," calling for renewed training efforts.[18] Likewise, Arthur Flemming, of the presidential Office of Defense Mobilization, called for training and employing women as scientists and engineers. Flemming rejected the preparation of women only as engineering aides or science teachers, insisting on their value as fully employed scientists. He reminded his readers that "all references to scientists and engineers make no distinction between the sexes or between racial groups, it being understood that equality of opportunity to make maximum effective use of intellect and ability is a basic concept of democracy."[19]

An important Rockefeller Foundation–funded report, *America's Resources of Specialized Talent*, also stressed women's potential as scientists and highly trained experts.[20] Dael Wolfle began this study during the Korean War but published it in 1954, after the immediate crisis had passed. However, after more than a decade of war such analyses were quite useful for clarifying national manpower needs. Wolfle's report went beyond merely analyzing the availability of highly trained specialists. Like Flemming, he pushed for including both women and minority students in training programs. And unlike many who blamed women for not entering science, Wolfle acknowledged that both women and minority students faced discrimination in collegiate and graduate training, financial aid, and professional opportunities. Although he stopped short of demanding federal action to remedy this situation, Wolfle supported the growing notion of women as a solution to manpower needs.

The profession of nursing exemplifies a specialized field where the call for "womanpower" was particularly acute and was articulated around the idea of women's patriotism. Early in the twentieth century nursing was oversupplied, leaving nurses underemployed during the Depression. However, World War II made huge demands on the nursing workforce in both military and civilian settings. Changes in health care, in nurse-patient ratios, and in expectations of where nurses could practice contributed to the demand for trained professionals. The onset of the Korean War exacerbated the need for experienced nurses.

In 1956, the field experienced a shortage of 70,000 nurses; in 1958, 11 percent of full-time nursing positions in hospitals went unfilled.[21]

In response, the American Nurses Association (ANA) created a Committee on Nursing Resources to Meet Civil and Military Nursing Needs, encouraging nurses to see themselves as civilian contributors to defense needs. Professional associations as well as government and the healthcare industry increased calls for married nurses to re-enter the profession. Employers added part-time jobs and flexible schedules, as they had during World War II. Maternity leave benefits, child-care provisions, and flexible refresher training were offered as enticements for skilled nurses to return to the workforce. According to ANA studies, wages (never very high in this feminized field) rose throughout the decade. In the five years between 1954 and 1959, staff nurses' salaries increased 24.5 percent, and head nurses experienced an 18.5 percent salary gain.[22]

Yet even with this public call for their "womanpower," nurses—many from the upper-middle class—felt the countervailing pressure of domestic expectations. The *American Journal of Nursing* and *Nursing Outlook* carried letters from nurses defending their decisions to work and asserting that their own families had not been harmed by their workforce reentry. One returnee, writing in 1952, explained her decision in womanpower terms: "I think it is the feeling we all have about our work, once we have been in active nursing—the idea of service to others—that draws us back into it."[23] Thus, even though married women were responding to patriotic needs, they found themselves caught between domestic expectations and economic opportunity.

One group was especially effective in advancing the womanpower notion. Throughout the 1950s, the Ford Foundation operated the National Manpower Council (NMC), a Columbia University study group on economic issues convening university presidents, heads of labor unions, and corporate executives, including a few women like Margaret Hickey of the Business and Professional Women's Clubs. Although not originally focused on women's issues, the NMC added them to its agenda when it recognized that "women constitute not only an essential but also a distinctive part of our manpower resources."[24]

A 1957 NMC report, *Womanpower*, surveyed the landscape for American women workers, concentrating on three issues: the *development* of womanpower (in schools, colleges, and private sector training programs); its effective *utilization* (in hiring, promotion, and working practices); and the enhancement of *knowledge* about women workers (through increased research). The book was notable in seriously considering women's workforce participation, outlining the characteristics of female employment, and acknowledging that women often faced discrimination when combining home and work roles. However, like Wolfle, *Womanpower* stopped short of recommending major changes, focusing on explicating the situation rather than on advocating new policies.

Shortly after *Womanpower* appeared, the October 1957 Soviet launch of Sputnik generated new evidence of America's manpower decline. As various reports had suggested, Americans already believed they lagged behind the Russians in technical fields; Americans, including women, were unfavorably compared to Soviet scientists, engineers, and physicians. The NMC assessment revealed that "about twice as many new engineers are currently being graduated in Russia as in the United States. . . . There are annually some 13,000 women graduating as engineers in the Soviet Union, compared to well under 100 in the United States.[25]

The Soviet audacity in launching Sputnik seemed a devastating demonstration of America's second-place status. However, many U.S. scientists were not, in fact, surprised by the Soviet achievement. They had anticipated the launch and were already preparing America's Vanguard rocket to carry a smaller, more sophisticated satellite. But the American public and some political leaders did not respond so sanguinely. Sputnik was frequently referred to as "the Pearl Harbor of the Cold War," suggesting a similar sense of surprise, vulnerability, and immobilizing worry.[26]

Sputnik greatly increased Americans' sense of crisis. First, more than a satellite, Sputnik represented the Soviets' possession of more sophisticated weaponry and the knowledge to employ it. Second, Sputnik highlighted an apparent deficit between American and Soviet scientific and engineering strengths. Third, such manpower shortages argued for an increased supply. Thus, education—both on the elementary and the higher levels—became a tool for solving America's technological crisis.[27]

Even before Sputnik, a focus on national security had encouraged increased federal support for university research. However, the Soviet launch provided a more direct impetus for addressing longstanding concerns over direct federal funding for education. Both the Eisenhower White House and Congress had previously pushed temporary and emergency measures to handle national security concerns about manpower, but a long-term role for federal funding defied consensus. Post-Sputnik, an accord finally developed between Democratic congressional leaders and the White House team, led by Assistant Secretary of Education Elliot Richardson. The result was the monumental National Defense Education Act (NDEA) of 1958, which broke the stalemate over federal aid to education.[28] NDEA's significant higher education provisions created undergraduate and graduate loan and fellowship programs to increase scientific and engineering training across a range of fields. NDEA's language was openly defense-oriented: "The present emergency demands that additional and more adequate educational op-portunities be made available."[29] NDEA explicitly encouraged young Americans to fulfill their patriotic duty by developing their scientific skills; women were included as equal sources of scientific expertise.

Over time, NDEA became a less science-specific program, but in the immedi-ate post-Sputnik context, it provided new sources of financial support for men and women seeking advanced scientific and foreign language training. Ten years after its passage, the act had supported 1.5 million undergraduates and fifteen thousand graduate fellows at a cost of more than $3 billion.[30] In the later years of the program, women received about one-fifth of the graduate fellowships.[31]

Ultimately, patriotic ideology sent mixed signals to postwar women who had options as trained professionals. While most women were being encouraged to defend America through supporting their families, calls for the workforce "womanpower" of highly trained females conflicted with these demands. Individual women had to choose between being successful domestic consum-ers in Richard Nixon's model middle-class home or becoming highly trained scientific specialists advancing the defense needs of their country. Studies like *Womanpower* understood this inherent conflict, and this partly explains its lack of strong recommendations. To argue against discrimination and for increased training for women would undercut the image of their primary role as wives and mothers. Such dual expectations for women also appeared around their overall economic contribution.

THE ECONOMIC IDEOLOGY

Married nurses returning to the workforce offer a good example of women caught in the disjunctions of postwar expectations. Their own comments about their choices reveal a mix of motives. Many nurses acknowledged the patriotic impetus in their return to the workforce; however, they also admitted that work-ing provided personal fulfillment and gratification by using their specialized skills and allowing them to support their families.

Nurses' responses mirrored the choices and the unreconciled expectations facing many postwar women. Even while women—particularly married, white, middle-class women—were lauded as guardians of the home, the actual par-ticipation of females in the job force grew at about 10 percent a year, continu-ing an upward trend observable since the beginning of the twentieth century.[32] The tensions resulting from differences between society's expectations and the reality of women workers confounded employers, policymakers, social observers, and even women themselves, with the result that women who did work were often treated as less-than-committed employees whose contributions were likely to be short-term, nonprofessional, and intermittent. The result was a lack of workforce advancement for women. Professional women were frustrated in both status and opportunities, while blue- and pink-collar women found their earning power limited.

The steady climb in women's labor force participation throughout the twentieth century challenges popular understanding of both World War II and the early postwar period. Even as Americans came to appreciate "Rosie the Riveter," they assumed that, at war's end, women either left the workforce voluntarily to start new families or were forced out in favor of returning veterans. In either case, the prevailing assumption has been that women's labor force participation dipped precipitously during the 1950s as the "feminine mystique" took hold, and that only the late 1960s women's movement rejuvenated women's workforce return. In this scenario, women's World War II work life was a lost opportunity on which women were unable to build.

However, the actual workforce story, including the ultimate impact of World War II, is more difficult to assess. On one hand, the surge of 6 million women into the wartime labor force suggests a new societal appreciation of them as effective and valuable workers. Certainly, contemporary analyses indicated this effect. *Womanpower*, for example, claimed that World War II produced a "revolution" in women's work, noting that the war "helped to alter the traditional approach of women, particularly married women, toward paid employment."[33] In this view, women's success confirmed their self-image as competent and adaptable, and showed employers they were reliable and efficient. However, later analysts have been more skeptical about the war's effects, noting that women's labor force behavior had already been changing, and resisting attribution of so much change to one event.[34]

How do we interpret the facts that women's actual behavior demonstrated increasing workforce commitment, but that women nonetheless were judged as less-serious, peripatetic workers? What explains the disjunction between behavior and reaction? Answering these questions requires a discussion of women's overall labor market behavior, including class differences as well as employers' reactions to female workers.

In terms of numbers of women employed, adult female labor market participation has increased with each decade since the early nineteenth century. The 1950s are no exception: the raw numbers of working women increased from 13 million in 1940 to 16.5 million in 1950 (Table 1.1). These numbers, however,

TABLE I.I
The Female Labor Force, 1890–1950

Year	Number of Women (in thousands)
	Workers aged 10 and over
1890	4,006
1900	5,319
1910	7,445
1920	8,637
1930	10,752
	Workers aged 14 and over
1930	10,396
1940	13,015
1950	16,552

Source: National Manpower Council (1957). *Womanpower.* New York: Columbia University Press. Table 9, p. III. Data is summarized from the U.S. Bureau of the Census, Decennial Census Reports. After 1930 the census shifted its definition of "gainful workers" and changed the age it measured.

conceal interesting facts. Economist Claudia Goldin, who has examined female labor force participation since the nineteenth century, concludes that the biggest transformation has been the long-term workforce substitution of older married women for younger single females.[35] Until about the time of World War I, most women workers were younger single females and new entrants into paid labor. From about 1920 to the 1940s, even during the Depression, married women's rate of employment grew, albeit somewhat slowly. Since World War II, however, the participation of married women has grown rapidly, with about a 10 percent increase per decade. Moreover, the increase has been greatest among married women over the age of 35.[36]

Table 1.2 breaks down the proportion of working women by marital status and racial background. Clearly, the overall percentage of women workers increased, from about one-fifth of adult women at the turn of the twentieth century to more than one-third by 1960. And while single women's proportions in the workforce shifted up and down over the decades, married women's participation grew steadily, jumping from 13.8 percent of the group in 1940, to 21.6 percent in 1950, and 30.6 percent in 1960. In other words, even during a supposed "feminine mystique" era, nearly one-third of married women worked. Given that nearly 90 percent of American women marry at some point in their lives—a figure remaining steady over many decades—this growth in married women working is significant, suggesting economic decisions made by women and families. Of course, the number includes women who worked by choice as well as those who worked by necessity.

TABLE I.2
Female Labor Force Participation Rates by Marital Status and Race

	1890	1900*	1920	1930	1940	1950	1960
Total	18.9	20.6	23.7	24.8	25.8	29.5	35.1
Married	4.6	5.6	9.0	11.7	13.8	21.6	30.6
Single	40.5	43.5	46.4	50.5	45.5	50.6	47.5
White	16.3	17.9	21.6	23.7	24.5	28.5	34.2
Married	2.5	3.2	6.5	9.8	12.5	20.7	29.8
Single	38.4	41.5	45.0	48.7	45.9	51.8	48.5
Nonwhite	39.7	43.2	43.1	43.3	37.6	37.8	42.7
Married	22.5	26.0	32.5	33.2	27.3	31.8	40.5
Single	59.5	60.5	58.8	52.1	41.9	40.0	39.7

*1910 labor force figures are omitted in original; see Chapter 2.

Source: Claudia Goldin, (1990). *Understanding the Gender Gap: An Economic History of American Women,* New York: Oxford University Press. Excerpted from Table 2.1, p. 17. Original sources are U.S. Bureau of the Census.

Table 1.2 also demonstrates differences by race. A much higher proportion of nonwhite than white women have always worked. The comparison between married women workers is especially pronounced. For example, in 1950 almost 21 percent of married white women were employed, while 32 percent of nonwhite women worked. Workforce participation by married women of color has been considerably and consistently higher since the turn of the century, doubtless reflecting the more limited incomes of both African American and recent immigrant families. For example, fully 40 percent of employed black women worked as domestics in 1950.[37]

Dividing working women by age, noticeable cohort effects appear, some of which are particularly interesting for the 1950s. Immediately after the war, women entering the workforce in the greatest numbers were older than 25. As Table 1.3 shows, young women left the labor force (presumably to start families), whereas older women increased their participation significantly. Mature women—those whose families were already grown—demonstrate the largest increase in labor force participation, from 19.7 percent in 1940 to nearly 30 percent of the age group in 1950.[38]

The data inform our understanding of the impact of World War II as well as societal encouragement for wives and mothers to stay home. Age differences among wage-earning women help explain why married women's labor force participation increased even while many responded to the draw of home responsibilities. Many women remaining or returning to work after the war were mothers

TABLE I.3
The Female Labor Force and World War II

Year	Age				
	14–19	20–24	25–44	45–64	Over 65
Number of women in the labor force (in thousands)					
1940	1,377	2,659	6,026	2,511	271
1940*	1,460	2,820	6,527	2,719	299
1942	2,370	2,900	7,020	3,420	400
1943	2,930	3,120	8,190	3,970	490
1944	2,900	3,230	8,220	4,320	500
1945	2,720	3,180	8,230	4,410	490
1946	2,160	2,780	7,370	4,020	450
1950	1,440	2,536	7,658	4,410	507
Labor force participation rate (%)					
1940	18.8	45.1	30.2	19.7	5.9
1950	22.6	43.2	33.3	28.8	7.8

*Goldin has adjusted the 1940 figures upwards by 7.7% for consistency with the Current Population Report figures for March of that year. See p. 153.

Source: Claudia Goldin, (1990). *Understanding the Gender Gap: An Economic History of American Women*, New York: Oxford University Press. Excerpted from Table 5.5, p. 153. Original sources are U.S. Bureau of the Census.

with grown children and with more lifetime work experience than their younger colleagues who had contributed labor primarily for the wartime emergency.

Clearly, women who joined the workforce during the war represented different ages, family circumstances, social class backgrounds, and prior work experience; and not all intended to remain working long-term. One analysis suggests that about three-quarters of these women had previously been in the labor force, and perhaps 1.5 million more would have entered "in the normal course of events."[39] Given the long-term trend of increased female labor market participation, and the natural maturation of the cohort, the increases of women working during the war were more predictable than is often assumed.

Another implication of this cohort analysis is that, contrary to the contemporary assumption that women moved in and out of employment frequently, they tended to remain working. In other words, the presumed intermittency of employment often used to challenge postwar women's commitment as workers was not nearly as strong as rhetoric suggested.[40]

Although Goldin's more recent analyses have clarified this view of the female labor market, postwar observers possessed neither the same perspective nor the advantage of hindsight, and they made strong assumptions about women as workers. The NMC's *Womanpower* report demonstrates how contemporary analysts viewed women's labor market behavior and its ultimate implications. Always overriding the analyses in *Womanpower* was the importance of women's role as wives and mothers; their labor market participation as well as employers' reactions could only be understood with this primary fact in mind. The following assumption was repeated frequently throughout the report:

> Women constitute not only an essential but also a distinctive part of our manpower resources. They are essential because without their presence in the labor force we could neither produce and distribute the goods nor provide the educational, health, and other social services which characterize American society. They constitute a distinctive manpower resource because the structure and the substance of the lives of most women are fundamentally determined by their functions as wives, mothers, and homemakers. (3)

Womanpower recognized that age, marital status, education, economic position, race, and residence all affected a woman's likelihood of wage-earning as well as influencing the job she would hold. In other words, "women" were hardly a monolithic labor market resource with equal needs and characteristics, as their sketches of working women demonstrate:

> The fifteen-year-old girl who takes a part-time job while in high school in order to earn additional spending money; the twenty-year-old wife who is willing to help her husband complete college by holding a secretarial job, but who looks forward to being a full-time housewife and becoming a mother; the woman of forty-five who took a job in an airplane factory during the war, and has since remained in the labor force; the mother who returns to the teaching profession when her children are of school age; the grandmother in her late fifties who has been practicing medicine throughout her adult life; the sixty-year-old woman who, having just lost her husband, takes a job as a housekeeper. (19–20)

Each example emphasizes women's balancing of workforce participation with family needs, leading to the conclusion that "the labor force behavior of women is characterized by discontinuity in work and by part-time work" (26). In such an analysis, labor market segmentation was a descriptive fact resulting from women's needs rather than a problem to be solved. For example, *Womanpower* showed that in 1950 nearly 30 percent of all women worked in clerical jobs and another 17 percent in semiskilled manufacturing. Only 8 percent of working women held professional posts as teachers or nurses (12). The authors offered little comment on the fact that such jobs were the least lucrative, although they did note the heavy concentration of black and Puerto Rican women in "undesirable jobs" (78–79). Rather than emphasizing women's poor earning and promotion opportunities, however, *Womanpower* pointed out the comfortable fit between women workers and female-oriented jobs involving care of the sick and the young or tending to food and clothing.

Generally, *Womanpower* reported rather than problematized labor market data. In fact, the report was criticized for its fact-based approach, leading to a second NMC volume in 1958. *Work in the Lives of Married Women* attempted a deeper explication of women's workforce concerns, particularly through the efforts of Eli Ginzberg, NMC's director of staff studies.[41] Looking at women's overall labor market difficulties, Ginzberg explored reasons that kept employers from fully utilizing women workers. First, he noted that the "influence of tradition" perpetuated job segregation through assumptions that women in "unfeminine" jobs might provoke negative reaction or lack of confidence in customers. In response, Ginzberg noted that "employers may be more prejudiced than they presume their customers to be."[42] Second, he explicated employers' beliefs about women, for example, that their manual dexterity and tolerance of repetition best suited them for clerical and lighter industrial work. Employers also believed that women needed time off to manage child care and home responsibilities. Here Ginzberg suggested that employers exaggerated women's problems and were more tolerant of men's spotty work records. Finally, he noted that women actually saved employers money because they would work for lower wages.[43]

Despite Ginzberg's overall advocacy, the NMC reports often blamed women for their workforce dilemmas, suggesting that their own lack of commitment and preparation prohibited advancement. Since workforce promotion required employees' ongoing investment, the reports decried "women who subordinate the claims of work outside the home to their obligations and functions in the home [and who] will not make the effort required to move up the ladder of skill and responsibility."[44] Ultimately, the report refused to blame "the low occupational status of most women exclusively in terms of the reluctance of male employers to promote them. No person achieves a high position without wanting and preparing and working for it, and the evidence is strong that women are, on the whole, less desirous of and less well prepared for promotion than men."[45]

Women thus faced complicated decision making. Middle-class women with freer choices clearly felt the draw of home responsibilities. Yet many women— whether in the workforce by choice or by necessity—found only lower-paying jobs that lacked the necessary flexibility to blend home and work.

Some economic change for women appeared in the 1950s, often as a result of women's own efforts. These changes signal a postwar activism on behalf of women that is often overlooked, especially when compared to later periods, but that in fact challenged the effect of labor market assumptions on individual choices. Labor unions became one site where women's postwar needs as workers were considered, particularly in blue- and pink-collar jobs. Unions had mixed relationships with female workers throughout the twentieth century, even as the organizations grew in size and influence. Earlier scholarship has focused on women's difficulties in male-dominated craft and industrial unions, especially as women's membership declined after the war.[46] Women's participation (22 percent of all unionized workers during World War II) dropped considerably, and the unions did little to keep women in the postwar workforce. However, focusing on female-dominated industries changes the picture of women's activity.

By the 1950s many female union activists shifted from the larger, male-oriented unions to those representing mostly female fields. Pink-collar jobs increasingly brought women into the Hotel Employees and Restaurant Employees Union and the National Federation of Telephone Workers, where women assumed leadership roles. In addition, some industrial unions—notably the United Auto Workers and the United Electrical Workers—offered footholds where women leaders pushed for labor market equity. There women advocated for the basic right to organize as well as for family-friendly policies like maternity leave, child care, and restrictions on mandatory overtime. Equal pay policies constituted a major focus, with union women pointing out how a strict definition of "equal pay for equal work" disadvantaged women. They argued instead for "compensatory work" provisions, and many of these unions supported passage of the Equal Pay Act of 1963.[47]

Some labor market changes came about through direct female activism. Others resulted from market operations that encouraged employers to adopt more supportive measures in areas where women's work was needed. Two such situations include the decline of the "marriage bar" and the rise of part-time work. The marriage bar primarily affected female-dominated fields like school teaching and office work. Remnants of older social notions about the impropriety of married women working, including the special influence of teachers on developing children, prompted many school districts to ban married or pregnant women teachers. Business firms, especially in insurance, publishing, banking, and public utilities, implemented such policies.[48]

Almost all firms and fields dropped marriage bars in the 1950s (with airline flight attendants an exception) at the same time that they increased opportunities for part-time work—two changes that considerably advanced opportunities for working women. The Women's Bureau showed that part-time work increased from 19 percent of all employment in 1950 to nearly 28 percent in 1960. In sales (a growing women's field), the increase occurred even sooner: 14 percent were part-time in 1940, 25 percent in 1950, and 40 percent by 1960.[49] Thus, the supply/demand ratio of certain fields, along with married women's increasing willingness to work, affected some segments of the labor market.

This increased flexibility did not apply equally to white and nonwhite women, however. Although black and other minority women workers experienced some improvements in job opportunities throughout the 1940s and 1950s, their real movement into expanded employment did not markedly change until after the 1960s.[50] As late as 1960, the majority of black women workers were still employed as household servants. In addition, formal and informal barriers against hiring minority women operated throughout the 1950s, even as other policies more beneficial to women appeared. Black women's lower educational attainment worked against their mobility into better-paying positions, but discrimination remained keen throughout the period.

By the end of the 1950s workplace barriers against women's employment began to lessen. Women workers from a variety of circumstances—married, older, experienced, committed—were becoming increasingly common and significant to the expanding economy. No longer courted solely for their patriotic contribution to a war effort, women were now necessary to sustain the industrial and service-oriented postwar economy as well as to maintain their individual household's standard of living. Throughout a century of economic changes, married women's contribution to household incomes had remained steady at about 26 percent since the 1920s.[51] Propriety aside, American women's income-producing labor was needed in homes across a range of social classes.

Hindsight shows that women's increased postwar labor force participation followed a long-term trend. However, the era's preference that women should be at home whenever possible had several consequences. First, it obscured the reality of women's *actual* labor market behavior, where many worked by choice and most by necessity. Second, by continuing to see women as non-continuous workers, it generated a legacy of discrimination—or at least a lack of attention to issues retarding women's progress. Third, by discouraging professional activity, it depressed women's use of advanced education for workforce advancement.

THE CULTURAL IDEOLOGY

As women increasingly joined the workforce, cultural expectations for full-time domesticity rose throughout the Cold War period. *Womanpower's* finding of the "stubborn fact" that women would always put home needs first captured the view of woman as keeper of the family. Yet postwar women clearly played public roles, both at work and in civic settings. Throughout the era, tension appeared over the definition of appropriate public female activities, especially for members of the middle class, who increasingly chose between labor force and home.

In paid employment, a cultural bargain was struck, recognizing women's participation but treating them as temporary, part-time, or non-competitive workers. Male-oriented professions attracted only the most dedicated women aspirants. More frequent female employment occurred in clerical or sales positions with weaker promotion ladders, lower wages, and less potential for advancement than male-dominated fields like law, medicine, and business. Recognizing that over time women had built strengths in public and civic arenas, few people believed that women should restrict themselves solely to the home. Instead, a Cold War version of the nineteenth-century "separate spheres" viewpoint developed, urging women into those public activities that seemed nurturant and "feminine."[52]

A number of factors promulgated the idealized portrait of white-collar husband, supportive wife, and several children residing in a comfortable suburban home. Certainly the end of the war rekindled family values. As millions of young men returned home, marriage and fertility rates boomed. Marriage rates peaked in 1946, with 118 women per 1,000 marrying, compared to just 79 per 1,000 twenty years earlier. Couples married at younger ages, with the median age for first-time marriages dropping from 21.5 to 20.3 for women, and from 24.3 to 22.7 for men.[53] The fertility rate rose sharply, producing the "baby boom" of 1946–64. In 1945, the last year of World War II, the birth rate was only 86 per 1,000; it jumped to 102 in 1946 and rose steadily throughout the decade. The number of families having three rather than two children increased across all income levels.[54]

Although many families struggled financially, the middle class grew in numbers. Particularly through the G.I. Bill, increasing numbers of young men (and some young women) completed college degrees and vocational training, swelling the middle class through their marketable skills. During the years of highest G.I. Bill participation, the rate of college completion by high school graduates went from 11 percent in 1946, to 27 percent in 1948, 36 percent in 1949, and 40 percent in 1950.[55]

A burgeoning consumer culture increasingly targeted middle-class families, eager to purchase the cars, household goods, and leisure items that signaled a booming economy. Wives contributed economically to families' consumption; although women of all backgrounds increasingly participated in the labor force, middle-class wives demonstrated the greatest increases in spending.[56] As *Womanpower* explained, in earlier "typical middle class families, the wife and unmarried daughters were not gainfully employed. Today, on the other hand, in such families the employment of the wife appears to be a characteristic way of achieving high consumption levels and social status simultaneously."[57] By 1957 nearly 40 percent of wives in middle-income families (those earning $6,000–$10,000) worked, a much higher proportion than in either lower- or higher-income families.[58]

New postwar households necessitated new housing stock, and the era produced planned communities and suburbs. With the help of G.I. Bill mortgages, areas like Levittown, New Jersey, epitomized safe, orderly, affordable communities, catering to middle-class families rather than urban dwellers or single people. Suburbs replaced cities as the fastest-growing residential sector: from 1950 to 1968, the percentage of Americans living at commuting distance rather than in cities grew from 24 to 35 percent of the population.[59]

Film, radio, magazines, and newspapers popularized suburban life, along with their widespread advertising of consumer goods. Television, however, quickly surpassed radio and magazines as the key image-maker for American families. Television spread rapidly in postwar America, with 19 million sets in American homes by 1952.[60] Television established its entertainment value quickly, with family-oriented vaudevillian programs taking immediate hold. Also quick to develop were light comedies depicting family life. A few shows like *The Honeymooners* featured the working-class, but programs like *Father Knows Best* and *The Adventures of Ozzie and Harriet* showed an idealized, comfortable, safe, suburban, and thoroughly middle-class home. As these latter programs grew in popularity, they established a familiar family prototype of a bemused but knowledgeable father, a devoted mother, and good-hearted children.[61]

I Love Lucy, with its cross-cultural marriage of housewife Lucy and Cuban bandleader Ricky Ricardo, was one of the few programs to stretch beyond white, middle-class suburbia. In real life, Lucille Ball was an effective businesswoman who pushed for a portrayal of her own family life. As the show's popularity grew, she and real-life husband Desi Arnaz gained more clout with the network, peaking with the program's coverage of Lucy's actual pregnancy in 1953. The episode portraying the birth of "Ricky Jr." drew 2 million more viewers than did President Dwight Eisenhower's inauguration the following day.[62]

Even as the suburban image predominated, however, social critics began to challenge its sufficiency for the postwar family, especially for fathers. By the mid-1950s, popular analyses such as William H. Whyte's *The Organization Man*, Sloan

Wilson's *The Man in the Gray Flannel Suit*, David Riesman's *The Lonely Crowd*, and Vance Packard's *The Status Seekers* suggested that the postwar push for conformity denied American men their individuality and quashed their personal development.[63] Commentators focused on the dangers to men of bureaucratic, noncreative work. Women, they suggested, could provide a solution. Harking back to the nineteenth-century view of home as a haven in a heartless world, postwar women were encouraged to bolster their husbands' self-worth through honoring their contributions to home and family. Men's job was to resist the alienating organizational culture, and women's was to use the family to ameliorate its effects. Such a balance supported "functionalism," a theory promoted by sociologists like Talcott Parsons that held that all parts of a system should perform a particular function to support the smooth running of the whole.[64] Although later analysts challenged its static view of gender and class roles, functionalism exerted a powerful influence in the 1950s.[65]

African American women—mothers or not—were considered to be outside the comfortable, suburban, middle-class image. Following the war, the largest residential movement for black Americans was not to suburbs but to cities. In fact, white relocation to suburbia often constituted a "white flight" away from cities as much as movement toward new housing. Racial segregation increased in postwar America, as did the containment of poverty in urban areas; and de facto segregation kept suburbs off-limits to most African American families.[66]

The mid-1950s proved an uncomfortable period for American race relations. Resistance to the 1954 *Brown* v. *Board of Education* school desegregation decision was often violent, particularly in the South. Armed confrontations at Little Rock High School and the rise of White Citizens' Councils demonstrated the emerging strain, while the civil rights movement simmered just below the surface of American life. The movement received a strong shock in 1955 with the murder of Emmett Till, a high-profile case offering a particularly poignant example of how the domestic ideal splintered along racial lines.

Till was only fourteen years old when he was kidnapped, brutally beaten, shot to death, and dumped in a Mississippi river by Roy Bryant and J. W. Milam, two older white men who alleged that Till had whistled at Bryant's wife. Till's youth, the horrifying manner of his death, and the nonviolent nature of his supposed "insult" combined to make his case a horrific symbol of the treatment routinely experienced by black Americans. Till's mother, Mamie Till Bradley, joined with male black leaders to publicize the horrors of her son's death, grieving in public and using Emmett's murder as a catalyst for civil rights activity.[67]

One analyst of the racial, class, and gender implications in Till's story explains that "motherhood itself was a battleground on which the meaning of Till's death was fought."[68] Americans were horrified at the brutality of the murder, made evident by Mamie Bradley's insistence on an open casket at a public funeral attended by thousands in Chicago. Emotions were heightened further at the murder trial. Bryant and Milam were rural men, described early on as "white trash," a designation making it easier for other white Americans to distance themselves from the men's actions and their own emotions.

Some observers suggested, however, that perhaps the defendants had a right to avenge Till's disrespect of Bryant's wife. Public presentations of Carol Bryant—the alleged victim of Till's insult—and Mamie Bradley—Emmett's mother—shifted repeatedly. Was Bryant, carefully attired for court in sedate black dresses, or Bradley, the stolid witness who had allowed her son to leave his Chicago home for a family visit to Mississippi, more a "real woman" and a "good mother"? Both sides accepted money, and outside supporters depicted them as victims and dependent women. However, as media coverage progressed and black protest increased, news reports shifted from supporting the "attractive, well-dressed" Bradley to criticizing her publicity-seeking and acceptance of outside money.[69]

Bryant and Milam were acquitted of Till's murder after a 67–minute jury deliberation. Key to the decision was the defense's effort to discredit Bradley's ability to identify her son's swollen, disfigured body. Many commentators were also uncomfortable with Bradley's stoicism and lack of tears on the witness stand. Faced with a racialized depiction of motherhood, many found it easier to abandon Bradley than to recognize her claims.[70]

Racial and class bias generated the particular critique of Mamie Bradley; however, many American women were challenged for their performance as mothers. Mothers who worked, especially those with professional ambitions, found their decision questioned. Along with sociological interpretations that women functioned best when supporting home and family, other experts asserted the "natural" differences between men and women and the roles they should adopt. Anthropologist Margaret Mead, for instance, was immensely popular in the 1950s, publicized through women's magazines and professional journals for her work on cultures far from the United States. Mead observed that, even in places alien to Americans, she found evidence of the primacy of women's incontrovertible reproductive role.[71]

Two sociologists who supported women's activities outside the home analyzed not the pre-industrial cultures of Mead's work, but four modern Western nations. Alva Myrdal and Viola Klein studied the United States, France, Great Britain, and Sweden in *Women's Two Roles: Home and Work*, advocating women's involvement in both venues. Myrdal and Klein argued that increases in women's life-span, the reduction of years devoted to childrearing, and the expansion of active maturity combined to give women two sequential lives: the first at home, the second at work. They challenged the "cult of Homemaking and Motherhood":

> The sentimental glorification which these activities receive may flatter many housewives, but in the long run it does more harm than good, for it encourages them to indulge in an irrational self-pity and prevents them from assessing their situation at its true value. . . . The sentimental cult of domestic virtues is the cheapest method at society's disposal of keeping women quiet without seriously considering their grievances or improving their position.[72]

Women choosing to work, even while their children were young, should not be made to feel like terrible mothers, Myrdal and Klein argued. Data on children's mental and physical health showed that as long as a mother assured her significant involvement during a child's first three years, she could safely share children's care with others. Their solution was allowing mothers more flexibility in public activities. Their socialist-sounding suggestions for shared housework, publicly supported child care facilities, and collective houses probably exceeded the comfort level of most Americans, but their call for women's participation outside the home was well-received.

Myrdal and Klein's analysis was unusual for the postwar period, when most people assumed that multiple roles produced strain and confounded women's attachment to the home.[73] Employment increases aside, the most culturally acceptable way for women to exercise their skills was as volunteers in civic-oriented organizations that bolstered American life. President Erwin Canham of the National Manpower Council extolled the importance of women's volunteerism in *Work in the Lives of Married Women*. Even as he advocated for women's work, Canham asked, "What is going to happen to the volunteer activities which constitute such an extremely useful and important element in our performance of our social responsibilities if women are, for the most part, in paid employment?"[74]

Canham was correct in highlighting women's public service niche. In the nineteenth century, temperance, abolitionism, education, and prison reform attracted women's energies; and in the early twentieth century, public health, immigration, and urban reform benefited from women's activism. In the 1950s, many of these same issues drew women's attention, sometimes in religiously affiliated groups like the Young Women's Christian Association, and the American Friends Service Committee; or in nonpartisan organizations like the League of Women Voters, the Parent Teachers Association, the American Association of

University Women; or in local politics.[75] Such opportunities proved comfortable for middle-class women, since they could participate without committing themselves to regular, paid employment. Mothers could fit activities around home responsibilities, and, most significantly, contribute to civic improvement.

Arguably, the most active volunteers devoted as much time as they would have to paying jobs, and generally, women active in these organizations were not those employed full-time. Rather, volunteer participation became a way to address social concerns while keeping family duties foremost. The organizations understood the pull of both aspects of women's lives. The YWCA, for example, distributed to 1950s college students a pamphlet called *Being a Woman*, in which author Fern Babcock acknowledged that "the most satisfying life for a man or woman is in a happy marriage." Babcock urged women to plan carefully before entering matrimony but also warned women against denying their own interests just to please a husband. Ultimately, she recommended that women shift in and out of the work force as family needs dictated.[76]

As in the past, many volunteers developed leadership skills and built strong female institutions commanding considerable local and national attention. Although groups like the League of Women Voters were later dismissed as too passive by critics like Betty Friedan, the League provided considerable opportunities for women's activism, and many members later pursued electoral politics and activist causes. In the mid-1950s, the University of Michigan conducted a study of the national and local League, revealing that 82 percent of members were married women using the organization as an outlet for their civic concerns. More than half were college graduates, drawn to the League's intense study of issues and its local political advocacy.[77]

Perhaps because the League of Women Voters remained a thoroughly white and middle-class organization, its function as a training ground for women's leadership is often overlooked. The Michigan study, for example, revealed the League's reluctance to expand membership to black and working-class women. Interviews with local members demonstrated their discomfort with anticipated necessary "adjustments" if more black women joined; one interviewer noted this "might require an adaptability on the part of both the local League and Mrs. C beyond that ordinarily required."[78]

Other volunteer organizations proved more comfortable with diversity, leading the way in cross-racial efforts. In fact, racial justice became a prominent goal of some progressive volunteer organizations. The YWCA was one of the few large-scale groups sustaining a mixed membership, with black women constituting about 10 percent of its members in the 1950s. Even though many cities supported separate black and white YWCA branches or separate programs within mixed locals, black YWCA members pushed the organization toward greater awareness of racial issues. In 1946 the national organization passed an Interracial Charter, committing the YWCA to combating racism, both in the wider society and within the organization. Despite this public commitment, black members shouldered most of the work of educating their colleagues.[79]

Besides their involvement with interracial groups, black women participated in their own traditions of volunteer activism. Historically, black women had worked outside the home in larger proportions than whites and had more openly connected their work and home lives. Black churches constituted the strongest sites of community support, and black teachers commonly assumed roles as community leaders. In the 1950s, civil rights organizations like the National Association for the Advancement of Colored People provided women with both paid and unpaid positions.

Most women's groups—whether white, black, or mixed—organized around concerns related to home and family, exercising a long-respected way for women to assert public responsibility. This maternalist approach proved especially prominent in peace organizations. Several "left feminist" groups advocated for peace in a Cold War milieu that readily suspected communist sympathies in such activism.[80] The short-lived Congress of American Women was, in fact, influenced by communist ideals; it supported health provisions and other working women's issues along with a peace agenda. The Women's International League for Peace and Freedom (WILPF) spent a decade defending itself against McCarthyist challenges as it advocated peace issues from its tradition of maternalist politics.[81]

One social critic who adjusted her behavior during the McCarthy era was Betty Friedan. Although in *The Feminine Mystique* and subsequent discussions Friedan painted herself as a suburban homemaker, recent scholarship shows that her earlier radicalism influenced her analysis of postwar domesticity. In the 1940s, Friedan worked as a reporter for labor newspapers, expressing strong radical sympathies. Over time, however, Friedan muted her radical voice, perhaps from ongoing wariness of McCarthyism, as well as to connect with her target audience. One historian commented on the strategy inherent in Friedan's self-presentation: "[I]f Rosa Parks refused to take a seat at the back of a segregated bus not simply because her feet hurt, then Friedan did not write *The Feminine Mystique* simply because she was an unhappy housewife."[82]

In fact, re-readings of 1950s magazines like *Ladies Home Journal*, *McCall's*, *Redbook*, and *Cosmopolitan* suggest that glorification of domesticity was neither as widespread nor as complete as Friedan asserted. Only about 2 percent of articles projected the single-minded "feminine mystique" that Friedan criticized. Rather, the magazines addressed an array of concerns, including women's employment and political activism, alongside discussions of married life, sexuality, and beauty.[83]

Like many social critics, Friedan might have exaggerated her findings to prove her point. She shared with other analysts a belief that the modern suburban ideal stifled American creativity. Her unique contribution lay in applying this analysis to women, specifically the white, middle-class, college-educated group. For all her nascent feminism, however, Friedan focused more on psychological than on political or economic explanations for women's concerns. The postwar ascendance of psychology brought considerable power to interpreting women's lives.

THE PSYCHOLOGICAL IDEOLOGY

Betty Friedan believed that contemporary cultural expectations produced increasing dissatisfaction, ennui, and lack of ambition among American women. Looking for the root causes, she blamed psychology and psychoanalytic theory for constructing the primary female identity as mother and sexual object.

The postwar era turned increasingly to psychologists as experts who could interpret people's behavior and their reactions to the change swirling around them. During World War II, psychologists had proved helpful in screening the mental health of military recruits, explaining the behavior of American soldiers, predicting the actions of America's military enemies, and advising on the internment of Japanese Americans. On the home front, psychologists interpreted public opinion polling and the spread of propaganda.[84] After war's end, their reach expanded as psychologists and other behavioral scientists began to address domestic issues, especially racial concerns and the mental health of ordinary Americans. As psychologists gained authority, their biologically deterministic views of women were accepted and shaped by popular discourse until women's aberrations were seen as problematic, deviant, and harmful both to the woman herself and to those around her.

Part of the reason for Friedan's omission of economic and political causes in her explanation for women's situation was that such understandings had not widely permeated American culture. In the early 1950s, French philosopher Simone de Beauvoir's *The Second Sex* had promulgated a radical view that women's condition was created, rather than inherent.[85] In explaining why women would remain voluntarily subservient amidst an array of available political rights, de Beauvoir highlighted social, economic, and psychological factors. At the same time, her existentialist views encouraged her to highlight women's own freedom to take action and responsibility for doing so.

Friedan had read de Beauvoir's work and admired those portions pointing toward economic, sexual, and power differences in men's and women's situations.[86] More powerful and immediate to her own understanding, however, was the influence of psychological experts who envisioned a subordinate role for women, ascribing their situation to the dictates of biology and personality. Friedan had studied psychology as an undergraduate at Smith College and during a year of graduate work at the University of California, Berkeley; her knowledge of both psychology and social theory influenced her analysis of women's postwar dilemmas.[87] Friedan had long been interested in the influence of Freudianism on modern understanding of women's lives. In *The Feminine Mystique,* both Freudian psychologists and functionalist sociologists attracted her ire.

In a chapter on "The Sexual Solipsism of Sigmund Freud," Friedan explains that Freud—whom she reads as a product of both his time and his personal psycho-sexual history—believed women to be a "strange, inferior, less-than-human species." She quotes Freud's discussion of "the inherent deficiency of femininity": "A man of about thirty seems a youthful, and, in a sense, an incompletely developed individual, of whom we expect that he will be able to make good use of the possibilities of development, which analysis lays open to him. But a woman of about the same age, frequently staggers us by her psychological rigidity and unchangeability. . . . There are no paths open to her for further development."[88]

In Friedan's analysis of Freudianism, women's biology determines her future, which is characterized by passive sexuality, stunted superego development, complete devotion to motherhood and reproduction, and avoidance of achievement-oriented work. Exhibiting these characteristics demonstrated to Freudians a woman's normal psychological development and sound adjustment to the female condition.[89]

Friedan correctly observed the power and pervasiveness of both Freudianism and psychology in general in mid-century America. Women drew the attention of experts, but not for any particular wish to emancipate them or to ameliorate their psychological dissatisfactions. Rather, a postwar focus on women developed because females—as mothers—were identified as key to the normal development of healthy young men and women. An instrumental view of adult women's mental health developed: without mothers as domestic linchpins, both local and national stability were threatened. Unfortunately, psychologists' assessment of women's progress toward mental health was neither encouraging nor flattering. Rather, women's lack of "adjustment" was viewed as an increasing problem, one requiring expert analysis. Over time, women were blamed for the bad behavior of children as well as for larger problems in the culture.[90]

Much of this negative assessment had a Freudian base. During the war, popular author Philip Wylie had blamed women's inability to separate from their sons for soldiers' lack of mental strength.[91] Wylie, who explained later that he purposely overstated his case in order to provoke argument, asserted that society overvalued motherhood, but he blamed women for not righting the balance.[92] Women, he explained, feared that relinquishing their role as mothers would leave only unbearable emptiness.

Other popularizers of Freudianism included Marynia Farnham and Ferdinand Lundberg, whose *Modern Woman: The Lost Sex* is cited widely as an example of the theory run amok.[93] *Modern Woman* is indeed provocative, for its authors blame feminism for most ills facing American society and working women's lack of adjustment as the cause of personal and family neuroses. For Farnham and Lundberg, feminism was "a deep illness," and women must understand that "it is not in the capacity of the female organism to attain feelings of well-being by the route of male achievement."[94]

Despite the appeal of *Modern Woman* for confirming later stereotypes about the 1950s, the book was less influential at the time than Friedan and some historians have assumed. Farnham and Lundberg did not represent the mainstream approach of either the wider culture or women's magazines. In fact, many magazine readers challenged such analyses, rejecting this narrow interpretation of their lives.

Even though popular magazines depicted a variety of women—from traditional mothers to working women, civic leaders, and political activists—their psychological interpretations of women remained narrow.[95] *McCall's, Ladies Home Journal,* and *Cosmopolitan* all painted marriage and motherhood as the natural state for adult American women. Simultaneously, they explored the difficulties, dissatisfactions, and disorientations of modern marriage. Through features such as "Can This Marriage Be Saved?" and "Making Marriage Work," editors acknowledged that many women found difficulty satisfying the domestic role. Regular advice columns allowed women to express frustration, and occasional features highlighted depression or confusion. Titles such as "How Do You Beat the Blues?" "Why Do Women Cry?" and "How to Recognize Suicidal Depression" recognized and normalized feelings of imbalance. As one historian concluded, "far from imagining the home as a haven, the women's magazines often rendered it as a deadly battlefield on which women lost their happiness, if not their minds."[96]

Many experts consulted by the magazines recommended adjustment as a solution to women's psychological dilemmas. Their advice urged women first to let off some steam ("It's Good to Blow Your Top," noted one article), but then to work at adjusting themselves to marital realities. A real contribution of such articles lay in their asserting the unrealistic nature of the romantic married ideal. Marriage, experts explained, required hard work and sacrifice. A woman could not expect immediate perfection in her wifely role, or thorough happiness with all its aspects. The solution: women should adjust their expectations, learn more about their husbands' work, recognize that his sacrifices benefited the family, cultivate their own talents, and by all means, not compete in their husbands' arena.

Even as women were encouraged to adjust themselves to their situation, they were also urged toward self-fulfillment. Alongside other psychological approaches, the era strongly promoted human potential theory, and popular advisers advocated women's right to fulfill their own needs. One magazine piece outlined five requisites for mental health: social approval, belongingness, mastery, need for love and affection, and sexual satisfaction.[97] In the thinking of the early postwar era, the two poles of self-fulfillment and motherhood seemed easily reconcilable; as the Freudians held, women would be happiest by choosing domesticity. But, as the era progressed and women made a variety of choices, the dilemma of harmonizing expectations produced ongoing difficulties, particularly for middle-class women with the widest set of options.

Throughout the 1950s, a few women challenged the general psychological contours. One group followed "The Beats," a collection of artists—mostly male—who flouted conventional mores, art, and literature. Jack Kerouac, Allen Ginsberg, and others wrote poetry and practiced lifestyles celebrating experience, sensuality, and adventure. Although these men enacted a kind of masculinity in "conscious contrast to the postwar image of feminized, middle-class men," they were less certain about including women in their nonconformist lives. For them, women remained adjunct to the Beat lifestyle, valued mainly for providing sexual satisfaction. Women drawn to such dissidence read Beat poetry, listened to rock 'n roll and jazz (with their clear roots in African American culture), and favored black clothing and unconventional attire. Other women led quieter lives while still admiring the sexual and experiential bravado of poets, singers, and actors. Yet women frequently seemed the followers rather than leaders of such rebellion.[98]

Sexual behavior offered another avenue for challenging psychological expectations. Contrary to later impressions, postwar discussions of sexuality were quite common. Freudianism familiarized talk of male and female sexuality. The two Kinsey reports, *Sexual Behavior in the Human Male* and *Sexual Behavior in the*

Human Female, brought this language further into popular parlance, highlighting the wide range of sexual attitudes and experiences among the American public.[99] The Kinsey studies revealed that nearly one-half of American women, across all socioeconomic backgrounds, had experienced premarital intercourse (even if soon followed by marriage). The reports described how the cultural ideal of "good" women fostered a sort of "sexual brinksmanship" whereby women engaged in certain sexual behaviors while technically protecting their virginity. Kinsey's work highlighted women's keen awareness that premarital sex tainted them as potential marriage partners.[100]

Kinsey also demonstrated that women could exercise freedom in their private lives, even while outwardly conforming to a more sedate image. He applauded this flexibility, demystifying women's sexual behavior and depicting their eroticism as normal. Kinsey also discussed the prevalence of homosexual behavior and refused to condemn lesbianism, noting that lesbians were often highly sexually satisfied. Homosexuality, although always extant in American life, became more prominent, more public, and more persecuted in the postwar era. Lesbian and gay subcultures had grown more obvious during the war, attracting additional attention afterward. Lesbianism offered the ultimate challenge to the postwar domestic ideal and was soon jumbled in with premarital sex, prostitution, and other presumed deviant behavior as causes for increased juvenile delinquency and misbehavior among American youth.[101]

Homosexuality was also linked to communism as a threat to American life. Strong efforts developed to uncover gays and lesbians in federal government and the military. A 1950 hearing before the Senate Appropriations Committee charged that ninety-one federal employees recently dismissed for moral transgressions were actually homosexuals.[102] Just as the era witnessed the ferreting out of supposed communists, an equivalent—and sometimes concomitant—investigation occurred around suspected gays and lesbians in public service. In popular media too, an effort to expose this lifestyle proliferated, with films and magazines demonizing lesbians and the danger they posed to "normal" American youth. Increasingly, lesbians were painted as "sexual predators," discontented with keeping their practices private.[103] A poignant example is a 1947 article in the *American Journal of Psychiatry* by self-identified lesbian Jane MacKinnon emphasizing the sexual aggressiveness of lesbians who, in their "need for relief from sexual tension" would flout any strictures of training or breeding to draw another woman "into her orbit of dominance."[104]

A more public acknowledgment of the gay female lifestyle began in the 1950s, along with growing comfort in discussions of sexuality. Widespread expectations of women's "normal" sexual behavior notwithstanding, lesbianism, premarital experimentation, and sexual gratification within marriage all existed in the postwar era; however, acceptance of such behaviors could differ across racial and socioeconomic lines. The treatment of "unwed mothers" provides a provocative example of how psychological experts chose approaches and explanations depending on the background—especially the racial identification—of the women involved.

Out-of-wedlock births had long been an issue in American life. In 1900, the approach to such women bore marks of missionary thinking. Unwed mothers were treated as misguided souls to be saved from their unbridled sexual urges and eased into a more normal lifestyle. By the 1930s, the rise of professional social work resulted in unwed mothers being viewed as "sex delinquents" who needed treatment for promiscuity. As Freudian theory took stronger hold, social workers and psychologists more frequently interpreted women's deviant behavior as neurotic and sought deep-seated causes for such self-destructive behavior.[105] By the 1940s and 1950s, approaches to unwed mothers shifted according to the race and class of the woman in question. Earlier, women's behavior was judged the same no matter who exhibited it; but by the postwar era, black women's actions were ascribed to racial "cultural pathology," whereas white women were seen as acting out individual neuroses.[106]

The general profile of unwed mothers changed in the 1940s: more middle-class white women appeared in maternity homes and social agencies, replacing the earlier preponderance of working-class cases. This new population seemed almost calm about their situation and were untouched by poverty or abuse. Initially uncertain about analyzing such clients, social workers applied Freudian understandings, determining a single woman's pregnancy as self-punishing behavior symptomatic of deep-seated dysfunction. This analysis not only ignored possible environmental influences but also painted women's behavior as a psychological problem being acted out through sexual conduct.

A different analysis was applied to black women. A long history of biological explanations for black women's sexual behavior, coupled with a belief in black "hypersexuality," overtook social workers' view of the problem as environmentally or socially based. Illegitimacy within the black community had been a growing concern for decades. In *The Negro Family in the United States* (1939), E. Franklin Frazier had pioneered a cultural explanation as an alternative to inherent biological deviance.[107] In the postwar era, however, Frazier's more positive explanation hardened into a belief that these women willingly chose unwed pregnancies. Their acceptance seemed to demonstrate a perverse matriarchal influence leading to an overall cultural pathology among black families. Whereas white women's behavior was an individual concern that could be ameliorated, black women's actions seemed representative of a wider and less correctable social and psychological problem.

Prevailing postwar expectations encouraged one best way for women to satisfy their psychological needs: as dutiful wives and mothers, taking satisfaction in preparing their children as the next generation of Americans. Such a model answered a number of needs for society, but it offered very limited flexibility for women who wanted more, sexually or culturally. Adjustment, rather than challenge, offered the more comfortable approach.

CONCLUSION

At first glance, the advice Kathryn Greeley gave her daughters seems like the ultimate stereotype of the "feminine mystique." "The most important goal," she told her girls, is "to meet enough men so that you will find the right one and not settle for anything less along the way."[108] On closer examination, however, Greeley's insistence on "the right one" shows a careful negotiation of her choices as a middle-class, educated woman. Greeley treasured her family's shared interests as well as her husband's support. He professed not to mind their "messy house" while she spent fifteen hours weekly on the League of Women Voters, the PTA, and the Kennedy presidential campaign. Together they pursued interracial concerns, including a joint presidency of the local Council of Human Relations. A non-employed mother of three who appeared stereotypically traditional on the surface was, in fact, finding ways to exercise her choices and interests.

Kathryn Greeley exemplifies ways in which many postwar American women—especially those with economic flexibility—respected the predominant ideologies while simultaneously stretching them. The four ideologies together set up huge expectations for women's behavior. The *patriotic ideology* declared that women should defend the home front against threats of communism and domestic disruption, sustaining the family with unique female strengths. Yet even as they valued roles as wives and mothers, women with specialized labor market skills were urged to answer the growing call for "womanpower." The *economic ideology* asserted that women should relinquish the jobs and economic status they had established as wartime workers. Where women's labor was needed, they were expected to take subordinate roles and lesser pay. However, this economic approach ignored the fact that women—especially wives—had increasingly moved into the labor force. It also consigned the majority of women to long-term expectations of low-status work and failed to bolster the interests of either professional employees or blue-collar women workers.

The *cultural ideology* touted women's family role, continuing a long tradition of valuing maternalism and domesticity. However, many women channeled energy into important volunteer and civic organizations. Achieving a good balance between domestic responsibilities and civic activism was difficult, but many women—whether of economic means or with lesser flexibility—devoted themselves to volunteerism and community. The era's *psychological ideology* supported the other three expectations with a Freudian interpretation that women were best fulfilled through acceptance of their reproductive role. However, this approach was challenged by a growing ease with sexual experimentation and publicity around healthy American sexuality.

Taken together, these four ideologies presented a potent set of expectations but did not universally determine women's opportunities or actual behavior, especially outside the middle class. Many women stretched their views of the economic, patriotic, cultural, and psychological expectations to create a balance that worked for themselves personally and for their families.

The situation of young, middle-class women raised a particular set of questions. Collegiate educators charged with preparing the next generation of educated women needed to consider a variety of possibilities. How would postwar women facing such a complicated mix of choices factor college into their plans? And, if they chose to attend college, how would educators formulate their curricular opportunities? Educators might continue to imitate men's training—an equality for which women had long fought—or they might accommodate societal expectations by preparing women to be wives and mothers. And when women left school to pursue marriage and family, should educators find a way to sustain their educational pursuits? Confusion around such choices permeated higher education throughout the postwar period, puzzling students, educators, and women professionals alike.

CHAPTER TWO

Educators Consider the Postwar College Woman

"Once I asked a professor for . . . a 'practical assistantship' . . . and he said to me, 'I can't, Beth. You're a very bright student but you'll have children and quit working in the field and not be publishing papers which redound to the credit and illustrious name of the university. So I will choose a male assistant.' He was quite correct."[1] So concluded Beth Isaacs, a subject (like Kathryn Greeley) in the 1966 study of former Columbia University graduate students. Isaacs, an economist, stopped just short of completing her Ph.D. in order to accompany her husband to his new teaching job in California. Her parents had emigrated from Russia to the United States, where her mother completed college and then pursued a 35–year teaching career. Inspired by her parents, Isaacs became a Phi Beta Kappa graduate of the University of Michigan and, in 1951, earned her master's degree in economics at Columbia. She had finished all the coursework toward her doctorate, plus one year of thesis research, when her husband received the California offer.

Isaacs and her husband soon had three children, and she chose stay-at-home motherhood. Of this decision, she explained, "I thought women could conquer the world, have children, and be great professors. Now I feel that expectation surely shattered. To be a warm, loving mommy you've got to be home with your kids." However, in 1966, with her children growing, Isaacs talked about the "definite ache" she felt for stimulating work, and she had recently taken a half-time research job. She found the work reasonably challenging but termed the lack of her Ph.D. continually "annoying."[2]

Did Isaacs harbor any regrets about her decisions? No, she explained, "not for what we've *had* together—but only for what *I* haven't completed and gone on with." Careers, children, and marriages all need careful tending, Isaacs noted, and it was unwise for a woman with family responsibilities to expect simultaneous success in all three.

Beth Isaacs exemplifies a large number of middle-class postwar women who, while drawn to intellectual work, chose home responsibilities over the workplace. Isaacs was unusual in progressing so far in her graduate training, but the choice to adapt her life to the demands of family matched the decisions made by thousands of women students. In the postwar era, the prevalence of a domestic ideology, the appeal of homemaking, and the cool reception women sometimes received in the job market joined professors' and employers' preferences for men, whose productivity—as Isaacs's graduate school professor explained—would be less affected by the challenges of family life.

In reality, however, postwar women did not abandon college. The absolute number of women in higher education rose throughout the postwar era, so that, by 1957, college attracted one in every five women between the ages of 18 and 21.[3] Just as the postwar labor market demonstrated a continuing upward trend in female participation, so did the numbers of women seeking college education. From 1948 to 1963, women's collegiate enrollments boomed from about 700,000 to nearly 1.7 million (Table 2.1). Only in 1950 and 1951 did the otherwise consistent annual increments temporarily reverse.

The widespread impression that women were forsaking advanced training was supported, however, by the fact that women's *proportion* of the postwar collegiate and graduate populations dropped markedly. Whereas women had constituted nearly half of all college students in 1920 (47.3%)—a historic high prior to World War II—their proportion dropped to 40 percent in 1940, 31 percent in 1950, and rebounded only to 37 percent by 1960.[4] This fact, when coupled with the visibility and numbers of the new male recipients of the G.I. Bill, diminished women's campus presence. Table 2.1 reveals a similar decrease in the proportion of women at the graduate level. The proportion of women earning graduate degrees, and thus qualifying to become collegiate faculty, remained low long into the postwar period. Later, in the 1960s, women's collegiate participation began a significant rebound, so that by 1980 women actually predominated on American campuses. However, in the postwar period, women's lessened collegiate participation matched cultural expectations that women would focus on home and family.

The four ideologies—patriotic, economic, cultural, and psychological—affected women across socioeconomic backgrounds, but they exerted a particular influence on girls and women who entertained the idea of college training. For

TABLE 2.1
Enrollments in Institutions of Higher Education, 1942–1965

	Undergraduate Enrollments				Graduate Enrollments	
			Women		Women as Percentage of Earned Master's Degrees†	Women as Percentage of Earned Doctoral Degrees†
Year	Total Enrollment	Number of Men	Number	Percentage		
1942	1,404,000*	819,000	585,000	41.6	42.4	13.1
1944	1,155,000*	579,000	576,000	49.8	57.4	18.4
1945	1,677,000*	928,000	749,000	44.6		
1946	2,078,000*	1,418,000	661,000	31.8	50.6	19.6
1947	2,338,000*	1,659,000	679,000	29.0		
1948	2,408,249‡	1,712,283	695,966	28.8	31.8	12.3
1949	2,456,841‡	1,728,672	728,169	29.6	30.6	10.3
1950	2,296,592‡	1,569,322	727,270	31.6	29.1	9.6
1951	2,116,440‡	1,398,735	717,705	33.9	29.0	9.1
1952	2,148,284‡	1,387,094	761,190	35.4	31.4	9.2
1953	2,250,701‡	1,432,474	818,227	36.5	32.8	9.5
1954	2,468,596‡	1,575,227	893,369	36.1	32.8	9.0
1955	2,678,623‡	1,747,429	931,194	34.7	33.4	9.3
1956	2,946,985‡	1,927,863	1,019,122	34.5	33.5	9.9
1957	3,068,417‡	2,003,424	1,064,993	34.7	33.2	10.7
1958	3,258,556‡	2,110,426	1,148,130	35.2	32.5	10.7
1959	3,402,297‡	2,173,797	1,228,500	36.1	33.3	10.5
1960	3,610,007‡	2,270,640	1,339,367	37.1	33.1	10.4
1961	3,891,230‡	2,423,987	1,467,243	37.7	32.3	10.5
1962	4,206,672‡	2,603,072	1,603,600	38.1	32.4	10.7
1963	4,419,000‡	2,743,000	1,676,000	37.9	32.7	10.7
1964	5,280,000*	3,249,000	2,031,000	38.4	33.6	10.5
1965	5,921,000*	3,630,000	2,291,000	38.6	33.8	10.7

Sources: *National Center for Education Statistics (1993). 120 Years of American Education: A Statistical Portrait. Washington D.C.: Office of Educational Research and Improvement.

†U.S. Bureau of the Census (1989). Historical Statistics of the United States: Colonial Times to 1970. White Plains, N.Y.: Kraus International Publications.

‡U.S. Department of Health, Education, and Welfare, Office of Education (1963). Digest of Educational Statistics. Washington, D.C.: U.S. Government Printing Office.

young women anticipating college, the ideologies dampened the appeal of education; aside from the opportunity to meet educated men, domestic life seemed unconnected to what college offered. For women in college, the ideologies produced confusion about which curriculum offered the best preparation for life, and they made college completion seem less necessary once a marriage proposal occurred. For women pursuing professional goals, the ideologies constrained educational and financial opportunities and often made professional success more challenging.

Even though women were, numerically, a large collegiate presence, they were treated as "incidental students" in terms of prominence, policy, and influence on postwar campuses. Three developments explain this reaction. First, women were generally ancillary at the institutions where the biggest growth occurred: the burgeoning research universities attracting new federal and corporate money. Second, women lost out to the attention directed at veterans on campus: a new group, mostly male, who excited the imagination of both the public and campus leaders. And third, faculty and administrators offered women confused curricular advice as they tried to balance women's preparation for domesticity with education for varied choices.

AMERICAN HIGHER EDUCATION AFTER
WORLD WAR II

Stereotypes of 1950s campuses as staid settings filled with quiescent students pursuing classical curricula belie the enormous changes confronting American higher education in the two decades following World War II. As the head of the Carnegie Foundation exclaimed rather breathlessly in 1950, "At no time in the history of this country has there been so much ferment and stir about the ends and means of education."[5] Most of these changes, however, involved women only incidentally, muting their particular concerns within a larger set of wide-ranging developments.

Following World War II, several higher education issues intertwined to provoke changes in clientele, in governance, and in curriculum. Throughout the early postwar period, significant shifts occurred in three areas: (1) the relationship between universities and the federal government, with notable increases in both government research funding and aid to students; (2) subsequent overall growth of higher education, including enrollments, size, and spending; and (3) new curricular responses to perceived educational needs.

The first educational change—higher education's strengthened relationship to the government—developed from the war-related windfall of federal research funding. The government directed enormous amounts of money to college-based research during World War II, and campuses retained this support at war's end. During World War I, university scientists had been recruited to work in federal laboratories and war-related bureaucracies. During World War II, however, the government used a different tactic, harnessing the talent of university scientists and engineers by developing a new contract and grant system that supplied research funds to universities.[6] Vannevar Bush, vice president at MIT and later president of the Carnegie Institution of Washington, led colleagues in arguing for peacetime applications of war-related technology. First through the White

House–based Office for Scientific Research and Development, and later through the new National Science Foundation, Bush, along with James Bryant Conant of Harvard, Karl Compton of MIT, and others, promoted partnerships between federal funders and campus laboratories. After the war's end, research centers shifted from war-related projects to expanded scientific and social applications. New types of collaborative relationships appeared on campuses, offering expanded avenues for federal and industrial research dollars as well as additional positions for researchers.[7]

Research had long been an important university focus, but the size and stability of the new funding catapulted research to the forefront of many institutional agendas. The new value affected all sectors of higher education, prompting even teaching-oriented colleges to compete for research dollars. As both the funding and its aura of prestige solidified throughout the 1950s, higher education scholar David Riesman described the collegiate scene as an "academic snake," where the middle and the end of the body tried to follow the same movements as the head, rarely recognizing that each part might more properly assume a separate function.[8] Not all institutions proved equally successful at winning federal largesse. By 1963 more than half of federal contract dollars were concentrated in just twenty institutions, the top ten receiving one-third of the funds.[9]

Another significant and long-term governmental shift came with the Serviceman's Readjustment Act of 1944, known as the G.I. Bill. The Readjustment Act provided unemployment insurance, low-interest loans for home ownership, and educational assistance through generous benefits. Veterans who had served at least ninety days received a full year of educational support, plus a day of schooling for every additional day of service, up to forty-eight months. They received a maximum of $500 for tuition, fees, and books, plus a monthly stipend that varied for married and single veterans (by 1948, $75 for single veterans, $105 for couples, and $120 for families).[10] Originally intended as an economic measure to slow the entry of nearly 16 million servicemen into the labor market, the G.I. Bill ultimately brought both new funds and new students to higher education, revising views about who could benefit from advanced schooling and how they could pay for it.[11] By the program's end in 1954, approximately 2.2 million veterans had attended college, far exceeding predictions. Many veterans were resuming interrupted college plans, effectively replacing the pre-war collegiate population. However, authorities estimated that about 20 percent of student veterans would not have attended college without the G.I. Bill.[12]

There had been little expectation that so many postwar Americans—with or without federal support—would turn to college. Before the war, college was a

TABLE 2.2
Higher Education Enrollment during the
G.I. Bill Era

| Year | Veterans Enrolled | |
	Number	Percentage
1945	88,000	5.2
1946	1,013,000	48.7
1947	1,150,000	49.2
1948	975,000	40.5
1949	844,000	34.4
1950	581,000	25.2
1951	396,000	18.7
1952	232,000	10.8
1953	138,000	6.1

Source: Adapted from K.W. Olson (1974). *The G.I. Bill, the Veterans, and the Colleges.* Lexington: University of Kentucky Press. Table 1, p. 44.

fairly elite proposition; only about 9 percent of the age cohort (18 to 24 years of age) attended.[13] In fact, institutional planners had worried about the long-term stability of higher education, finding finances and enrollments particularly vexing problems. The veterans changed the financial picture, however, bringing thousands of new students and a new source of tuition support. In 1946 and 1947, the peak years of G.I. Bill attendance, veterans constituted 48 percent and 49 percent, respectively, of all collegiate enrollments (Table 2.2).

All sectors of higher education benefited from G.I. Bill funding, but the veterans' choices proved somewhat surprising. Prestigious institutions, both private and public, attracted the greatest interest. With the government providing tuition, many veterans pushed for the best institution they could find, including the Ivy League schools, state universities, and well-established liberal arts and technical colleges. In 1948, male veterans predominated at private institutions, and non-veterans at public schools. Community colleges, teachers colleges, and small institutions also drew high numbers of veterans, although not always by the former soldiers' choice.[14] Two-year schools benefited from those veterans either less well-prepared for four-year schooling or seeking quicker, job-oriented programs. Similarly, teachers colleges were not the first choice of many veterans but were often the local institution best able to accommodate the student influx. Unquestionably, many smaller and less-prestigious schools enjoyed enrollment stability and tuition support from the program.[15]

Although the G.I. Bill benefited a wide range of students, it is not clear how well it served black veterans.[16] Many African Americans were welcomed into white institutions, especially in the North. In some cases, special provisions facilitated their entrance, including waivers of admission requirements or credits for special military training. However, black veterans also encountered resistance from the Veterans Administration, the American Legion, and the Veterans of Foreign Wars, organizations influential in creating and administering the G.I. Bill. As one analyst concluded, "Staffed almost entirely by whites empowered to deny or grant the claims of black GIs, the Veterans Administration became a formidable foe to many blacks in search of an education."[17] Charles Rangel, future congressman from New York, was counseled to use his benefits at a trade school; instead, he pursued law at St. John's University. Most G.I. Bill–era enrollment increases by African Americans occurred in historically black colleges and universities. One estimate suggests that by 1947 predominantly white institutions had grown by more than 29 percent from G.I. Bill usage, but historically black colleges had grown by 50 percent.[18]

The experience of female veterans has not been widely studied. However, findings suggest that eligible women used the G.I. Bill in slightly lower percentages than men, about 35 percent for women compared to 41 percent for men.[19] When asked why they had not used benefits more fully, many women said they were unaware of their eligibility (the Veterans Administration made little specific outreach to women) or that they had not needed financial support (especially those who married and started families immediately). Another frequent explanation was that women "did not consider their service equal to that of men, and therefore, they did not expect equal benefits."[20]

The effects of the G. I. Bill support the view of women as auxiliaries to male veterans, especially in their role as students. The story of the veterans' campus influx proved irresistibly appealing. Newspapers and magazines abounded with tales and photos of the G.I. on campus, relishing the image of these older men strolling the campus or studying at night, surrounded by their young families. Women were usually portrayed as wives of college-going veterans rather than as students themselves. Ironically, although the pictorial coverage of postwar campuses depicted a wide variety of men as students, it limited women's image to helpmate, muting their presence as self-directed students.[21] The influx of male veterans had other effects on women students' access to higher education. Some institutions created admissions quotas for women and non-veterans, hoping to free up space for G.I. Bill recipients. Many women were rejected from schools that, five years earlier, would have welcomed their presence.[22] At the University of Michigan, freshman women's enrollment was reduced by one-third in 1946, with a quota remaining in effect until 1952.[23]

A second major development occurred alongside—and partly as a result of—higher education's enhanced relationship with the government: overall growth in colleges and universities. During the twenty years after World War II, higher education expanded in all directions, including size of enrollments, numbers of institutions, predominance of the public sector, and overall spending.

The veterans clearly inflated enrollments in the early postwar years, but even this huge influx failed to replenish the number of college degrees not achieved during the war. Rather, G.I. Bill–fueled enrollment increases marked the beginning of expanded interest in higher education, soon exacerbated by the baby boom. At the start of the war less than 10 percent of the age cohort (18 to 24 years) attended college. By 1950, however, more than 14 percent attended, and a decade later, nearly 24 percent attended college.[24] In raw numbers, about 2.3 million attended college in 1950, but 3.6 million in 1960 and 5.2 million by 1964.[25] The veterans' success on campus solidified the growing belief that a wide variety of Americans could enhance their life chances through higher education.

Many higher education institutions increased in size, and the postwar period evinced a new tolerance for large universities. In 1947, the peak enrollment year for veterans, eight institutions enrolled more than 20,000 students. By 1967, baby boom enrollments produced fifty-five universities housing more than 20,000.[26] The size increases supported the growth of research-oriented universities, allowing economies of scale at the largest schools that could, concomitantly, pursue undergraduate teaching alongside a research focus.

Besides increases in size, the number of colleges grew by several hundred, especially in the 1960s, and there was a sharp turn toward enrollment at public institutions. In 1950 public colleges and universities attracted about half of all students. That proportion increased to 59 percent by 1960, continued throughout the decade, and grew to 73 percent by 1970.[27] As enrollments, size, research capacity, and sources of funding all grew, overall spending expanded accordingly. One summary statistic reflects the enormous growth: "Aggregate spending by all institutions of higher education rose from $2.2 billion in 1950 to $21 billion by 1970."[28]

The third educational change grew naturally from shifts in clientele and mission, focusing on the appropriate nature of the curriculum. Since the mid-nineteenth century, especially with the growth of land-grant universities, schools had struggled to balance liberal learning with market-oriented specialization. Concerns about anti-intellectualism were growing before World War II, with critics attacking the "life adjustment" education that apparently had seeped from

progressive schooling into the collegiate curriculum.[29] Critics worried that, in trying to make college increasingly relevant to students' futures, faculties were dilut-
ing the traditional academic core. The pressures of wartime further enhanced the
appeal of "practical" courses. All these concerns prompted a rejuvenated interest
in general education as the war ended.

In 1945 a Harvard University faculty committee staked out a postwar response
to the anti-intellectual sentiment in *General Education in a Free Society.*[30] The report
emphasized the importance of liberal values for well-educated people, asserting
the necessity of broad training in humanities, social sciences, and natural sciences. Harvard's recommendations—adopted by many universities—countered
the nonintellectual work that predominated at many schools, usually in the name
of preparing youth for citizenship.[31] Even with this attention to liberal education,
institutions were well aware of the increasing democratization of higher education and its new clientele like the veterans. In addition, wartime and postwar developments heightened awareness of the increasingly global aspects of modern
life. Language and "area studies" proliferated on campuses as educators encouraged students to consider America's expanded role in the world. From language
courses to behavioral sciences, college students studied those global cultures that
might affect America's future.[32]

A different curricular issue developed from a more wary encounter with internationalism: a concern that in science and technology, America must compete
with the Soviet Union. The National Defense Education Act (NDEA) of 1958 symbolized American commitment to strengthen its technological base; science and
mathematics increasingly took precedence over broad-based general education.
Over the next several years, graduate student funding from the National Science
Foundation, the National Aeronautics and Space Administration, the National
Institutes of Health, and the Atomic Energy Commission augmented NDEA fellowships. In 1958, federal agencies spent $219 million sponsoring university
programs; by 1964, the figure had climbed to $866 million.[33] Although funding
went to languages and area studies as well as to science and technology, the pur-
ported benefit of these fields helped secure overall high support.

Curricular issues appeared in many forums, and all of them—general education, citizenship training, internationalism, and curricular balance—were highlighted in 1947 by the Truman administration's President's Commission on Higher
Education. The Truman Commission was the first presidentially sponsored group
to study higher education on a national scale, and it touched on nearly all the issues facing postwar higher education in a six-volume report, *Higher Education*

for American Democracy. The commission declared that the United States, and in fact the world, was "in a time of crisis." It called on education to remedy modern concerns, acclaiming three educational goals for the postwar nation:

— Education for a fuller realization of democracy in every phase of living.
— Education directly and explicitly for international understanding and cooperation.
— Education for the application of creative imagination and trained intelligence to the solution of social problems and to the administration of public affairs.[34]

The President's Commission viewed higher education as a social solution for the nation's problems and encouraged wider distribution of educational benefits. Among its best-known recommendations, the commission declared that, unlike past assumptions that college best suited the elite, 49 percent of the population could beneficially complete two years of college, and 32 percent could complete four-year degrees.[35] The commission based these calculations on results of the Army General Classification Test that had been administered to World War II servicemen. This test of mental ability encouraged the commission to argue that the nation's "inventory of talent" was much wider than previously assumed and that the country should extend its higher educational capacity to accommodate new students. Accordingly, the commission supported the burgeoning junior colleges already serving the new clientele, predicting a remarkable junior-college growth rate that was, in fact, reached by the early 1960s.

Without explicitly acknowledging the veterans' experience, the Truman Commission forecast that more older, married, and middle- and working-class students could successfully attend college. In strikingly straightforward language, it also called for elimination of racial, religious, and gender barriers discouraging less-traditional students and recommended a program of federally funded fellowships for new clientele.

Its call for eliminating racial segregation was the most internally contentious pronouncement, with four commission members dissenting. Although President Truman had already recommended military integration, and the NAACP was pushing desegregation cases through federal and state courts in 1947, integration was neither inevitable nor uniformly supported. The commission demonstrated, using 1940 census data, that only 7.3 percent of blacks over age 25 had completed high school, while 28.8 percent of "native whites" and 11.6 percent of "foreign-born whites" had done so.[36] College statistics were equally discouraging: by 1947, only 4.3 percent of black men and 5.2 percent of black women were completing some years of college, compared to 13.4 and 12.1 percent of white men and women.[37]

The President's Commission stressed the long-term effects of racial discrimination, noting that black students pursued graduate and professional degrees in very small numbers, a situation exacerbated by segregation. Nearly one-quarter of the nation's medical schools were located in the South and therefore closed to black students. At the Ph.D. level, in 1947, only eight doctorates were awarded to African American students by non-segregated institutions.[38] In calling for change, the commission relied on an equity argument: "The basic social fact is that in a democracy [the black American's] status as a citizen should assure him equal access to educational opportunity" (2:30–31). Four members dissented, explaining: "We recognize the high purpose and the theoretical idealism of the Commission's recommendations. But a doctrinaire position which ignores the facts of history and the realities of the present is not one that will contribute constructively to the solution of difficult problems of human relationships" (2:29).

Commission membership, which included three clerics (one a rabbi) and two women, also denounced discrimination experienced by Jewish students, particularly through quotas. Here the commission acknowledged a slippery slope. Having called for higher collegiate representation of black students to match their numbers in the general population, they recognized that Jews were over-represented: more Jewish students sought entrance to colleges than their population percentages justified. The commission finally concluded that "the only defensible basis is that total ability and interest—rather than quotas or ratios, however determined—be the criterion of admission" (2:36).

Compared to the strong statements on African Americans and Jews, discrimination against women received only three short paragraphs in the report. Treated under "Other Arbitrary Exclusions," the report decried "antifeminism in higher education" as unfairly limiting women's options. The commission explained that women's collegiate opportunities were fairly recent, concluding optimistically that "the denial of opportunity has largely disappeared in the present century except at the professional school level." Although citing a precipitous drop in women's presence as graduate students, the President's Commission offered no specific recommendations beyond a generalized call for attention (1:40).

Ultimately, the recommendations of the President's Commission, although noteworthy and prescient, did not greatly influence the higher educational landscape in the late 1940s or 1950s. The federal fellowship program was never funded, the desegregation issue was larger than one group's advocacy could secure, and the support for junior colleges—although significant to those institutions—

met with reserve from other foundation-sponsored committees and collegiate associations less sympathetic to this growing educational sector. Nonetheless, its wide-ranging examination represents a significant benchmark of the postwar educational scene.

INCIDENTAL STUDENTS: UNDERGRADUATE WOMEN IN THE POSTWAR LANDSCAPE

The Truman Commission's lack of consideration for women students and faculty was typical of the era. Without the participation of the commission's sole female members—Sarah Gibson Blanding, previous president of the National Association of Deans of Women and new president of Vassar College, and Agnes Meyer, journalist, philanthropist, and women's advocate—women might have been left out entirely. The larger movements affecting higher education—especially growth in the research mission and new connections to the federal government—proceeded with little acknowledgment that women constituted nearly one-third of undergraduate enrollments.

The G.I. Bill left a mixed legacy for women. It did, of course, provide benefits to female veterans. It also expanded the notion of who could benefit from college, easing the way for older, married, and non-elite students. Such a change seemed to predict a more comfortable road for women, who might wish to start their families without completely abandoning higher education. However, the more frequent image of married women at college was as support to student-husbands, rather than as students themselves.[39]

A negative aspect of the G.I. Bill occurred around enrollments and campus space. Even as schools increased housing, staffing, and capacity, the concentrated onslaught of veterans displaced many non-veteran women (and some non-veteran men) who had constituted stable sources of enrollments before and during the war. As Table 2.1 shows, from 1945 to 1965 the number of women pursuing a college education tripled, from 749,000 to 2,291,000. However, the pattern of increases shows variations in a long-term upward trend. From 1945 to 1946, the first year that G.I. Bill benefits were available, a steep increase occurred in men pursuing higher education—a natural result of war-delayed attendance and generous educational benefits—but women dropped considerably. Women's enrollments rebounded a bit over the next few years, but men continued to outnumber them. In 1950 and 1951, during the Korean War, women's actual numbers decreased again (as did men's). By 1952, with the Korean situation stabilized and a new G.I. Bill (smaller than the 1944 version) in place, enrollments throughout higher education began another rise, with women rebounding first, then men.

Examining women's *proportion* of the collegiate enrollment demonstrates these effects more dramatically. Here we see how the availability of veterans' benefits dampened women's participation in the years immediately following the war. From a high of 49.8 percent of all students during the war, women dropped to only 28.8 percent in 1948. As the initial effects of G.I. Bill funding eased, women slowly reclaimed a stronger share, moving from under 30 percent of enrollments in 1948 and 1949 to 38.6 percent by 1965. In other words, two decades after the conclusion of the war, women had still not reached their earlier levels of participation; they returned to 40 percent only in 1967.[40]

Another characteristic of the era—with a long-term trend newly influenced by the G.I. Bill—was women's differential representation across higher education. As Table 2.3 shows, teachers colleges and liberal arts colleges (four-year institutions without significant graduate programs) claimed the largest share of female enrollment, and universities the smallest. Teachers colleges attracted student bodies more than 50 percent female (a number that might have been higher without the attendance of many male veterans). These institutions, along with women's colleges, had traditionally served high proportions of female students, given the attraction of teaching as a profession for women, as well as women's propensity to use general collegiate training for preparation as teachers. As the *Womanpower* report explained, "almost two out of every five women who graduated in 1954–55 majored in the field of education, and an additional one out of seven prepared for teaching, even though she specialized in some other field."[41] Although women's proportion as students at the university level grew as the 1960s approached, in 1957 they constituted less than one-third of enrollments.

By the early 1960s, public community colleges claimed a growing share of the student population as well as the attention of higher education planners.[42] Community college growth in the 1960s was nothing short of phenomenal. Analysts (including the Truman Commission) had predicted that community college enrollment gains would double in the 1960s; the actual growth rate was closer to quadruple. A much-quoted statistic noted that "America had built nearly one community or junior college per week for a decade."[43]

Several decades later, community colleges became a prime entry point for both women and minorities, especially nontraditional students. By the late 1990s, one-third of community college students were non-white. Forty percent of all African American students and 55 percent of all Hispanic students began their

TABLE 2.3
*Distribution of Women Undergraduates by Type and Control
of Institution*

	1957	1962
Women Undergraduates		
Number	1,064,993	1,603,600
Percentage	34.7	38.1
Women	%	%
In junior colleges	35.6	38.0
In 4-year schools	34.5	38.1
In universities	28.3	32.3
In liberal arts colleges	44.0	45.8
In teachers colleges	52.0	51.7
In public institutions	35.4	38.3
In private institutions	33.7	36.9

Source: Adapted from U.S. Department of Health, Education, and Welfare, Office
of Education (1963). *Digest of Educational Statistics.* Washington, D.C.: U.S. Government Printing Office. Table 44, p. 58.

higher education careers there. Furthermore, these institutions served women
well: females constituted 45 percent of all full-time community college faculty in
1992, and 58 percent of the student body in 1998.[44]

As Table 2.3 shows, women represented 35.6 percent of community/junior
college clientele in 1957—only one percent higher than their percentage across
all sectors. That relationship continued: in 1962 women moved to 38 percent of
community/junior college students, but this still matched their overall collegiate
participation rates. In 1957 women faculty constituted only 28 percent of new
full-time hires at these institutions.[45]

The general diminution of women's collegiate presence also affected black
women, who traditionally lagged behind their white counterparts in college
attendance. By mid-century, nearly twice the proportion of the white college-
age cohort attended college as did black (Table 2.4). Two factors characterized
African American women's college-going in the postwar era. First, unlike white
students, black women outnumbered black men in both college attendance and
graduation. In the early postwar years, while women completed degrees started
during wartime, black women consistently outnumbered black men as college
graduates; in 1949, for instance, African American women earned 6,618 degrees
to men's 4,692.[46] When G.I. Bill benefits started, however, men's percentages
grew, so that by 1960 nearly identical percentages of African American men and
women attended some college and completed degrees. Jeanne Noble, author of

TABLE 2.4
Years of College Completed by Race and Sex

	Male population		Female population	
	1–3 years	4 years or more	1–3 years	4 years or more
Whites				
1940	5.2	5.8	6.4	4.0
1947	6.9	6.5	7.3	4.8
1960	9.1	10.3	9.5	6.0
Blacks				
1940	1.6	1.4	2.1	1.2
1947	2.0	2.3	2.6	2.6
1950	2.8	2.0	3.1	2.3
1957	3.0	2.6	3.3	2.9
1960	4.4	3.5	4.4	3.6

Source: U.S. Department of Commerce. Bureau of the Census. (1989). *Historical Statistics of the United States.* White Plains, N.Y.: Kraus International Publications. Part 1, p. 380.

The Negro Woman's College Education (1956), attributed the greater percentage of collegiate black women to the appeal of teaching, a highly regarded profession within the black community and a way for women to exercise leadership.[47]

Even though black men's college-going rates caught up to black women's by 1960, African American women's participation rate increase surpassed that of white women from 1940 to 1960. At the start of World War II black women attended and completed college at less than one-third the rate of white women—a fact reflecting their limited financial and academic opportunities. By 1960, however, although black women's participation still lagged behind their white counterparts, they had closed the gap to about one-half. In other words, the *rate* of their increase surpassed that of white women. The prohibition against de jure segregation after the 1954 *Brown v. Board of Education* decision might have encouraged and permitted more African American women to attend college.

WOMEN'S PARTICIPATION AS
GRADUATE STUDENTS AND FACULTY

Women's movement into graduate training and then onto collegiate faculties followed a different path than undergraduate trends. Although some graduate schools accepted women on the very campuses that refused them as undergraduates (e.g., Princeton and Yale), women's overall ability to enter the professions was limited by cultural expectations. As historian Patricia Albjerg Graham noted,

"The twentieth century female virtues were seriously at odds with a career."[48] While the public grew increasingly comfortable with females as college students, envisioning them as professional equals conflicted with images of both the American woman and the American scholar.

By the time of World War II, women had made steady advances into graduate schools, establishing a foothold on the collegiate faculty. In the late nineteenth century, women had pushed American universities to open graduate training to them; and many women had pursued doctorates in Europe because of U.S. inhospitality. Once American graduate schools opened, women made slow but steady progress (Table 2.1). They earned more than one-third of master's degrees by the start of World War II; and during the war, with many male students absent, women earned up to 57 percent of these degrees. Doctoral degree attainment was not quite as dramatic. Nevertheless, women earned 13 percent of the Ph.D.s at the start of the war, and as their wartime studies culminated, their share of doctorates rose to nearly one in five by 1946. By 1948, however, the adverse effects of veterans' funding showed on women. In two years, female master's candidates dropped from half to less than one-third of the total, and women's doctorates began a slide to less than one-tenth of all degrees earned, a low continuing almost all through the 1950s.

Because not all collegiate teaching posts required the doctorate, women held faculty jobs in higher proportions than their share of the Ph.D. population. For most of mid-century, women held just over one-quarter of collegiate jobs; by the start of World War II, they held 27 percent of all teaching posts and gained a few points during the war. However, the decline of women in graduate school during the 1950s affected their ability to move into academe and other professions. Just at the time when higher education expanded, in the 1950s and the 1960s, fewer women were positioned to take advantage of the growth. Numbers tell one side of the story: women constituted only 22 percent of all full-time faculty in 1954–55;[49] they had not budged past 22 percent by 1960; and they had grown to only 25 percent by 1970,[50] after two decades of unprecedented collegiate growth. Admittedly, this small advance represents an increase in actual numbers of women entering the professoriat. As with undergraduates, however, the distribution of faculty women across types of institutions shows that they did not markedly benefit from the rise of the research university and were rarely sought after by this increasingly important sector.

The Research Division of the National Education Association (NEA), which had long studied the elementary and secondary teaching force, decided to examine collegiate faculty out of concern for the enormous expansion in higher education. Their 1955 study concluded that "college teaching is not exclusively a man's job," noting that 36 percent of faculty in teachers colleges and 33 percent in the small nonpublic colleges were female. However, by disaggregating the data, the NEA showed where women fared least well: in nonpublic universities, with 13 percent women, and in public universities, with 16 percent. In total, women constituted 21.8 percent of the teaching force, but their participation varied with the prestige level and size of the employing institution.[51]

Large gender differences also appeared in fields of specialization. Women constituted 96 percent of home economics professors and 71 percent of library science teachers, but only .5 percent of engineers and 1.7 percent of law professors. Women found strong representation, although not parity, in physical and health education (38%), general education (36%), and health sciences (32%).[52] In larger universities, women had made few inroads beyond home economics, library science, and education. Two fields, religion and agriculture, were 100 percent male; and engineering, philosophy, and the physical sciences were more than 95 percent male.[53]

Surveying the changing scene, NEA argued for recruiting women as new faculty. Employing the familiar "womanpower" theme, the study enumerated the difficult issues facing higher education planners: enrollment was rising precipitously; the present teacher corps could not meet increased demand; the weak group of newly available teachers tended to "pull down rather than to upgrade the average level of preparation"; and a full quarter of current teachers were over age 52, adding replenishment needs to expanding enrollment demands. Challenging current assumptions about the teaching force, NEA suggested that women might fill some of the gaps.[54]

NEA repeated its study biennially for several cycles, and in 1959 queried whether women had joined higher education's new recruits. The results were not encouraging. From 1953 to 1959 the percentage of women among newly employed college teachers moved only from 23.5 percent to 25.2 percent.[55] Registering some surprise, the researchers reminded readers that women had long proved themselves capable scholars and teachers, noting that one-half of high school teachers and one-fourth of college teachers had always carried their load "in able fashion." Yet, the authors concluded, "there is no unanimity of opinion" on the use of women as resources. One question had asked employers if they might recruit women for short-staffed fields. A substantial portion (28%) felt that women should be considered for any field, especially social sciences, English, mathematics, and foreign languages. However, 23 percent said that women could fill no shortages on their campuses.[56]

The NEA reports contrast sharply with two contemporaneous studies that ignored women as significant academic resources. A 1959 Office of Education study examined recruiting practices at nearly two thousand institutions, outlining twenty-one techniques used to expand the teaching pool. Choices included employing faculty who were retired, less-qualified, or part-time; sharing jobs among institutions; raising faculty's retirement age, salaries, ranks, or fringe benefits; enlarging individual courses; or reducing the overall number of courses. However, the report never suggested that employing women could help the situation and never inquired about institutional recruitment of females. A short note indicated that eight schools hired "professors' wives," but that these women were not eligible for tenure and worked more cheaply than new recruits.[57]

The study's single positive reference to women came from the president of a small women's college, who explained how he found no trouble staffing his institution with female faculty: "We pay not less than $5,000, with the schedule rising to $10,000 at step rates of approximately $300 per annum. We have a tenure and retirement plan. Our faculty members average 14 hours per week, with l full day or 2 consecutive half-days off during every 5–day week (we have no Saturday classes). We have had no faculty change—except for additions, death, or retirement for 5 years. Meanwhile, we receive more than 200 applications yearly from instructors to full professors from as many major as minor colleges."[58]

Another study of faculty hiring was openly negative about women's academic career opportunities. Theodore Caplow and Reese McGee's *The Academic Marketplace* became a classic for its analysis of the market's operation. In terms of women, however, the interpretation was discouraging, finding female faculty to be mere ciphers, or even abnormalities, in their attempts to join the academic guild. In demonstrating how academic recruitment worked, particularly in tight times, Caplow and McGee explained why decision makers were likely to avoid or ignore women:

> [W]omen tend to be discriminated against in the academic profession, not because they have low prestige but because they are outside the prestige system entirely and for this reason are of no use to a department in future recruitment.
>
> With the exception of a few disciplines which enjoy the privilege of hiring in a truly international market (Spanish studies, for example), the importation of scholars from abroad is a sign of a very tight market in a specialty. The major universities may seek men from abroad before they will seek them from the minor league at home. Failing to discover a candidate

to their taste in a foreign land, they may decide not to hire at all; or they may even hire a woman, who, being outside the prestige system, cannot hurt them. Not even as a last resort will they recruit from institutions with prestige levels much below their own.[59]

Because of the market's focus on prestige, the authors noted that "women scholars are not taken seriously and cannot look forward to a normal professional career." And the reason was beyond the scope of academe to repair: "This bias is part of the much larger pattern which determines the utilization of women in our economy. It is not peculiar to the academic world, but it does blight the prospects of female scholars."[60]

Caplow and McGee never claimed that the way the market *did* operate was the way it *should* operate; their goal was merely to explain it. In fact, they criticized the market's effect on the flexibility and enhancement of higher education. In a 2001 reissue of their work, the authors acknowledged that subsequent changes in the academic marketplace—particularly the influence of federal legislation and more open processes—had resulted in greater representation by women and people of color on collegiate faculties.[61] They also attributed the longer-term change to increased willingness by elite universities to hire more widely, including bringing as faculty women who had earned degrees on their campuses. In the postwar era, however, at the very time that research universities were growing in prominence and the prestige hierarchy was solidifying, marketplace preferences often excluded women as both students and faculty.[62] Women's overall presence as faculty held steady in the postwar era, but their movement into new areas of institutional prestige, strength, and influence was negligible.

WOMEN'S EXPERIENCE AS STUDENTS AND FACULTY: NOT A MONOLITHIC VIEW

Women's uneven distribution across types of institutions suggests that not all women experienced college and graduate school the same way; not every female entered college with the same expectations. The greatest range appeared among undergraduates, as earning the bachelor's degree became more commonplace for women. Although popular literature highlighted socially oriented college "coeds" sharing campuses with men they viewed as potential marriage partners, collegiate women actually employed a range of approaches to schooling—a variety that has been termed the "subcultures" of higher education.[63] A closer look at how postwar women approached college complements and enhances the quantitative analysis.

In *The Feminine Mystique,* Betty Friedan offered an intriguing—if intentionally overdrawn—view of the 1950s college woman. By portraying vacuousness among contemporary students, Friedan hoped to shock readers into angry protest against the devolution of women's ambitions. Friedan decried the effect of the domestic ideology (her "feminine mystique") on college women, causing them to drop out before completing college. She cited a study of Vassar students which found that "strong commitment to an activity or career other than that of housewife is rare." At her alma mater, Smith College, Friedan saw her worst fears confirmed by professors resorting to tricks to grab students' attention and by her chats with students who explained that "you learn freshman year to turn up your nose at the library." Friedan found these students flocking to courses like "Family Living," resisting majors that appeared too intellectual, and focusing on dating and sorority life. Fearing celibate futures, they especially worried that overinvestment in scholarship might result in the life chosen by their professors. One student explained why she abandoned an honors program in history: "Suddenly, I was afraid of what would happen. I wanted to lead a rich full life. I want to marry, have children, have a nice house. Suddenly I felt, what am I beating my brains out for?"[64]

Friedan, however, ignored a positive aspect to students' more social approach to college life. These students supported campus extracurricular activities such as student government, continuing an old tradition of collegiate women working to create and sustain rules of self-conduct.[65] At the University of Kansas, for instance, the Associated Women Students assisted the dean in promulgating rules and adjudicating lapses.[66] On coeducational campuses, they staffed student newspapers and women's athletic teams. Although some women shunned intensive intellectual participation, they also demonstrated a shifting, broader use of college in an era moving toward mass higher education.

Another group of students were distanced from this socially oriented life, sometimes by their own choice (a greater scholarly temperament) and sometimes involuntarily (through religious, racial, or ethnic difference). Havemann and West, studying nearly 10,000 college graduates, noted Catholic students' lesser likelihood of marrying shortly after college. Whereas nearly 70 percent of Protestant graduates had eventually married, only 52 percent of Catholics had done so, whether they attended non-sectarian or Catholic campuses.[67]

Both religion and ethnicity affected Jewish students. Sociologist Pepper Schwartz recalled her discomfort during an alumni admissions interview for the University of Pennsylvania: "He was extremely wealthy, and he received me in the paneled study of his home on Lake Shore Drive along Chicago's gold coast.

He radiated old money (to which new money has a profound attraction and re-
pulsion), and I suddenly felt very Jewish, very nouveau riche, too made up, and
generally unworthy. He evidently thought so, too. And I felt discounted and shut
out during the entire interview."[68]

Although rebellious college students seem more a feature of the 1960s, the
postwar era featured a small but growing group of nonconformists. These rebels joined civil rights protests, and many responded to new currents in the arts
such as Beat poetry, folk music, and abstract painting. Sociologist Wini Breines
traced the experience of Beat students in what she termed "the other Fifties."
Although women were not readily welcomed into the Beat circle, many turned
there to differentiate their dress, speech, attitude, and lifestyle. Beat aficionado
Joyce Johnson described her college life at Barnard in the 1950s: "Moving back
and forth between antithetical worlds separated by subway rides, I never fully
was what I seemed or tried to be. I had the feeling that I was playing hooky
all the time, not from school, but from the person represented by my bland
outward appearance.[69]

Perhaps the most conspicuous nonconformists were African American wom-
en who desegregated Southern white campuses in the late 1950s and early 1960s.
Women were often picked to challenge barriers in hopes that their femininity
would lessen the shock and mitigate the violence. Autherine Lucy and Pollie Ann
Myers sued to integrate the University of Alabama in 1952, successfully taking
their case to the U.S. Supreme Court. Lucy finally entered the university in 1956,
although repeated campus protests made the school uncomfortable and even
dangerous for her. Alabama administrators suspended Lucy "for her own protection." After she sued to gain readmission, Lucy was expelled by the trustees "for
libeling the university's intentions."[70]

Even when admitted to campuses, black women found numerous social
barriers. Joanne Smart Drane and Bettye Davis Tillman were the first African
American women to integrate the Woman's College of North Carolina. Since
mixed housing was a major administrative worry, the two students were assigned
an entire wing of a women's dormitory, with the rest of the floor vacant. Tillman
later joked that she "often wondered how many white girls were denied on-campus housing that year because two black girls had been given an entire section
of a dorm."[71]

By the time women reached graduate school, they exhibited fewer behavioral
differences. Women choosing graduate work had already committed themselves
to intense study and were less likely to pursue rebellion. But, whether or not they
chose to be outsiders, women graduate students and faculty often found them-

selves treated as such. Sociologist Schwartz, who constantly felt her class and religious differences at college, realized that gender transcended these characteristics once she started graduate school at Yale: "Yale was virtually all male at the time; there were no undergraduate women and relatively few women graduate students or faculty. At first it was exhilarating to be one of the only women on the street. That experience became less sweet, however, when it became clear that a woman had to fight to be a first-class citizen of the university."[72]

Carolyn Heilbrun, later a full professor of literature at Columbia, found in graduate school no clear place for women scholars and no real models. Women professors who had succeeded seemed "honorary men; they presented themselves and their ideas in male attire." Eschewing the "half-life" of such women, Heilbrun found models in male professors who constituted the real "union of thinkers." They allowed her briefly into this group while she was a student but offered no conception of (or interest in) how she might continue her intellectual life after graduation. Before the women's movement, Heilbrun asserted, her only option was the "romance"—not the reality—of vocation.[73]

As Patricia Graham analyzed and Carolyn Heilbrun corroborated, the characteristics valued in postwar women rarely matched those required of professionals or scholars.[74] Many of the academic women interviewed by sociologist Jessie Bernard confirmed others' discomfort in the "role confusion" of seeing a woman in an unfamiliar job. She quoted a male professor discussing his female colleague: "There she stands. A beautiful woman. Above her neck she is talking about the most abstruse subject. From the neck down her body is saying something altogether different. She wears good clothes. They show her body off to good advantage. And yet she acts as though she were completely unconscious of it. She acts as though she were a man, like the dog who thinks he is a human being."[75] Although more blatant than most, this man's discomfort likely explains the treatment and lack of acceptance many women found as graduate students and professionals. Historian Margaret Rossiter cumulated the negative graduate school experiences of several women who pursued postwar academic careers:

> Leona Marshall Libby, for example, decided to work with someone other than the University of Chicago's great Nobelist James E. Frank after he informed her that since she was a woman, she would never amount to much in science, and that like many Jews, she would starve to death! Archaeologist Emily Vermeule left Radcliffe Graduate School for Bryn Mawr after one year because six or seven of the thirty-five or forty faculty members in her department at Harvard did not talk to the women students and the library was very hard to use. When marine biologist Ruth Dixon

Turner's professors at Cornell were so overwhelmed by veterans in the late 1940s that they had no time for her, she transferred to Radcliffe, partly because she already worked in a museum at Harvard.[76]

Women's experience as faculty differed by field, by department, by type of institution, and, of course, by individual. Both Jessie Bernard and Bernice Cronkhite of Radcliffe College peppered their studies of academic women with quotations by those who had experienced both positive and negative reactions. Generally, women teaching at all-female colleges reported more positive relationships with colleagues and administrators, although some complained that promotions were slower for women, even in these settings. One woman flatly stated, "Most women's colleges prefer men to women on their faculties."[77] At the same time, both authors found women at coeducational schools who reported good support for their work.

In the end, many faculty women remained ambivalent or resigned about the continuing ambiguities of their situation. Said one full professor: "I have been considered for positions for which men were also considered. In one case I received the appointment and in the other case the man did. In general I have not found being a woman presented as great obstacles as I expected, either in my professional work or in my work in the Church. It has, of course, been an advantage in my work as Dean in a woman's college though it has closed the academic deanship in anything other than a woman's college."[78]

RESPONSES TO WOMEN'S EDUCATIONAL STATUS

The irrelevance of women to many of the postwar changes relegated their interests to a small group who, as educators, held direct responsibility for women's training, or who, as analysts, studied women's advanced training and workforce performance. Three types of responses characterized their analyses of women's postwar higher education: *economic utilitarians* highlighted the "pipeline" implications of women's reduced attendance, and pushed for wider professional support; *cultural conformists* blamed an inappropriate curriculum for women's lack of collegiate interest, and advocated for domestically-oriented education; and *equity-based planners* argued from a concern with equal opportunity, advancing the need for balance in women's curriculum, lives, and thinking. This complex trio of responses indicates the variety of thinking about women's educational and career options in the early postwar period.

Economic Utilitarians

This first group of researchers, the economic utilitarians, analyzed women's contributions to the labor market and encouraged them to pursue careers. What distinguished these analysts was a focus on women as potential economic resources equal to men. They rarely apologized for women's differences, but instead, they outlined their contributions, analyzed the differences in women's career choices and pathways, called attention to discrimination when they saw it, and supported labor market accommodations to women's family needs.

Along with the NEA's work on women faculty, the most prominent economic utilitarian advocacy appeared in Dael Wolfle's *America's Resources of Specialized Talent*, in Marguerite Zapoleon's reports as special assistant in the U.S. Women's Bureau, and in the NMC's *Womanpower*.[79] All of these efforts highlighted the nature of women's economic contributions.

Wolfle directed the Commission on Human Resources and Advanced Training for the Conference Board of Associated Research Councils. This postwar program, funded by the Rockefeller Foundation, examined the future of the nation's specialized professional talent—both men's and women's. Understanding the significance of the growth in higher education, Wolfle advocated for building university capacity that would train scientists and other professionals. He presented data on men's and women's participation in the labor force, in advanced training, and in use of graduate education. Recognizing that women had a lower employment rate even after earning advanced degrees, Wolfle declined to blame women for their choices or accuse them of squandering their training. Instead, he analyzed what hindered women, first in their decisions to pursue advanced training, and later in their movement through careers. Stressing that many manpower analysts posed the wrong questions, he explained how his study included female and minority professionals: "Instead of asking *How many jobs are there for scientists?* it asks *How much scientific talent is not being utilized?*"[80]

Wolfle examined characteristics influencing college-going, some direct and others more tangential. Issues directly connected to college choice included the student's "mental ability," record of school success, available resources, and motivation. Indirectly important were the student's gender, "cultural background" (social class), geographic location, and ethnic and religious background. Wolfle demonstrated that girls matched boys in basic mental abilities, but that as they proceeded up the educational ladder, more boys than girls of all intellectual levels stayed in school; fewer girls even attempted advanced education.

Because of his focus on "specialized talent," Wolfle analyzed the top-level group of high school students—the nation's highest scorers on the Army General Classification Test. Of this top group, he found that girls and boys finished high school in about the same numbers, "but thereafter a large sex difference appears. Nearly two-thirds of the boys enter college and 55 percent graduate. But only 42 percent of the girls enter college and only 37 percent graduate" (182). Following this group into the doctoral level, Wolfle found that "one in 30 [top-scoring men] receives a Ph.D.: of women of equal ability, only one in 300 receives that degree" (184). The very brightest female students were lagging behind men.

In analyzing possible discrimination, Wolfle attended more to job market concerns than to barriers in the academic world (such as a lack of fellowships), wondering whether women's expectations of professional pathways inhibited them from investing in advanced training. He cited a 1950 Women's Bureau study of men's and women's hopes for their professional situations five years hence. Opportunity for advancement was the number one priority for men, but only the fifth for women. Women sought "steady work, comfortable working conditions, good working companions, and good bosses" (234–35). Although such responses did not bode well for women's professional investment, Wolfle acknowledged their realism in making these choices: "Perhaps the evidence should not be accepted at face value. Women are handicapped in many lines of work. They know it. Their attitudes as expressed in such studies as those cited may constitute a defensive reaction against hard reality, and not a reflection of the behavior which might be expected if there were no sex discrimination in the labor market" (256).

Wolfle's specific suggestions for supporting women and minorities turned to those that had offered increased flexibility during the war, including available child care, higher salaries, and special training opportunities. His clearest message was that female scholars were being overlooked as potential specialists and that continued prejudicial assumptions about their performance could affect the country's economic opportunities.

Marguerite Zapoleon, a longtime Women's Bureau analyst trained in both engineering and economics, matched Wolfle's approach of providing data about women's participation and then encouraging more women to pursue advanced training and professional work. After the war, Zapoleon published a series of reports on women's prospects in various professional fields, including medicine, health service, social work, general science, chemistry, and biology.[81] A frequent speaker and contributor to women's educational conferences throughout the 1950s, Zapoleon assured listeners that no conflict need exist between marriage and career. Her statistics emphasized the number of women choosing to work at various points in their lives: after graduation and before marriage; before children arrived; after children's birth, perhaps part-time; or after children had grown. She also demonstrated a path of continuous professional work by many women graduates, carefully disaggregating the female work force.

Zapoleon focused less on job-market discrimination than on other elements in women's lives that could affect their own and their families' satisfaction. Expressing confidence in her data, she explained: "The statistics and opinions given so far should have exploded the marriage-career myth. But if it still appears plausible, I am willing to leave it to be destroyed by individual observations and experience. I am certain it is utterly safe and not at all contradictory for young women to continue to prepare themselves for the industries of this age and for marriage."[82]

Unlike Wolfle, who often took a neutral stance on how best to increase the pool of specialized talent, the authors of the NMC report *Womanpower* mirrored Zapoleon's approach of explicitly advocating for women. They connected women's historical involvement in education to their present dilemmas. Thus, *Womanpower* included a section summarizing past resistance to women's college-going, from worries over their physical stamina to challenges about their mental capacity. *Womanpower* noted women's tendency to cluster in traditional fields like education, home economics, and nursing, and agreed with Wolfle's findings that bright girls declined college in disproportionate numbers: "Young women probably account for about 3/5 of those who have the ability to graduate from college but do not, and for slightly over half of those who could obtain a doctoral degree but do not."[83]

Although Wolfle absented himself from the era's most popular educational debate—over the best curriculum for women—*Womanpower* tackled the question of "whether higher education should serve primarily the needs and interests of women as homemakers, as workers, or as citizens." With a sentiment that appeared regularly in contemporary educational treatises, *Womanpower* asked: "Should the primary emphasis in the college education of women be given to preparing them for adult responsibilities and functions which essentially differ from or resemble those of men?"[84] Its answer—which became the litmus test of contemporary educational analysis—was that, although a liberal education was probably best overall, the wide variety of choices facing women made any single approach self-defeating. Ultimately, economic utilitarians sought broad liberal education to complement and fortify women's training for the job market.

Cultural Conformists

Unlike economic utilitarians seeking to expand women's labor market participation, cultural conformist analysts believed that the most important feature of women's education—at least on the undergraduate level—was a suitable curriculum. They worried less about how women might contribute their resources to nontraditional professions and more about how such specialization could threaten their roles as wives and mothers. Although subsequent scholarship has often painted these analysts as anti-feminist martinets desperate to keep women in antiquated roles, they were responding to prevalent ideologies by trying to create an attractive collegiate alternative to early marriage.

In actuality, the widespread concern over women's apparent exodus from college was overblown. Friedan, for example, repeatedly said that only 37 percent of 1950s women students were finishing their bachelor's degree, suggesting that this meager success rate resulted from the cumulative effect of the feminine mystique.[85] In fact, this statistic came from Wolfle's examination of the top-level group of men and women undergraduates.[86] Other studies showed that the overall college attrition rate did not appreciably worsen during the 1950s, either for men or for women. John Summerskill summarized extant knowledge about collegiate dropouts in 1962, noting that, overall, approximately half of all students who entered American colleges—men and women—left before completing the bachelor's degree, and that furthermore, this figure had long been stable. Recognizing that "attrition" can constitute a number of measures (those who leave higher education permanently, those who leave for just a year, or those who graduate within four years or some other period), Summerskill summarized: "American colleges lose, on the average, approximately half their students in the four years after matriculation. Some 40% of college students graduate on schedule and, in addition, approximately 20% graduate at some college, some day. These have been the facts for several decades in American higher education."[87]

Examining factors associated with dropping out, Summerskill noted that gender played little part. He cited a 1957 nationwide study finding attrition rates of 61 percent for men and 59 percent for women; other studies had found few attrition differences at men's, women's, or coeducational schools. However, Summerskill did focus on the issue of most concern to cultural conformists: women's apparent predilection to drop out for marriage. He explained that the female collegiate population was more selective to begin with, since fewer women than men begin college and those who do were "characterized by better grades and less academic failure." The similar attrition rates meant, then, that more capable women were leaving college, a fact matching Wolfle's findings for the top student group.[88]

However, anecdotal evidence abounded that women were abandoning higher education in order to marry, a concern exacerbated by the number of women who lamented the irrelevancy of college training to their post-college lives as wives and mothers. Lynn White Jr., the Mills College president who best captured the cultural conformist analysis in his book *Educating Our Daughters*, organized his entire analysis around such a complaint. He opened a chapter on "The Frustrations of Feminism" thus: "On my desk lies a letter from a young mother a few years out of college: 'I have come to realize that I was educated to be a successful man and now must learn by myself how to be a successful woman.' The basic irrelevance of much of what passes as women's education in America could not be more compactly phrased."[89]

White began from a different vantage point than the economic utilitarians. Where they saw a positive, linear increase in women's workforce participation, White saw deep dissatisfaction around women's use of collegiate education. In addition to the letters and comments he had received, White cited a 1946 poll by *Fortune* magazine in which men and women were asked whether they would like to be born again as the same sex. Whereas 90 percent of men said yes, only one-third of women would wish to be born female.[90]

Ernest Havemann and Patricia Salter West also focused on women's dissatisfaction with collegiate training. Havemann, a former journalist with *Time* magazine, and West, an analyst with Columbia's Bureau of Applied Social Research, popularized data gathered by the Bureau in a *Time*-sponsored study, *They Went To College*. Their breezy analysis examined women's lives after graduation. In sections devoted specifically to "former coeds,"[91] Havemann and West offered several facts about collegiate women: they had disproportionately majored in the humanities but were more recently choosing varied majors; parents of more women than men supported their children through college; most women professionals were schoolteachers; jobs for women tended to cluster in low-paying fields; and women overall earned considerably less than men.

Havemann and West's main interest was the relationship of college to graduates' later lives, especially the connection to marriage and motherhood. Although much of their analysis focused on "working wives" (19 percent of the total group) and unmarried "career women" (another 31 percent), the authors took as a benchmark of success—for both men and women—the cumulative achievement of getting married, staying married, having children, and purchasing a home. They created a rating scale to judge this success, starting from a possible high of 7 points, which "represents the ideal family situation: married to the original spouse, owing a house and having three children or more." Twenty-three percent of men achieved this level, but only 12 percent of women. More lopsided, however, were women's scores at the scale's low end, where 2 points or less meant "practically no family success at all; the majority with this score have never married or have made one attempt never repeated, which ended in divorce or separation." Only 6 percent of men wallowed here, but a full 34 percent of women did. Such results led the authors to conclude: "For many coeds, it would appear, college amounts to an education for spinsterhood."[92]

Havemann and West did note, however, that the relationship of "spinsterhood" to college was waning over time; the oldest college grads were the ones least likely to have married. In addition, they asked respondents about overall satisfaction with how college had prepared them for life. In chapters filled with testimonials from men and women about how they used collegiate training, the authors concluded that 58 percent of women (including full-time homemakers) found college helped them "a lot" in their current work, and only 4 percent said it had not helped at all. Yet the number of critical women graduates led the authors to conclude that "college life is a poor investment for a very considerable number of students."[93]

Such commentary fueled cultural conformists' worry that women were deeply unhappy. Some writers followed the Freudian analysis advanced by Farnham and Lundberg, who argued in *Modern Woman: The Lost Sex* that women pursuing professional lives at the expense of families were destined for unhappiness.[94] However, Farnham and Lundberg represented the extreme end of the conformist viewpoint, and subsequent treatment of this collection of work as representative has skewed understanding of this position. White, for example, argued that his thinking came from deep appreciation of women and their role in contemporary society, not from any denigration of their contributions. He maintained that modern civilization had undermined women's self-respect by inappropriately encouraging them to hold the same values as men, thereby not recognizing women's special attributes. Foreshadowing later debates over whether women should be treated the same or differently than men, White advocated for recognizing women's unique social and psychological skills.

The cultural conformists faulted an unsuitable curriculum for women's dissatisfaction. In fact, similar concern over inappropriate curricula had occurred at other times in educational history. In the early twentieth century, educators had decided that "the boy problem" of fewer boys than girls graduating from high school resulted from a curriculum unappealing to males. These educators crafted a report called the Cardinal Principles of Secondary Education, which reorganized schooling, not around academic concerns, but rather on health, command of fundamental processes, worthy home-membership, vocation, civic education, worthy use of leisure, and ethical character.[95] Although critics argued that this reorientation made high school less intellectual, advocates averred that the wider variety of students attending high school (including many immigrants) required a different approach to schooling. Offering curricula that seemed better suited to these students' futures was, they argued, more "democratic."

This debate between traditional studies and more practical curricula had characterized American education since the mid-nineteenth-century rise of common schooling. Generally, when smaller, homogeneous populations attended school, an academic or traditional curriculum was noncontroversial. But when more than 60 percent of the age cohort was graduating from high school (as it was by the 1950s), or when one-third attended college (as it did in the 1960s), institutions needed to do more than prepare all students for the same economic future.[96]

Just as a "life adjustment" curriculum surfaced in the high schools after World War II, the idea of adjusting collegiate women to their family-oriented role became the main concern of some college educators.[97] White laid out three objectives for a proper female curriculum: (1) to prepare women to meet the crisis of their twenties (whether to marry) as well as the crisis of their forties (how to rejoin the labor force or civic world); (2) to understand the situation they faced in modern society and help them make necessary changes; and (3) to create an atmosphere that valued and respected women for their differences.[98]

Some cultural conformists like White focused on undergraduate schooling; others studied graduate school and women's subsequent professional careers. These researchers focused on three issues: explaining women's apparent lesser success as graduate students and faculty (measured by rank, productivity, and salary); determining whether discrimination really operated against women; and suggesting what might improve their situation.

Two studies, written almost a decade apart by well-known academic women, were disheartening. Bernice Cronkhite, dean of the Radcliffe Graduate School of Arts and Sciences, was primary author of a 1956 report by the Radcliffe Committee on Graduate Education for Women, summarizing the experiences of several hundred holders of Radcliffe Ph.D.s.[99] Eight years later, in *Academic Women*, sociologist Jessie Bernard of Pennsylvania State University used quantitative and qualitative data to examine women's status in the collegiate world.[100] Both studies—important because of their rare focus on academic women—initially had difficulty interpreting their findings that women were unproductive and unsatisfied. Both Cronkhite and Bernard doubted the operation of widespread discrimination and ultimately faulted women for many of their career difficulties. They wondered about women's poor research productivity, generally placing them on the fringes of academic life.

Although Cronkhite studied just one institution, Radcliffe was important because it had graduated more women doctorates (over 500) than any school in the country except Columbia University and the University of Chicago and because its connection with Harvard suggested a ready audience for Cronkhite's findings. The study was not encouraging about the long-term success of Radcliffe doctorate-holders. Having polled women who graduated since the school began awarding the Ph.D. in 1902, the study included both women new to academe and longtime participants. Statistics showed that each year only about 10 percent of enrolled women finished the doctorate. Overall completion rates were strongest in astronomy, biology, and economics (more than 10 percent), but low in classics, philosophy, and mathematics (less than 6 percent).[101] Furthermore, women were taking longer to finish, an average of six years among the most recent classes.

Cronkhite reported women's own comments about their experiences, including whether discrimination had affected their careers. The group most satisfied were full professors, the vast majority of whom worked in women's colleges. Yet half reported encountering obstacles there, most commonly slower promotions and lower pay than men. As the self-reports moved from associate to assistant professors, and then to instructors and part-timers, dissatisfaction rose. Cronkhite compared full and associate professors: "The older women [full professors] are much more likely to express a feeling of satisfaction in their work for its own sake, a joy in cultivating their professional gardens regardless of rewards in terms of academic recognition. But then, the full professor is older, possibly more mellow, and she may have lost sight of her earlier obstacles once she has scaled the academic heights. The associate professor is more likely to express a sense of discrimination, and with bitterness" (29).

Single academic women seemed the most disaffected. Cronkhite noted their "defensiveness" and "insecurity," worrying that they "show a severe psychological handicap for the single academic woman" (51). For married women, whom Cronkhite, like others, saw as the wave of the future, the keys to success included domestic help, supportive husbands, and a favorable geographic setting.

The report found one positive element in women's pedagogical accomplishments: "They give the impression of having performed their obligation as teachers with devotion and competence." However, women's publication records paled in comparison to that of men of similar age and rank, and Cronkhite concluded that "the record of their work in publication does not suggest that they work twice as hard, or even as hard, as male competitors" (34).

In analyzing women's lower productivity and satisfaction, Cronkhite suggested that some of the fault was self-imposed: "These women's own comments seem to reflect a certain pervading consciousness of their position as women, a defensiveness which probably constitutes a psychological impediment to full enjoyment of their work and perhaps to major achievement in it" (34). Although she acknowledged some job market discrimination against women, Cronkhite felt that dwelling on disadvantages would distract efforts that could more profitably go toward research: "No one can do first-rate work, a lot of it and over a long period of time, if she is obsessed or seriously bothered with problems of status and discrimination" (51).

Like many cultural conformists, Cronkhite advocated individual rather than collective responses for women, arguing that harder work by women faculty would solve the problem. Unlike economic utilitarians, she did not propose the creation of more flexible policies for expanding the pool of potential faculty. Instead, she highlighted her work as Radcliffe's dean in reducing the number of part-time students, arguing that such approaches brought only the best students. Ultimately, she explained, the "solution is for women to do work of such high quality that no question of 'competition' arises. It would take a very prejudiced anti-feminist to refuse to employ, on the ground of sex, a woman who has demonstrated ability and achievement clearly superior to that of the men available" (108).

One of only two female professors of sociology teaching at a major university, Jessie Bernard followed Cronkhite's advice by working harder and ignoring discrimination.[102] Bernard published one of the era's few serious works on academic women. Although she identified with feminism in later decades,[103] in her 1964 book Bernard struggled to understand the issues facing women colleagues, especially the differences between successful female scholars and those she called "fringe" academics. Bernard felt that women often made choices and followed interests that kept them peripheral, but she rarely acknowledged that socialization influenced such choices. For her, "rank and file" women filled an important role in academe, even if their lesser skills and ambition detracted from focus on top-flight female scholars.

Bernard, believing that women made their own circumstances, rejected discrimination as a cause for their lesser academic roles and weaker research production.[104] She doubted that prejudice could explain the decline in female faculty, noting that women's colleges and teachers colleges were experiencing the greatest drops, an analysis that ignored the fact that these institutions, from the 1930s onward, often replaced women teachers with men in an effort to "upgrade."[105] Bernard concluded that "It was not a situation in which men were slamming the doors of academia in the faces of eager, ambitious women scholars but rather one in which, despite the lures of fellowships, women turned their backs and ran to rock the cradle.[106]

Explaining female career trajectories, Bernard concluded that the majority of women—including those with long service in academe—preferred less competitive situations. "The modal picture of the academic woman that emerges," she noted, "is of a very bright person so far as test-intelligence is concerned, but compliant rather than aggressive" (83). By temperament, most women preferred to teach rather than write, and to serve as "academic mothers" to their students rather than as research advisors. Bernard suggested that many women pursued the doctorate less as "the result of a decision and much more the result of drift" (59). Women were lulled by early success in school, but acted out of compliance rather than ambition.

Although trained as a sociologist, Bernard turned to a biological explanation for women's choices:

> The brains of men and women are packaged in different containers. The brain packaged in a woman's body has different muscular and glandular equipment at its disposal; it is sensitized to different kinds of stimuli; it is protected from exposure to certain other kinds of stimuli. Even though there were originally no intrinsic differences between it and a brain packaged in a man's body, it inevitably becomes different because of its different packaging, and this quite independent of cultural or social factors. (168)

Bernard recognized that some women avoided the trap of compliance; these she labeled "professionals" in contrast to the "fringe benefit" women in lesser academic posts. Her analysis of the fringe role proved insightful, outlining a situation where, as everyone recognized, colleges saved money and lessened their long-term commitment by employing women as part-time teachers, research associates, and even volunteers rather than providing full-time, tenure-track posts. However, in an environment valuing research universities, such choices limited women's long-term contribution.

Bernard acknowledged that marriage restricted women's options for mobility and job choice. With anti-nepotism rules frequently forbidding employment of husbands and wives on the same campus, many women settled for associate positions. Or, like Beth Isaacs in the Ginzberg and Yohalem study, they moved to accommodate a husband's career, whether or not something suitable appeared for the wife.

Bernard ended with stories of three married academic women who had created compatible and productive research and teaching careers. She analyzed factors leading to their success as marrying a supportive academic husband and finding complementary research areas. Two couples planned parallel research agendas to avoid competing. Household help, including from husbands, enabled these women to remain professionally active after their children's birth. She also highlighted one woman's uncanny skill of being able to write amid domestic commotion.

Equity-Based Planners

Whether examining women's undergraduate experience or their subsequent professional lives, cultural conformists valued fit and continuity for educated women. Equity-based planners, on the other hand, suggested the power of "productive discontinuity."[107] These educators valued the emancipatory aspects of education, trusting liberal education to support students in pursuing something new. They advised women to prepare for a variety of roles, envisioning combinations of marriage, work, motherhood, and continuing education. While acknowledging the vital role of the home, they advocated the integration of domestic futures with other goals.

Even these observers, however, differed over how women should prepare for and combine future choices. Some, like President Harold Taylor of Sarah Lawrence College and David Riesman of Harvard, shied away from specific advice, believing that liberal education itself would provide guidance.[108] Others, including Vassar's Mabel Newcomer, were more specific, alerting women to the sequential nature of their lives: while a career might not suit the early married years, it might be feasible as children grew.[109] Another group disaggregated the population of college women, recognizing that different advice suited different situations. State university dean Kate Hevner Mueller was one of few to acknowledge that socioeconomic differences affected women's choices and that many students could benefit from vocational education.[110] Jeanne Noble, an African American analyst, recognized differences between black and white collegiate populations, emphasizing black women's longstanding work balancing vocational with liberal training.[111] Mirra Komarovsky used a sociological approach to acknowledge the impact of societal demands on individual choices.[112] At the far end of the continuum and latest in her analysis, was Betty Friedan, who challenged much of what she viewed as too-timid advice and encouraged women from their earliest college years to prepare themselves for continuous professional lives.[113]

Taylor and Riesman took the most philosophical and least practical approach to women's education, decrying what they saw as narrow prescriptions from both the economic utilitarians and the cultural conformists. As Taylor proclaimed, "The true purpose of education is to develop one's inner self and one's capacities to serve the needs of other people." Like fellow president Lynn White, Taylor denounced the tendency of women's colleges to accept "the external standards of competition and competitive success as a substitute for deep personal satisfaction on the part of the student in the work she is doing." The problem for women, as Taylor analyzed, was that they could not know in their early college years how their lives would develop in terms of service to others. Calling on the patriotic ideology, Taylor argued that only a deep commitment to national values and one's own beliefs would sustain women and men in the modern world.[114]

David Riesman also decried education that restricted women to current possibilities. He cited vast changes during the two recent wars but also compared women's sense of opportunity to that which African Americans were instigating through the civil rights movement. Riesman explained how educators had long advocated for Booker T. Washington's practical philosophy, aimed at educating black students for the jobs at hand. However, Riesman noted, this approach had actually limited the growth of a black professional class as new opportunities grew. Citing this cautionary tale, Riesman warned educators against restricting students to the "role definitions provided by even such quite loose garments as our sexual and ethnic identities," and argued for an education that prepared students for "discontinuities" in their future lives.[115]

Vassar College economist Mabel Newcomer took a more practical approach, even while supporting liberal education. Her book, *A Century of Higher Education for American Women*, struck a balance between a history of women's education and a plan for its future. Newcomer stressed the historical significance of women having won the right to classical training, implying that current educators had drifted in their planning for women rather than carefully considering students' needs. *A Century of Higher Education* was one of the few books to demonstrate the sharp decline over time in women's academic participation. Newcomer culled statistics and invented creative ways (such as studying marriage announcements in the *New York Times*) to study the progress of college graduates. However, she found it hard to convince contemporaries that women had constituted nearly half of all students in the 1920s; the current situation seemed so natural that many observers questioned her statistics.[116]

Trained as an economist, Newcomer explained that college-going women responded logically to available choices but worried that their decisions limited future opportunities: "Women are now faced with a new handicap of their own choosing—increasingly early marriages and large families" (204). The challenge was getting women—and their parents—to see that options could change over time. Newcomer asserted that "the problem today for women is lack of motivation. The women themselves are not convinced that higher education is as important for them as for the men" (236). This attitude, combined with parents' propensity for under-investing in girls' education, made it much harder for college women to look beyond the idea of schooling primarily as training for homemaking.

Sympathetic to women's situation, Newcomer tried to maximize education for as long as women could persist. Her formula relied on understanding women's life cycle: "Our real concern should be, then, not whether college women will ever use their college education, but whether the women will get the education they need before they marry, in order to bring up their children according to the best advice of the specialists; and then, when the youngest child is in school, to follow the children to school and teach, or to establish themselves in some other profession without too long a period of training" (181). Unlike the course prescribed by most conformists, Newcomer advocated a curricular middle ground where women could get some vocational preparation, some training for life as a civically responsible homemaker, and some liberal education for a personal sense of fulfillment. The ideal plan combined all three.

Newcomer raised the notion of different education for different students but often reverted to her Vassar experience in explicating collegiate women's situation. Kate Hevner Mueller brought a less typical and less elite experience as a longtime state university dean. Mueller's *Educating Women for a Changing World* stands out as a rare book written by a state university practitioner. Aimed at fellow educators as well as parents, Mueller's book had a casual tone that belied her thoughtful analysis of the differences among college women. She cautioned against an oversimplified recommendation of identical education for all. "The first step," she argued, "is to differentiate the sociological layers and the psychological differences of the women for whom these curriculums will be needed."[117] More cognizant than many of the changes produced by mass higher education, Mueller clarified differences not only among students but in jobs available to them. Nearly 50 percent of all women workers would find clerical or service work, leading her to ask, "For how many of these jobs do women need specific training in the schools and colleges?" (75).

Mueller analyzed the varying needs posed by socioeconomic difference and highlighted "Jeffersonian" versus "Jacksonian" philosophies to explain the differential education of the talented and the average. "For the serious and able college woman, as for her counterpart among college men, the campus years are the most significant in her intellectual development," she explained, and they should be filled with strong academic content and professional preparation. But for the "vast majority of students who are not so generously endowed," a curriculum stressing home economics along with basic liberal preparation might be the best plan (140, 143). Mueller did not see this approach as diminishing women's options, but rather, as keeping them flexible during a time of societal role transition. Ultimately, she supported the liberating aspects of education, arguing that "a woman needs an independent spirit much more than an independent income" (283).

Jeanne Noble explored these qualities of independence in a national study of 400 African American women college graduates, *The Negro Woman's College Education*. Her book brought rare attention to black women's education. Unlike educators who viewed the liberal/vocational issue as dichotomous, Noble saw them as appropriate, successfully-paired educational goals for black women.

Writing during an expanding civil rights movement, Noble was sensitive to readers' potential misunderstandings of black collegians. She cited historical reasons for African Americans' high esteem for women's education, recognizing both utilitarian and liberal functions for this population. Given continuing social and economic discrimination, black women much more than white women expected to work and raise families simultaneously rather than sequentially. Noble cited the notion of "working citizen" that characterized the expectation for black women's civic, economic, and cultural contributions. Without denying the importance of job preparation, black leaders insisted that women be more than narrowly focused workers. Noble cited one community leader's explanation: "The whole business of segregation has given the Negro woman—and the Negro in general—a sense of responsibility toward solving community problems. The Negro college has done a good job of this. The difference in the white and Negro sorority is that the Negro sorority feels that it ought to do something for the community."[118]

Noble's utilitarianism differed from "womanpower" analyses by acknowledging black women's frequent lack of choice in whether to work or not. Unlike white collegians, 90 percent of black women indicated that vocational preparation was their main reason for college, and they were supported in these goals by parents and families to a far greater degree than white women. Rather than pursuing a narrow focus on landing a job (the fear of many of the equity-based planners), these black graduates were attuned to combining the facets of their lives. As Noble explained, "Work, family life, and citizenship are their greatest concerns, and they demand of their colleges the kind of education that will contribute to their preparation for effective living in these areas" (66).

Noble was not averse to criticizing black colleges, as well as white schools with large black populations, for addressing only some aspects of students' lives. The tendency for strict discipline that Noble observed in some black colleges struck her as adolescent and disrespectful of students' adulthood. Likewise, she encouraged more flexibility in pushing students into racially integrated experiences as better preparation for the world they would find upon graduation.

Although she keenly recognized the differences affecting black women in postwar American culture, Noble declined to recommend either a distinct "black philosophy of education" or a "women's philosophy of education." She called, instead, for the sort of education for "self-fulfillment" that she found in her subjects' experience: "The ultimate outcome of education as it touches upon the individual's life is to strengthen her freedom to become what she is willing and able to become. It would include a daring to dream as well as to labor, a daring to pursue as well as to conform, a daring above all else to be true to herself, or to strive to realize what trueness to self could mean, what it will involve, and what it will cost" (141).

Mirra Komarovsky agreed with both Noble and Newcomer in recognizing that differences among women might require varied educational approaches. However, as a sociologist, she focused on how societal expectations and mechanisms affected women as a group. Komarovsky felt that women's experiences, especially the contradictions surrounding their collegiate education, offered a barometer of confusions in the wider society. "New goals have emerged without the social machinery for their attainment," she explained.[119] Unlike the black women in Noble's study who had clear expectations for their futures, Komarovsky believed that most American women received inconsistent messages while young: prepare for an economic future, but not at the expense of your family, and not if such preparation makes you seem too smart or too unfeminine. She wryly noted that the "best-adjusted girl" was one who recognized constraints: "[She] is intelligent enough to do well in school but not so brilliant as to get all As; . . . capable but not so . . . in areas relatively new to women; able to stand on her own feet and to earn a living but not so good a living as to compete with men; capable of doing some job well (in case she doesn't marry or otherwise has to work) but not so identified with a profession as to need it for her happiness" (74).

Pointedly disagreeing with both White and Freudian analysts, Komarovsky stressed that women could make healthy choices by balancing work, family life, civic duty, and personal fulfillment. Instead of blaming women when housework proved unsatisfying or when combining work with motherhood became unmanageable, she outlined the psychological, economic, and sociological reasons why such issues confounded postwar women. Yet Komarovsky also worried that students held unrealistic expectations of marriage and family life. Examining transcripts of interviews with married women having trouble balancing home, family, and intellectuality, half of Komarovsky's undergraduate students expressed "indignation" at the women's complaints, calling them "self-pitying, neurotic women" who simply seemed spoiled and uncommitted to family. "The tendency to attribute the housewife's discontent to personal deficiency is widespread," Komarovsky explained (116).

Helping women understand the nature and impact of these societal effects directed Komarovsky's curricular solution. In her approach to home life, Komarovsky resembled the cultural conformists, but she welcomed a home-oriented curriculum only if such education provided "intellectual coherence through its focus upon human relationships within the institutional framework of the family" (217). In her view, educators should treat the family as a social institution, examining modern values and exploring the roots of personal and interpersonal conflicts, an approach that would elevate the "family living" course to a respectable academic enterprise. In Komarovsky's view, pairing this education with preparation for a vocation, whether for immediate or later use, would create a sensible curriculum. Above all, she added, men must be similarly educated so that women did not bear the entire responsibility for balancing work and family. In the end, Komarovsky asserted, "The sense of irrelevancy to life is a mark not of a 'masculine' education but of an *inferior* one" (285).

Writing nearly a full decade after Komarovsky, Noble, and Mueller, and absent their responsibilities as educators, Betty Friedan lost patience with repeated calls for carefully balancing women's collegiate offerings with cultural expectations. Her *Feminine Mystique* was inspired by educational observations—especially her recognition of graduates' dissatisfactions and students' ennui—but was never intended as a curricular response to women's problems. However, the book's final chapter claims education as women's best hope: "The key to the trap is, of course, education. The feminine mystique has made higher education for women seem suspect, unnecessary and even dangerous, but I think that education and only education, has saved, and can continue to save American women from the greater dangers of the feminine mystique."[120]

Friedan rejected a sequential approach to women's lives (calling it "separate layering"), even though she recognized that it might be necessary for women to make choices that varied with their situations. Relying on the idea of layering, she felt, gave both women and educators an "out": rather than educating women for serious work over time, colleges could allow themselves to focus only on the short-term, home-oriented goal. Instead, Friedan argued, women must develop a "life plan" early on: "Educators at every women's college, at every university, junior college, and community college, must see to it that women make a lifetime commitment (call it a "life plan," a "vocation," a "life purpose" if that dirty word *career* has too many celibate connotations) to a field of thought, to work of serious importance to society. They must expect the girl as well as the boy to take some field seriously enough to want to pursue it for life" (336).

Friedan's call for an "educational G.I. Bill" for women, and her plan for six-week summer courses for housewives ultimately seemed rhetorical rather than pragmatic (370–71). In addition, her vision appeared limited to the socioeconomic group of women's college graduates and suburban homemakers with the most options. However, Friedan moved farther than most educators—even equity-based planners—in her call for seeing the universal "core of autonomy" that liberal education offered to collegiate women, and preparing them for serious, committed, and fulfilling lives. For Friedan, higher education had already found the answer for women and men in its strong liberal base; educators and students alike now needed to reaffirm confidence in that training. "I discovered that the critics were half-right," she noted. "Education was dangerous and frustrating—but only when women did not use it" (357).

CONCLUSION

The 1963 publication of *The Feminine Mystique* is often taken as the start of the 1960s women's movement. Indeed, the resurgence of feminist argument, the use of data to confront the status quo, and the challenge to women's lesser participation that marked the new women's movement are all nascent in Friedan's work. However, Friedan was hardly the only thinker raising these concerns in the 1950s and early 1960s. As this review of womanpower analyses, conformist explorations, and equity-based planning suggests, many postwar educators and observers struggled with reconciling women's current situation and their potential. They wondered how to support women's choices without limiting their opportunities.

Most postwar educational leaders worked within a familiar system that had allowed them to succeed. Even though higher education was changing rapidly in size, mission, and clientele, advocates' explorations on behalf of women were often limited by the era's expectations and by the recognizable educational structures around them. As Carolyn Heilbrun explained, "Men were the only models I had."[121] Neither feminist analysis nor inclination was prevalent among their approaches.

At the same time, many postwar educators did raise concerns about the incidental nature of women's experience. Over the two decades, they gathered information, they assembled groups, they reconsidered curricula, they fostered research, and they examined policy. Although their efforts proceeded more quietly than did the wider feminist challenges of the late 1960s and 1970s, they nonetheless reveal activism on behalf of women that persisted throughout the early postwar era. In both traditional women's organizations and in newer study commissions, advocates for women worked to keep women's concerns from becoming ever more incidental in the midst of higher education's growth. With support from such organized efforts—spanning research, practice, and policy on behalf of women—some structural changes eventually appeared in higher education.

PART TWO

Explorations

CHAPTER THREE

Research

The American Council on Education's Commission on the Education of Women

In 1955 Esther Lloyd-Jones, professor of education at Columbia University and founding chair of the Commission on the Education of Women, worked hard to craft an enthusiastic fundraising appeal for this fledgling project of the American Council on Education (ACE). She wrote to the Phillips Foundation, a family philanthropy that had provided the initial $50,000 gift to create the commission. Lloyd-Jones began with flattery, noting how significant the commission's work had become as it grew from Kathryn Phillips' original idea. "The Commission on the Education of Women has a bear by the tail," she explained to Phillips and her son, Ellis. "The American Council on Education identified the animal as a bear when it accepted the generous gift made two and one half years ago by the Phillips Foundation to get the study under way. It is doubtful whether the Council or the Commission—or even Mrs. Ellis Phillips, whose vision sparked the whole project—realized what a big, fierce, thrashing bear this one would turn out to be."[1]

In her letter, Lloyd-Jones was optimistic and upbeat. However, the Phillips family declined to offer further support, arguing that it was time for other foundations to take a role in launching this important effort on behalf of women. Unfortunately, Lloyd-Jones and her colleagues had already spent two years approaching numerous other sources, receiving at best expressions of interest but with no money attached.

Notwithstanding such rejections, Lloyd-Jones was accurate in her metaphoric description of the commission's work. The bear she described was certainly "big": it represented the complicated question of how higher education could best serve

America's female postwar citizens as they responded to patriotic, economic, cultural, and psychological expectations. And clearly it was "thrashing": in an era marked by the preeminence of family, educators differed over the relationship between women's likely futures and the type of education they should receive. However, the bear seemed more "fierce" to commission members than to their audience of funders and higher education administrators. The commission spent ten years between 1953 and 1962 trying to clarify issues, encourage research, and generate funds, but few philanthropies committed to the project, and most collegiate leaders expressed only mild interest.

Created at a time when women were receiving mixed messages about their responsibilities to family and nation, the Commission on the Education of Women (CEW) accepted the task of translating these expectations into educational programming for women. They turned to the new tool of social science research, often finding psychological explanations for women's educational choices the most convincing. Generally, such postwar research suggested that women's decisions were explained by gender-based differences in their aptitudes, attitudes, and motivation. Given these differences, only the exceptional female pursued graduate education or professional status.

Over time, however, researchers perceived structural and cultural explanations for women's under-investment in education. Some argued that women's frequent choice to forego advanced schooling in favor of marriage and family made sense, given continuous societal messages about the benefits of education and the cost of professional pursuits. Such analyses began to suggest a collective rather than a merely individual explanation for women's lack of advancement. However, the limited analytical tools of the era, the power of cultural expectations, and the variety of choices facing women left advocacy groups like the Commission on the Education of Women reliant on the notion of "womanpower" to advocate for them: each individual woman must decide for herself how to respond to her family, civic, and personal responsibilities.

Ultimately, lack of agreement about the needs of postwar women's education, a weak research base on women, female leaders' lack of influence, and the indifference of foundation and higher education executives hampered the commission's efforts. Compared to its initial hopes for directing a million-dollar research agenda on women, the devolution into a research clearinghouse was a pale realization of early potential. After ten years, a new ACE president closed the commission in 1962.

However, the ACE Commission on the Education of Women became the most visible national research effort on women's collegiate education of the early post-

war period. Spanning a decade when women's collegiate and professional participation were stagnating, the commission spurred inquiry, disseminated research,
and fostered a network for women's advocates. The four statements it published
on women's collegiate education—issued under the auspices of the prestigious
ACE—demonstrate an emerging analysis of women's postwar education as a collective concern.

CREATING THE COMMISSION

Kathryn Phillips was a frustrated woman in 1952, but she was also a woman
with resources. After four decades advocating for women's collegiate interests,
including as a dean of women in Nebraska, Phillips felt that "women were losing
their identity" in postwar higher education. As the founder and first president
of the National Association of Deans of Women (NADW), Phillips had been instrumental in professionalizing deans' work. Now Phillips lamented that many
postwar female deans were being replaced by men.[2]

Phillips was a senior and influential member of the deans' network. By the
1950s the group she had founded with 26 colleagues in 1915 was a thriving organization with an annual meeting, a journal, and a membership of over 1,500.[3]
Nevertheless, many members agreed that lack of information and publicity about
the dean's role was leading to women's diminishing influence. Phillips decided to
focus her energy and money specifically on this concern.

Phillips tapped the family foundation she and her husband had created following his successful engineering and management career.[4] Their philanthropy
had long supported NADW, and in 1952 they offered that group $50,000 to study
and publicize the educational work of women. The question for NADW was
how to use the money. NADW president Ruth McCarn had recently created an
internal committee on the Status of Professional Women in Higher Education
and decided to use the Phillips gift to reorient its direction. The committee con-
templated whether NADW should keep the gift or donate it to a larger organization better equipped for a nationwide study. They considered both the National
Education Association (NEA) and the American Council on Education (ACE),
but Phillips encouraged the latter, recognizing its influence across the field of
higher education.[5]

Creating the commission within ACE was an important move. Organized after World War I to coordinate collegiate responses to national emergencies, the
ACE had grown in prestige and influence. As the largest "umbrella group" of
higher education organizations, ACE held a unique and comprehensive view

of collegiate concerns. It served as catalyst, facilitator, convener, and publisher on higher education interests, connecting government and the public with collegiate institutions.[6]

Although not usually focused on women's issues, ACE had supported a precursor to the commission: its 1951 Committee on Women in the Defense Decade. When the Korean War had followed so closely on the World War II recovery, many Americans, nervous about the country's vulnerability, had once again considered women's potential civic contributions. The Defense Decade committee explored ways that women could help the nation, including military service, industrial work, and the home.

Connecting women's civic role to their education, the Korean-era group argued that a modern woman's most important task was educating herself to be "politically literate and . . . conscious of her responsibilities as a citizen in a democracy."[7] Whether as mother or worker, the true American woman must welcome the preeminent responsibilities of citizenship and should use higher education to prepare herself. More than 900 educators, government representatives, business people, and concerned citizens demonstrated their agreement by attending the committee's 1951 conference in New York City.

In 1952 four educators were serving both on this ACE Defense Decade group and on NADW's committee on the Phillips gift. They believed that a focus on women's citizenship could combine the rather diffuse ideas of the Defense Decade committee and the more focused interests of NADW. These deans thought that citizenship would be served by improving the educational experience of women students, pushing for attention to the dropout rate, encouraging adult education, providing better statistics on college women, and enhancing the status of women leaders in higher education.[8] Applying the Phillips gift to this agenda, they reasoned, could further both groups' interests.

The charge this small committee drafted for ACE's vote on the new women's commission indicates the profusion of expectations facing postwar women. They recommended that the group "explore the current and long range needs of women as a result of the impact of changing social conditions upon them. This should include a consideration of women as effective individuals, as members of families, as gainfully employed workers, as participants in civic life and as creators and perpetuators of values." Women were expected to fulfill all five of these roles, although the committee could not yet explain how. It asked for "a compilation of the known facts of this impact on [women's] lives, an analysis of what higher ed is doing to meet their needs and what is necessary to free and utilize their highest skills and contributions."[9]

With backing from NADW as well as from ACE's Defense Decade committee, the new commission won support from ACE president Arthur S. Adams. With start-up money already in place, Adams gained easy approval from ACE's governing group, the Problems and Policies Committee. Their only reservation was expressed by the secretary general of the National Catholic Education Association, who worried that the new commission seemed "to be influenced heavily by certain materialistic considerations," paying too much attention to divorce, women's unhappiness within the family, and work outside the home. His challenge was only the first of many that, over time, accused the commission of encouraging women to disregard their family responsibilities.[10] Evenhanded attention to five sets of female responsibilities proved difficult to manage.

With ACE approval in hand, Adams turned to finding a chair and a director for the commission. Kathryn Phillips and NADW president McCarn strategized in advance, unifying support for the chairmanship around Esther Lloyd-Jones, a professor of guidance and counseling at Columbia University Teachers College, and for director, Althea Hottel, a sociologist and dean of women at the University of Pennsylvania. These two served the commission during its most vigorous years, organizing an agenda and pursuing foundation support.

Mindful of initial challenges to the commission's focus, both Adams and the group's new leaders recognized the potential for public and professional objections to focusing specifically on women's needs. Although some organizations had sponsored earlier committees on women, 1950s practitioners did not commonly regard women's professional or educational needs as special.[11] ACE's own Defense Decade group had always emphasized attention to women as citizens rather than as individuals. Adams himself repeatedly stressed commitment to the patriotic ideology. From his first comments about the commission, to his summary of its work ten years later, Adams underscored that the group "is not interested in securing special privileges for women. We are concerned with the welfare of the United States and by better definition make it clearer how every person in our population may more adequately contribute to our society."[12] In an era increasingly focused on civil rights, he further advised the commission never to "look at women as a race apart or as an underprivileged minority for whom special pleadings shall be made."[13]

Nor did commission members contradict Adams about seeking "special privileges." The era's expectations for how women contributed to the national welfare emphasized their service as wives and mothers and only secondarily their economic contributions. Psychologically, it was understood that women's acceptance of supporting roles promised the smoothest operation of both society and individual families. Thus, someone like Adams—a longtime supporter of women—could advocate increased attention to their education while still resisting an implication that women were disadvantaged or discriminated against.

Many, like Adams, saw women's lack of postwar advancement primarily as a "pipeline" issue rather than as resulting from any discriminatory intent. To them, women's lack of prominence resulted from too few of them being ready—either through education or experience—to assume top faculty and administrative posts. Prominent labor market analysts supported this view. Caplow and McGee, experts on the academic market, had found women existing outside the "prestige system" of academe, providing no benefits to institutions who might hire them. Sociologist Jessie Bernard had also placed women on the periphery of academe, finding a potential fringe benefit in women's willingness to fill less-secure jobs.

The commission's Lloyd-Jones and Hottel understood this prevailing view but wondered whether it presented the entire picture for women. Although they lacked a full understanding of how labor market operations affected women's progress as students and faculty, they surmised that data might influence collegiate leaders, echoing a feminist approach from earlier in the century. As commission director Hottel argued, "the best approach will not be to 'burst in' but we must develop a way to get at the root of the major problem and secure the cooperation of the top administrators." And although she appreciated Adams' skill in commanding national attention, she felt that getting him and others to "realize 'the fact of life'" about the job market was a necessary step to changing views.[14] The first task, then, would be to assemble and assess the extant research base on women's higher education.

ORGANIZING A RESEARCH AGENDA

Outlining the issues and gathering pertinent research proved a difficult task for the commission, which was composed of practitioners across a variety of settings. The thirteen original commissioners—ten women and three men—were carefully chosen for geographic, gender, racial, religious, and disciplinary diversity. NADW was well represented through Lucile Allen (Chatham College), Anna Hawkes (Mills College), Eunice Hilton (Syracuse University), and Ruth Brett Quarles (Dillard University).[15] Quarles was the commission's sole African American member. Working at Fisk University when first invited, she moved to a deanship at Dillard, another historically black institution. Mother Eleanor O'Byrne represented the Catholic viewpoint as president of Manhattanville College of the Sacred Heart. In addition to these deans, two male college presidents served, representing institutions quite different in size and scope: Louis Benezet of Allegheny College and Harlan Hatcher of the University of Michigan. They were joined by two female presidents, Katherine Blyley of Keuka College and Katharine McBride of Bryn Mawr. The other male commissioner (besides the ex officio Adams) was Robert Sutherland of the University of Texas Hogg Foundation.[16]

The diversity of the members affected their views about the commission's goals and the best focus for their work, revealing the era's confusion about how best to address women's concerns. The influence of the patriotic ideology led some to address the particular role of women within a democracy; others argued for treating women first as members of society, and only secondarily as females. Some thought that older women deserved primary attention, others that the needs of youth should predominate. There was also disagreement over whether to include non-college women, adult education, and drop-outs in the work of a commission devoted to higher education. On issues of psychology, some members believed that individual factors such as personality and attitude explained differences among women, while their colleagues argued for the influence of social factors or labor markets.[17] The diversity in the commissioners' views mirrored contemporary variations in educational research.

Working from the charge approved by ACE—with its list of women's five roles—the commissioners turned to crafting a statement of purpose. They recognized the political value of incorporating ideas from the Defense Decade committee, ACE's only other group focused on women.[18] Members of that panel had strong advice for the new commission. First, they expressed surprise at the limited focus on higher education. They argued that, since not all of women's contributions to society came through work, and since many women focused their lives only after leaving college, limiting the commission's scope to collegiate concerns would actually shrink attention to women's issues. Above all, the Defense Committee warned the group not to focus on research at the expense of action.[19]

However, the new commission saw the potential of using research to clarify issues and educational directions. In the long run, its lasting contribution would be clarifying and enhancing the era's research base. Although it had never publicly identified itself as a funder of research, scholars soon sent research proposals for their consideration. Recognizing the dearth of information on women, even with several proposals in front of them, the commission deemed it premature to support particular projects. Given the visibility of ACE's platform, they hoped to do more than merely fund research; they decided the first step was to understand and summarize extant research on women's education.

At a March 1953 meeting, the commissioners looked at ten research proposals, most by scholars known to them. The influence of these ideas—as well as the variety they represented—led the group to adopt a disconnected initial agenda that seemed to endorse nearly every possible research direction. In the first draft of a statement, the commissioners imagined "a study of the contributions which women are making and can make to society, including a study of the influence of personality, attitudes, aptitudes, education and culture which have affected them, and of areas wherein informed people of both sexes feel that women have been adequately or inadequately prepared for the expanding responsibilities which they must assume to themselves, to their children and families, to their economic status, and to their communities and nation."[20] This omnibus statement not only reflected disparate thinking about women's education but also showed the commission balancing its attention to women in the home, the community, and the job market.

To explore further the nature of research findings, the commission arranged a two-day meeting to consider reports and recommendations from established researchers in the field. They engaged seven prominent scholars to contribute papers formulating "the most important problems referring to the influence that education, social attitudes, and culture patterns have had upon women in the development of their personalities, use of their aptitude, and the nature of their contributions to American Society." And they asked contributors to suggest conceptual approaches for studying the issues.[21]

The researchers' recommendations provide a snapshot of scholarly understanding about women's education in the early 1950s. Frequently, the work mixed demographics with sociology and psychology, trying to understand the effects of women's choices on their development. Psychologist Marie Jahoda, for example, studied women's morale, satisfaction, and achievement, comparing career women with families, career women without families, housewives, and older widows. Harvard sociologist Florence Kluckhohn offered a historical view of women's roles, focusing on the lack of prestige for housewives, the "limited scope" of careers for women, and the effect of these conditions on women's choices of schooling and career. In an era with inconsistent expectations for women's labor market contributions, such research investigated how they fared in different situations.

Sociologist Robin Williams examined the effect of education on women's choices, goals, and reaction to societal pressures. In a period when community agencies and private arrangements were not well organized to support working women, he hoped to discover whether "nascent social institutions" could address the pressures on women. Berkeley educator Mary Jones looked at how women met their needs for "creative self-expression" in the home, the community, and at work. Similarly, W. Lloyd Warner examined communities, wondering how the "social characteristics of different types of women and the roles they play" related to the country's different social systems (size, complexity of social life, work opportunities). Sociological understandings of women's choices were frequently matched to their psychological development as individuals, family members, and community participants. In all these studies, the researchers balanced concern for the individual with her ultimate contribution to a larger milieu.

Cognitive psychologist Robert Blake echoed some of the labor market studies about academic women by focusing on women's tendency toward "chronic yielding," which he defined as "avoiding clash, by being docile, by withdrawing and by being agreeable" in response to societal norms. Like sociologist Jessie Bernard, Blake wondered whether women's need for social integration overwhelmed their capacities for critical thinking, independence, and inner security. Theodore Newcomb, who conducted some of the era's most prominent studies of college women and men, looked at women's choice of roles in terms of their own "clarity v. ambiguity, rigidity v. flexibility," wondering how these might affect women's approaches to professionalism.

Overall, the researchers focused on women's status, roles, aptitudes, motivation, creativity, and developmental differences, generally emphasizing effects on individuals. They all recognized that higher education could lead women in a variety of directions, although none offered sweeping conclusions about the effects of different choices on collegiate women's performance, satisfaction, or general development.[22]

FUNDING THE WORK ON WOMEN

The 1953 meeting with researchers helped organize the commissioners' thinking and their plans. Since ACE's charge permitted a wide-open agenda, they decided to focus in two directions: defining the research base, and securing financial support. Because research on women's education was relatively new and amorphous, the commission proposed to gather, clarify, stimulate, and disseminate work in the field. To do this, the commissioners educated themselves through meetings, conferences, and requests for proposals. Yet the group also recognized the need to secure outside funding, both to cover operations and to finance an expansive research agenda.

ACE was not itself a philanthropy; its role was to organize efforts, provide a prestigious imprimatur, and bring together advocates, researchers, and funders.

Therefore, a good part of the commission's early efforts focused on raising money for research on women. Unfortunately, although the group began with great enthusiasm for the power of research to expand women's opportunities, lack of financial support stymied its success over the next ten years. The history of the commission alternates between the internal story of thwarted fundraising and the external effort to foster and publicize research on women.

Before the commission could begin its formal appeal to foundations, it needed a deeper understanding of both the research base and directions that seemed fruitful. Using the ideas outlined by the visiting researchers, they organized into five subcommittees. One committee undertook a grand literature review on what was known about women and education. The other four groups organized around specific methodologies encouraged by the scholars: community studies, national studies, developmental and laboratory studies, and "change procedures." The commission developed an ambitious five-year plan with a proposed budget of $1 million to fund new studies and sponsor public reports. Director Althea Hottel—an admitted newcomer to fundraising—found the scope of this proposed effort "staggering," but her colleagues urged her to tell foundations how important and potentially valuable the work would be.[23]

The funding appeal that the commission crafted in 1953 centered on seven major needs:

> to study the roles of women in American society and the sources of confusion in these roles; to observe the influences that education, social attitudes and cultural patterns have had upon women in the development of their personalities, the use of their aptitudes, and the nature of their contributions; to ascertain the differentials in child rearing and their effects on the personality, the aptitudes, attitudes and responses of both sexes; to examine the motivation and basic processes that affect the intellectual growth of men and women; to determine what social factors inhibit, permit or encourage the larger participation of women in the familial, economic, civic, and cultural life of this country; to determine what changes in roles men and women view as desirable and how these are related to definable trends; and from all of the above to make recommendations for change for the thoughtful consideration and action of the American people.[24]

The proposal clearly tapped a wide variety of research directions and approaches. It also emphasized that, although considerable "speculative" work existed, there was very little empirical research on women; thus, the commission sought support as the first national-level group to foster such a program.[25]

Fundraising soon dominated the commission agenda. Highest hopes rested with the Ford Foundation's two programs in Adult Education and the Advancement of Education. Arthur Adams worked his ACE contacts carefully; however, Ford's director Alvin Eurich declined the appeal, saying that his foundation preferred to support "programs of action rather than studies."[26] Lloyd-Jones approached the General Education Board of the Rockefeller Foundation as well as the Kellogg, Guggenheim, and Hazen foundations. She continued personal stewardship with the Phillips family, but Kathryn's son, Ellis Jr., found the proposal "abstruse."[27] The Social Science Research Council criticized the project's "vastness," disparaging Hottel's claim to be "looking for another Gunnar Myrdal" to do for women's education what the Swedish sociologist had done for America's understanding of race.[28]

None of the major funders was drawn to the commission's widespread consideration of women's concerns. As fundraising dragged on, Lloyd-Jones expressed frustration to her friend Paul Anderson, president of Pennsylvania College for Women, noting that "while it is easy to get a lot of research under way, and it is comparatively easy to get funds for a specific piece of research, it does not seem so easy to persuade people to sustain the planning, on-going body that is the Commission itself."[29]

Philanthropic foundations in the 1950s were not attuned to deep attention to women's issues. The era's higher education growth had occurred in the research universities, places where women's participation was not prominent either as students or scholars. With the exception of certain technological needs spurred by the Cold War, women generally were not seen as vital contributors whose participation should be increased. Certainly, the movement of the "baby boom" generation into schooling raised the need for more school teachers, but drawing women into teaching hardly seemed to demand special research attention. Overall, unless women's diminished participation was identified as a solution to a specific and important problem, it remained unconvincing as an issue for foundation and government support, and the Commission on the Education of Women was notably unsuccessful in changing that view.

How Fare American Women?

Although CEW members were pleased when the *New York Times* published a supportive article about their work in March 1954, they lamented education editor Benjamin Fine's mistaken implication that its five-year plan had secured full funding.[30] The reality was that the group spent a considerable part of every meeting and most of its behind-the-scenes time trying to generate support for any part of the commission's agenda.

Both to incubate interest and to pursue the goal of publicizing research, the commission decided in 1954 to publish a report discussing the available research on women. *How Fare American Women?* became the first of the commission's four published statements on women's education, each of which serves as a noteworthy example of postwar thinking. Commissioner Robert Sutherland recalled the impact of ACE's own 1938 Youth Commission report, titled *How Fare American Youth?* and recommended a similar approach for the assessment of women. After considering potential authors, the group decided on their director Althea Hottel, promising to provide an advisory board to help her analyze and interpret the research.

How Fare American Women? appeared in 1955.[31] Its compilation of demographic facts and research findings stressed three points about women and their education. First, college training had not kept pace with changes in society, leaving women unequipped for the social and financial realities around them. Second, the research base, although not extensive, was beginning to encourage women to pursue wider career and educational choices. And finally, even with expanded choices available, women should understand that it was unrealistic to manage all roles at once and should always consider home and family as their primary duties. The contradictions among these views—encouraging women to seek wider educational and career options while also heeding the primacy of home and family—did not trouble the commission at this early point in its work. The group saw its task as outlining issues for future consideration, hoping that subsequent research would clarify women's dilemmas. Thus, the book is useful for exploring how postwar advocates thought about managing the mix of societal expectations.

The opening chapter of *How Fare American Women?*—seen as key for convincing people of women's needs—discussed the various and complicated choices facing postwar women. It reviewed significant demographic developments, including the younger age of marriage, the growth in U.S. population, and the fact that fully one-third of women—half of them married—now worked outside the home. Thus, women's multiple roles, simultaneous or sequential, were nonarguable facts. However, neither education nor society's expectations for women's accomplishments had yet caught up with this reality. Too often women received "contingency education" to fall back on as necessary, rather than carefully planned preparation for a complex life. The inconsistencies in expectations and their translation into educational curricula created problems for educators and for women themselves. As Hottel explained, "Apparently, we have not yet decided in this country whether women in their functions are to become first-class or second-class human beings. Is it any wonder, then, that the education of women, wavering between the primary and the secondary roles and some vague ideas of compromise, presents a confused and confusing picture?"[32]

The book also reflected the era's assumption that women's issues were individualized concerns. That is, each woman would make a calculus of her choices and craft a personalized solution; there was little cognizance of systemic problems or solutions. With this individual approach as a base, the important educational task was to assure that women students and their teachers possessed good data for their decisions. At the same time, one overall assumption remained: women's primary role was in the family. The commission did not wish to be seen as encouraging choices that devalued family life, noting that "the chief task is neither to free more women to work as and where they choose, nor is it to persuade more women to work less and housekeep more. Once again the task is rather to help her work out her plans in a seeing way that will contribute to her partnership with man as well as helping the healthful individuality of each."[33]

During the drafting of *How Fare American Women?* commission members recognized the delicate balancing act that women faced in an era with such varied expectations. Louis Benezet, president of a women's college, worried that educators too often misled women about the feasibility of simultaneously addressing home, career, and community concerns. He called this view of women's unlimited freedom "twaddle" that ignored the pressures facing women in the real world. Believing that each woman must make her own choices work, he condemned those who suggested that women's "chief task is now to adjust the environment to her own liking, rather than adjust herself to the environment."[34]

Benezet's discomfort with urging women to challenge norms was shared by many commissioners, who argued that the task was not "to challenge the culture so much as to bring clarity, aid to understanding, and promote wiser choice."[35] Overall, the idea of accommodating rather than disregarding society's needs appeared the wisest course. Even Hottel, who expressed a need for expanded choices, argued that "our times call for some changes in attitudes, emphases, and perspective in the education of women students. This does not, in my estimation, require an educational revolution."[36]

How Fare American Women? turned to research to explain how women might respond to societal expectations. One of the era's primary research directions was understanding women's motivation. Differences in females' educational participation—both their lesser attendance at college compared to men, and their tendency to drop out—had long been explained by their supposed weaker motivation. But *How Fare American Women?* presented findings that within-sex differences

(differences among women) often trumped the presumed differences between men and women. That is, not all women made choices for the same reasons.

In examining how and why women made decisions about educational investment and job choice, newer research suggested that the cumulative effect of their individual, continuous, and specific decisions affected their ultimate investment in education. John Anderson and Lester Sontag had shown that girls often made inconsistent decisions as they considered the separate developmental paths of career and motherhood. Exploring the issue of motivation, Sontag found that by age ten, girls' "feminine motive" dominated, leading them away from college and career. Other work demonstrated that girls' grades and IQ test results actually decreased when they perceived that being smart lessened their popularity and femininity. Some suggested that society's valuing of masculine traits such as self-expression and individualism, rather than female virtues of supporting others and "bearing the culture," also depressed women's choices.[37]

How Fare American Women? offered a good presentation of research findings but did not take the next step of using them to recommend particular approaches for female education. The book—and the commission, at this point—took a middle road in the era's major curricular debate, siding neither with the cultural conformists who advocated training for home and community, nor with the equity-based planners who sought ways to extend the reach of the curriculum. In the end, *How Fare American Women?* blandly urged that women receive "broad educational opportunities with a spiritual emphasis," rather than offering any specific program. Perhaps confident that its forthcoming program of research would provide more clarity, the commission used this initial public presentation more to address future goals than to make current recommendations, and it offered no specific ideas for changing women's education.

LIMITED FUNDING SUCCESS AND A NEW RESEARCH STATEMENT

How Fare American Women? succeeded better as a publicity effort for the Commission on the Education of Women than as a fundraising tool. The American Association of University Women (AAUW) adopted the book as a program guide for local chapters; thus, through AAUW alone, thousands of women studied the book's analysis of societal change and its summary of educational research.[38] Such enthusiasm did not, however, convert into foundation support. Acutely in need of operating funds, the commission turned to ACE for carry-over funding until more substantive help arrived.

Two years into the commission's work, with *How Fare American Women?* its sole tangible product, Althea Hottel felt pressured to return to her dean's job at the University of Pennsylvania. With only basic financing for the commission in hand, Esther Lloyd-Jones appealed to her home institution for support, convincing Columbia University to advance her sabbatical by two years and to headquarter the commission at Teachers College. For nearly two years Lloyd-Jones was CEW's mainstay, managing its daily work while continuing to seek foundation funding for the research agenda.

In May 1955, Lloyd-Jones and Adams added some strategic new members to the commission, notably, representatives from the Carnegie and Ford foundations, the National Manpower Council, the Labor Department, and the Brookings Institution. These participants helped reorient the commission toward two issues: how to enhance the nation's "womanpower" (particularly important to the NMC), and how to support a growing interest in continuing education for women.

Acknowledging that the funding drought prohibited any deep investment in research projects, and recognizing the public success of *How Fare American Women?* CEW decided to create a regular publication to summarize studies, describe experimental programs, and define issues about women's education. This effort would draw attention to the commission's program even as it disseminated knowledge more widely. At the same time, it launched a consultation service to help institutions plan women's curricula and influence schoolteachers who worked with girls and young women. Commission leaders gamely presented these new efforts as longstanding interests, although in fact they represented a quiet recognition that foundation officers were not inspired by the research program.

Although the new plans failed to impress the Carnegie, Mellon, or Russell Sage foundations, spring 1957 brought the first good fundraising news.[39] The Lilly Foundation—a new source for the commission's appeals—awarded $75,000 for three years' support of the research bulletin and consulting service. Simultaneously, the Carnegie Corporation provided $9,900 for a research conference to "assess the present status of research on the education of women." The modest grant felt like a consolation prize, following Carnegie's rejection of its larger appeal. Although clearly a positive development, the new funding dictated a much-diminished agenda for the commission. Early goals had envisioned $1 million for a creative range of research and dissemination efforts. Yet the combined $84,000 from Lilly and Carnegie—two of the more likely prospects—did not even cover costs of the new bulletin and consulting service.[40]

Commission leaders recognized the potential influence that could be generated by a Carnegie-sponsored research conference, and the effort reinvigorated their energies. At the same time, the tight budget prohibited meetings of the full commission during 1956–57. Actual planning for the conference occurred behind the scenes, led by Lloyd-Jones at Columbia, Lucile Allen, dean of Chatham College, who arranged the program, and Katharine McBride, the influential president of Bryn Mawr, who served as conference chair.

CEW's conference on women's education, held at Rye, New York, over three days in October 1957, was attended by thirty-six practitioners and scholars on women's education, including representatives from foundations and educational organizations.[41] Speakers included longtime ACE participants like Judge Mary Donlon, past chair of the Women in the Defense Decade conference; current and former commissioners Louis Benezet, Anna Hawkes, and Robert Sutherland; new commissioners, including Dean Mary Bunting of Douglass College (soon to be CEW chair); activist presidents such as Margaret Clapp of Wellesley College and Harold Taylor of Sarah Lawrence; and researchers on women, including Elizabeth Douvan of the University of Michigan, Marguerite Zapoleon of the Women's Bureau, and Dean Kate Hevner Mueller of Indiana University. The participants included some of the most prominent scholars of women's educational and economic concerns. Most supported the economic utilitarian and equity-based approaches, although some cultural conformists attended.[42]

Whereas *How Fare American Women?* primarily documented women's status without much commentary about the future, the Rye conference tried to offer both. The conference marked an advance in interpreting research on women, adding the understanding that cultural and sociological influences—along with individual psychological differences—could explain women's choices. In particular, it introduced the idea of "life phases" in women's development that paralleled and explained their educational choices. This notion, along with its recommendations for continuing education programs for women, became a future direction for commission efforts. The Rye conference proceedings, published as *The Education of Women: Signs for the Future*, constituted the commission's second research statement.[43]

The background information about women's needs presented at Rye differed little from the 1954 report. By 1957, however, many speakers were more precise in connecting women's educational concerns to their wider participation as citizens as well as to the effects of discrimination on women's performance. Mary Donlon, for instance, provided a wider context for American women's situation, referring both to Hitler's racial policies and to the recent use of the U.S. National Guard to quell racial disturbances in Arkansas as examples of denying citizens full participation. Acknowledging that prejudices surrounding women were "more subtly exercised" than those around race, Donlon nonetheless argued that both educators and the public must recognize the consequences of denying women their fair opportunities.[44]

The late 1950s lacked a widespread interpretation of how discrimination affected women as a group, including the combined operation of economic and cultural forces. For many researchers, differences in individual motivation seemed the most convincing explanation for why some women pursued education and careers while others chose the less intellectually demanding (although more immediately satisfying) role of motherhood. Work on women's educational motivation had assumed increasing importance within the commission over the years, and the Rye conference highlighted the work of several researchers in that field. Psychologist Elizabeth Douvan presented her findings that college women were drawn early to the "typically female professions," finding little attraction to other fields. Douvan found that 87 percent of girls intended to use college to prepare for fields like teaching and nursing or for purely "social" reasons that barely acknowledged the intellectual aspects of college. Only 13 percent presented what she called any real "academic focus" for college attendance.[45]

The persistence of psychoanalytic explanations for women's choices was supported by a theory of women's career development advanced by psychologist David Tiedeman. While recognizing that women experienced different pressures than men do, Tiedeman's Freudian analysis held that only by satisfying their "feminine core" could women free themselves for intellectual pursuits, a conclusion highlighting the stalemate facing women who felt forced to choose between college and marriage. His analysis confirmed other findings—for example, that the adult "identity crisis" typically hit men in their sophomore year of college when deciding on a major, but it confronted college women in their senior year when marriage or further study posed their difficult choice.[46]

Whereas *How Fare American Women?* stopped short of applying research findings to curricular recommendations, Rye participants speculated on how research might prompt change. Planning the best course of study to prepare women for a variety of futures was the most pressing issue facing collegiate leaders. But as in the field at large, the vibrant discussion at Rye produced little agreement on the best approach. Some speakers believed that only the liberal arts, with their strong general focus, could prepare large numbers of women for the widest set of possibilities. Less clear, however, was the precise amount of vocationalism that should guide any such program. Home economics had long been touted as a sound curricular complement to liberal education, and even some of the most prestigious women's colleges had included home economics—or its variants, political economy and public health—as important parts of the collegiate plan. Other speakers advocated the service ideal as the most important aspect of women's education, finding there a culturally comfortable notion of women serving others. For some, especially the Catholic educators at the conference, this commitment to service emanated from religion; for others, it came from a social service impulse, such as the early twentieth-century settlement houses. An appealing feature of using service to guide women's curriculum was that it could address both volunteerism and careers. College women who chose to focus on community and home rather than on career and profession could still provide educated expertise to the world around them.[47]

A new idea appeared toward the end of the Rye conference, ultimately affecting the direction of the commission's work and signaling a new development in women's collegiate education: the notion of "life phases" for women that might explain—and support—their educational choices. Rye speakers introduced the idea of continuing education as a new option for women who had left college but who later wished to return and complete their education. Such programming might offer a solution to women's under-investment in schooling and their inability to provide sufficient "womanpower."

While not a planned element of the conference, the ideas behind continuing education—rearranging institutional requirements, timing, schedules, and expectations to meet the needs of married and "returning women"—attracted enthusiasm as attendees compared their concerns. Some ideas grew from a spontaneous discussion about married female students. Kate Mueller, dean of women at Indiana University, expressed her concern about the lack of attention to married women on public campuses, where they constituted nearly 20 percent of all students. Mueller's 1954 book was one of the few to consider women's needs on a large public campus; more frequently, scholars wrote with smaller, private institutions in mind.[48] Mueller argued at Rye that colleges should smooth the way for married women, noting the egregious loss of womanpower when young wives and mothers were discouraged from trying to continue their educations. However, her practical approach did not convince other deans, who saw instead an obligation to dissuade students from early marriage.[49] Nevertheless, the discussion edged the idea of continuing education onto the commission's agenda.

In the end, Rye's *Signs for the Future* placed researchers' analysis of women's decision making alongside practitioners' interpretations of their actual choices. In doing so, the book demonstrated the era's lack of agreement on women's education, as well as the continued potency of "womanpower" reasoning in arguing for women's needs. It also suggested some new directions for CEW's attention.

A SHIFT IN COMMISSION FOCUS

Following the Rye conference, after five years' service, Esther Lloyd-Jones turned the duties of commission chair over to Judge Mary Donlon, a longtime participant in ACE activities. With money now available from the Lilly Foundation, CEW again hired an executive director to assist the chair. Opal David became the second director, bringing considerable Washington experience from stints at the Civil Service Commission and the Commerce Department. Donlon and David turned the group's attention to its new grant-funded research bulletin, *The Education of Women*, which allowed a wider distribution of the commission's findings.

Pursuing leads from the Rye meeting, the commission focused its interests—for both research and practice—on the phases of women's lives and the role education played in each. They identified five developmental stages, each raising separate educational issues. The first stage, the pre-high-school years, actually provoked little concern because research showed few differences between the genders at that point in children's lives. However, the commission acknowledged the continuing importance of supporting grade school teachers who could influence girls at early ages. The high school years—the second phase—attracted more concern for their role in motivating women to attend college; of special interest were high-performing female students who, as Dael Wolfle's data had shown, could become discouraged before committing to college.[50]

The college and graduate school years, the third stage, were key periods for women's choices, where differences in their motivation as well as in curricular and personal choices affected long-term options. A newly defined stage called "post-college, through middle age" drew attention from educational planners because of the necessity of preparing women for motherhood as well as providing continued intellectual stimulation during these "at-home" years. The last period of a woman's life, beyond middle age, also grew in significance as practitioners and researchers recognized women's increasing return to the work force, often with insufficient training. The commission observed an unfortunate cycle wherein young women who nonchalantly left college for early marriage later found themselves inadequately prepared for work. Labor market studies like *Womanpower*, as well as the commission's own work at Rye, had impressed educators with the needs of these adult students.[51]

This view of women's lives having sequential stages with different educational demands was a new conceptualization for educators. Based on both research findings and observations from practice, this new thinking revealed a growing awareness that individual psychological issues as well as wider cultural and economic factors influenced women's interests, choices, and investment in education. As research presented at Rye suggested, women's behavior often reflected their understanding of the rewards and challenges that particular decisions would bring. Yet the new approach also showed how decisions made early could produce unfortunate long-term results.

As the commission moved to study these developmental stages, it experienced another change in leadership. Mary Bunting of Douglass College (the women's branch of Rutgers University), succeeded Donlon in 1959. Bunting's personal situation demonstrated the wisdom of being educationally prepared for unforeseen circumstances. Her husband had died unexpectedly at a young age, leaving her to raise four children. Bunting also attracted respect in an era of scientific manpower due to her doctoral training as a bacteriologist and her role in creating a program at Douglass to retrain female college dropouts in mathematics.

Bunting proved somewhat more directive than previous CEW chairs, and although she headed a woman's institution, she often resisted exploring educational change tailored solely for women. Instead, Bunting moved the group to consider two particular adult education options, neither of which need serve women only. First, she advocated the creation of nationwide educational guidance centers to serve adults who had left college. Second, she introduced the notion, quite new at the time, of what became the College Level Examination Program (CLEP), a series of achievement tests allowing both women and men to accrue credits for courses and other studies pursued outside the regular collegiate curriculum. In these recommendations, Bunting acknowledged the peripatetic nature of many adult lives as well as the difficulty of convincing colleges to accept scattered credits. Her own proclivities as a scientist led Bunting to explain these efforts as "a valuable framework for important curriculum experimentation."[52]

During Bunting's one-year chairmanship, a more decentralized commission pursued four interests: the educational bulletin, the consultation service, the guidance centers, and the achievement test. Interest in the latter two faded when Bunting left the commission in 1960 to assume the presidency of Radcliffe College and Wichita's dean Margaret Habein assumed the chair's role. With funding from the Lilly Foundation, the bulletin and the consultation service continued with modest success.

A THIRD PUBLIC STATEMENT

By 1960, after seven years of effort, CEW's original commitment to a wide-spread research program had been replaced by a sense of itself as catalyst and publicizer for women's education, roles benefiting from the power of ACE sponsorship. Recognizing their opportunity to focus educators' attention, the group issued a short statement summarizing what they had learned since Rye and highlighting their interest in women's developmental stages. They distributed their work in a policy statement, *The Span of a Woman's Life and Learning*, a much-reprinted four-page endorsement for seeing women's educational needs as continuous and changing.

The statement began by acknowledging and supporting women's interest in marriage, but it encouraged a simultaneous recognition that "the role of home-maker can well be combined with other creative endeavors and responsibilities." They would not deny that family life produced unique and keen satisfactions, but, the statement argued, many people "have not been informed that major responsibilities in bearing and rearing children under modern conditions may consume less than two decades in a woman's life." Thus, educational planning, guidance, and careful curricular choice became key to both the "full mental development" of individual women and the "total intellectual potential of the United States."[53] Once again the twin notions of individual and collective womanpower supported attention to women's educational investment.

Although the statement was short and precise, it had provoked considerable commission discussion and disagreement during the drafting stages. An early version emphasized women's "special needs" as compared to men, but deference to Adams' recommendation against special pleadings reduced the idea in the final version to "special deterrents" affecting women's choices. Also, the importance of women's role in the family figured much more prominently in original versions of the statement; the final document discussed family as only one aspect of women's complicated lives. Third, a heavy push for the importance of achievement tests in helping women (Bunting's idea) was muted in the final statement, which advocated more generally for the role of sound educational guidance. In the end, the *Span* statement presented strong but general advocacy, fulfilling the commission's role of raising awareness but without specific programmatic recommendations.

The Span of a Woman's Life and Learning represented the crispest summary ever offered by the commission. It relied heavily on the arguments of the patriotic ideology that fulfilling the potential of individual women would inevitably lead to enhancing the nation. "Womanpower" had provided the commission with its clearest justification for women's education. It was no longer acceptable to allow women's contributions to stagnate with marriage; a longer-term approach, bolstered by educational options, would benefit women, families, and society.

PRECIPITOUS FINALE

The year 1961 brought quick change to the Commission on the Education of Women. Arthur Adams retired as president of ACE and was replaced by Logan Wilson, chancellor of the University of Texas. Wilson, previously dean of Sophie Newcomb College (the women's branch of Tulane University), inherited a commission program that had produced less than its original potential.

As executive director, Opal David had pursued commission work under less-than-ideal circumstances from 1958 to 1961. The fundraising challenge remained as constant and minimally successful as ever; the ten-year uphill effort had raised less than $200,000. Lack of funding meant lack of space. When David's husband transferred to Stanford University for a year, she received approval to move CEW's office temporarily to California and the next year to Charlottesville, Virginia. David presented these choices—arising from her role as what would later be called a "trailing spouse"—as opportunities for ACE to showcase its commitment to women's issues. Adams had seized the publicity opportunity, praising his organization for "practicing what it preaches with respect to the need for flexibility in dealing with the education of women and the different patterns of their lives."[54]

Along with publishing *The Span of a Woman's Life and Learning* in 1960, the commission had focused on collecting and disseminating information, applying that knowledge to the counseling of women and girls, and encouraging experiments in continuing education. Long-term goals included convening a conference on continuing education, preparing a summary document of research on women, locating a steady funding source for the bulletin, and sponsoring a revision of *How Fare American Women?* The only new funding during that period, however, was another small ACE infusion, a mark of Adams' continuing support.

As Adams' retirement neared, and with Wilson's support less certain, David and others recognized the precarious situation facing CEW.[55] David wrote to commissioner Robert Sutherland that the project was "fresh out of foundation support and will need his [Wilson's] sympathetic attention very promptly if we are not to have a serious break in the continuity of the program."[56] When Wilson arrived, David prepared thoughtful, positive memos on the commission's work and its plans for the future. For his part, Wilson undertook a review of all ACE programs. Within a few months, however, his concern about CEW's continuing lack of funding became clear, and Wilson recommended closing it in 1962.[57] David tendered her resignation for September.

In the meantime, however, the commission's interest in continuing education had won a friend at the Carnegie Corporation. Through the influence of corporation secretary Florence Anderson, CEW received a grant of $23,000 to sponsor a conference on continuing education. Carnegie's commitment to this issue had grown in the past few years, mostly through Anderson's efforts. The corporation had funded three projects that quickly became national models: programs for returning women undergraduates at the University of Minnesota and Sarah Lawrence College, and one at Radcliffe (created by Mary Bunting) to reinvigorate the careers of doctorate-holding women.[58] Carnegie intended these as demonstration projects and wished to foster their visibility through the conference as well as in various ACE and Carnegie reports.

Although Wilson remained unconvinced about the long-term need for CEW, he acknowledged that Carnegie's grant presumed some sort of ongoing ACE involvement with women's concerns. Having already decided to disband the commission, Wilson reconstituted it as a special advisory committee just for the conference. Carnegie support thus allowed CEW to complete its work with a flourish, hosting an invitational three-day meeting at Itasca State Park in Minnesota. Eighty-six educators and researchers—drawn by Carnegie's influence—shared information about the burgeoning continuing education movement and its role in advancing women's concerns.

The Itasca meeting produced CEW's fourth and final statement, *Education and a Woman's Life,* emphasizing the idea of life phases and the role of continuing education in enhancing them.[59] Like the Rye conference, the Itasca conference mixed educational research with examples of practice. Researchers updated findings about women's motivation, career development, and curricular choices. Practitioners discussed a variety of educational projects, emphasizing both the array of women's needs and the range of institutions that could respond, including public universities, private colleges, and professional organizations.

At Itasca, the predominant theme was educating women over a lifetime, rather than stressing their single chance for a four-year college degree. Gordon Blackwell, president of Florida State University, promoted the image of an "educational bus trip" allowing women to get on and off as their personal situation changed. Foremost among conference analyses was the strong womanpower emphasis that "the needs of women and the needs of our society are not in opposition."[60]

Aware that Itasca represented the commission's last chance to dramatize women's educational needs, conferees concluded with specific explorations of new administrative arrangements, curricular plans, and research approaches that could best serve women. Publication of the proceedings gave their ideas further currency, encouraging campuses to strengthen guidance programs, review hiring procedures, ease transfer requirements, provide more creative scheduling, and offer more support to married students.[61] The commission's last public statement emphasized the ways in which "womanpower" promoted women's ongoing educational opportunities.

UNFINISHED WORK

The ACE Commission on the Education of Women concluded its work with the Itasca conference in 1962. The group passed a resolution thanking ACE for a decade of support and encouraging the creation of a subsequent committee on women's issues. President Wilson pursued a different direction, however, folding women's interests into a new Commission on Academic Affairs, where women no longer appeared as a separate concern or attracted much attention.[62] In fact, ACE did not institute a new office on women's issues until 1973, after the feminist movement prompted many organizations and educational institutions to reexamine their commitment to women.[63]

The commission's history reflects many of the changes and opportunities of the early postwar era. As the 1950s progressed, a new appreciation for civil rights as well as new opportunities for women's careers in teaching and other fields contended with expectations for ever-earlier marriage and motherhood. Women's decisions in a climate of such diverse expectations ultimately affected their participation in colleges and universities, and educators responsible for female students struggled to find the right balance in curriculum and programming.

The ten-year period of CEW activity witnessed increased public and professional attention to women's issues. Adams commented at a 1960 commission meeting that the very idea of helping women "realize their true capacity" was much more acceptable now than when CEW was formed in 1953. Chair Margaret Habein concurred, offering the example of how "natural" she felt addressing women's needs at a recent Rotary Club meeting, noting that "ten years ago, [I] would have felt like a feminist."[64]

Few of the women and men who served on the commission, in fact, identified as feminists, although they certainly saw themselves as advocates for women's concerns. The 1950s still equated the term "feminist" with the more radical push for women's suffrage of the early twentieth century, or with the pointed advocacy of the Equal Rights Amendment by the National Women's Party. Neither of these stances appealed to educators who had themselves succeeded in a mainstream world and who hoped to assert a place for women in a collegiate world rarely attuned to their presence. Their advocacy of continuing education projects suggests a preference for refining and improving women's place in traditional institutions rather than significantly changing those settings. As Hottel had written early on, their work did not seem to "require a revolution."

Supporters of CEW's decade-long work, although committed to better planning for female students, were constrained by the era's limited understanding of women's issues, the under-developed research base, and the dearth of foundation interest. They managed a delicate balancing act of addressing women's concerns while heeding Arthur Adams' call for "no special pleadings" on behalf of women. Overall, reliance on the idea of collegiate womanpower remained the commission's most effective argument for attention to women's concerns.

Within a decade of the commission's closing national sentiment shifted dramatically, with deeper change demanded for women and minority students. The decade-long work of the Commission on the Education of Women was key to this new advocacy. Although a full-fledged analysis had not yet developed, the commission moved from a conception that women's situation resulted from individual, psychological choices to an awareness that structural, economic, and cultural influences also played a role. Its ten-year project provided a touchstone for those involved in women's education, and its effort to gather, foster, and disseminate research constituted an important phase in advancing women's postwar concerns.

CHAPTER FOUR

Practice

*Advocacy in Women's
Professional Organizations*

When Northwestern University students returned to their campus in fall 1948, many were surprised to realize that the year's leave of absence taken by their dean of women, Ruth McCarn, resulted from her dismissal. They had assumed that McCarn was merely taking time off. But in fact, Dean of Students F. B. Seulberger, acting for President Franklyn Snyder, had arranged for McCarn's leave, even as he hired her replacement.[1] Pushed by student newspapers for more information, President Snyder said merely that "the change in the position of counselor to women is one of these administrative changes which take place from time to time in any big organization." Touching on a more subtle issue, he added: "It reflects no discredit of any sort on the preceding incumbent, and no connection with politics, religion, or social attitudes."[2]

In fact, Ruth McCarn had posed problems for Northwestern administrators since joining the university in 1937. McCarn had repeatedly protested racial and ethnic discrimination at Northwestern, especially in student housing and social life. In 1941 she had annoyed Snyder and business manager Harry Wells by securing acceptance for the prestigious black sorority Alpha Kappa Alpha to Northwestern's Panhellenic Council. Her advocacy for AKA—the nation's oldest African American sorority—coincided with her backing of an appeal by Northwestern's Interracial Commission for more on-campus housing for black students, who faced restrictive local options. McCarn's chastisement by the president and dean in 1941 festered over several years, peaking with her dismissal in 1948. In the interim, McCarn continued to advocate publicly for changes in

Northwestern's treatment of black and Jewish students, prompting alumni and financial supporters to complain to President Snyder.

McCarn's story is in some ways unique and dramatic. Students rallied to her defense, claiming they had discovered transcripts of potentially embarrassing administrative conversations. Moreover, the daughter of Robert Maynard Hutchins, prominent president of the University of Chicago and a rival of Northwestern's Snyder, was a student advisee of McCarn's. Her public defense of McCarn enticed newspapers in Chicago and nationwide to carry the story, embellished by unfavorable racial and administrative comparisons between the city's two leading universities.

On the other hand, McCarn's story typifies the experience of many women deans as they encountered postwar changes in campus organization, curricular decisions, and gender and race relations. Female professionals experienced challenges as campuses changed to accommodate more men and as society debated appropriate roles for educated women. Members of professional associations lamented the frequency with which women deans lost their jobs, often to men who had honed administrative skills in the military and who seemed impressive new leaders for postwar campuses teeming with G.I. Bill recipients.

This chapter tells a parallel story to the research advocacy of the ACE Commission on the Education of Women. Several prominent deans also served as ACE commission members, enhancing the networking opportunities. Through the commission, they explored how research could help explain and improve women's situation. Simultaneously, in their membership organizations, these women dealt with their own specific situations as they faced economic, patriotic, cultural, and psychological strictures that required careful balancing of expectations and ambition.

The story traces women's advocacy in two organizations: the American Association of University Women (AAUW) and the National Association of Deans of Women (NADW), the first a general membership group for college graduates, the other a specialized professional organization. Within these organizations, women confronted challenges in three areas: clarifying an appropriate collegiate curriculum, confronting issues of diversity within their own organizations, and defending their sense of professionalism as educators. First, working on the front lines of educational practice, they tried to craft curricula to prepare young women for a wide variety of futures; like the era's educational planners, they did not always agree on the best course. Second, within their organizations, these women faced cultural challenges around their own elitism and racial homogeneity, finding that an appreciation for the importance of integration did not automatically smooth the way to its enactment. Finally, the deans' own professionalism faced challenges as women's roles were debated and, as in McCarn's case, circumscribed in favor of more "modern" approaches. In confronting these challenges, women practitioners often took an individualized approach, offering explanations and remedies. Only as the challenges grew did they recognize patterns and systemic concerns that pushed them toward more collective action.

"THE FELLOWSHIP OF THE CONCERNED"

Women's work within professional and membership organizations offers a distinctive lens for investigating how they approached societal expectations. Anne Firor Scott, who studied women's use of such organizations over time, found that women often used activity in voluntary groups to "evade the constraints" of domestic roles. In times of limited opportunity for public or professional activity, women turned to such organizations to exercise public power, trade "self-absorption for community influence," and create alternative career ladders in nonprofessional settings.[3]

Postwar America teemed with volunteer and civic groups that provided leadership outlets for women. Many of the longstanding organizations targeted women both as members and as subjects; the most prominent included the League of Women Voters (LWV), the General Federation of Women's Clubs (GFWC), the Young Women's Christian Association (YWCA), and the Business and Professional Women's Clubs (BPWC). Two groups focused specifically on college women: the American Association of University Women (AAUW) and the National Association of Deans of Women (NADW).[4] AAUW and NADW, situated on opposite ends of the membership spectrum, one large and one small, one open widely to college graduates and one limited to college deans, were complementary partners in advocating for women's collegiate concerns.

AAUW constituted a large-scale membership group (112,000 members in 1950) for female graduates with liberal arts training; as such, it represented a wide scope of interests and experiences. NADW represented a much smaller, more focused professional organization; its membership (1,570 in 1951) was composed of deans of women in colleges and secondary schools.[5] Both groups served upper-middle-class members, but they represented collegiate leaders' thinking about education for women in a range of circumstances. As stalwarts in monitoring and supporting women's collegiate concerns, these groups became what one colleague dubbed "the fellowship of the concerned."[6]

The "fellowship" grew from a history of interrelationships in which women professionals moved between groups and issues. Such networks had long characterized women's work both within and outside education. Early efforts to open higher education to women, to encourage coeducation, and to expand the professions had all benefited from mutual support and activity between women and their organizations.[7] The postwar era continued such mutuality. In fact, many women leaders participated in AAUW, NADW, and the ACE Commission on the Education of Women (CEW). Ruth McCarn offers a good example of such professional networking. In the early 1950s, McCarn organized the NADW committee that eventually delivered Kathryn Phillips' $50,000 gift to start the ACE Commission on the Education of Women. She and Phillips had hoped that NADW could help ease the deteriorating situation for academic women. After discussions, however, they decided that focusing Phillips' money solely on deans was "too selfish and limited," reasoning that ACE could have more influence and a larger impact.[8] Although scholars disagree about the long-term wisdom for NADW in transferring the Phillips gift rather than using it to build its own influence, the donation clearly strengthened connections between the deans' group and the influential ACE.[9]

Several NADW members held seats on CEW. Esther Lloyd-Jones, first commission chair, was a longtime NADW member and author of key texts in student development.[10] Althea Hottel, who directed the commission during Lloyd-Jones's chairmanship, served as the University of Pennsylvania's dean of women, NADW member, and later president of the AAUW. McCarn became president of NADW following her dismissal from Northwestern. Other ACE commissioners, including Katherine Blyley, Ruth Quarles, and Eunice Hilton, moved easily among AAUW, NADW, and ACE, alternately using the distinctive strengths of each organization.

Besides sharing members, AAUW and NADW shared a history that began when AAUW lent office space and pages in its journal to the fledgling deans' group in the 1910s and 1920s.[11] NADW was just starting in 1916, but AAUW boasted nineteenth-century origins as the Association of Collegiate Alumnae (ACA). Bostonian Emily Talbot had created the ACA in 1881 to provide fellowship and mutual support for the era's scattered female college graduates. In 1921, ACA merged with the Southern Association of College Women, creating the new AAUW with a national and—via membership in the International Federation of University Women—even a global reach. As a membership organization for female graduates of approved colleges, AAUW existed to support higher education for women, encouraging its members to "continue their own education; further the advancement of women; and discharge [the] special responsibilities of college educated women."[12]

By the post–World War II era, AAUW was an influential organization with hundreds of local branches and a national office in Washington, D.C. Serving more than 100,00 members via a tripartite national, state, and local format, AAUW covered a wide array of interests. Its headquarters operated through committees: international relations, legislation (with a full-time lobbyist), status of women, program development (including fundraising), and social concerns. Its active education program included an important standards and accreditation board that promulgated guidelines for women's collegiate programs.

In the early twentieth century, when accreditation for colleges and universities was new, few administrators worried about standardizing programs for women, often leaving their interests unattended. AAUW assumed a monitorial role for women's education, creating a template that assessed programming for women, particularly in the liberal arts. Although it had no formal authority, AAUW tried to pressure coeducational institutions to devote more attention to their female students and faculty.[13] The accreditation program provided an important tool during the postwar era when focus on women waned. In addition to its accreditation effort, AAUW supported a committee on education, staffed by a higher education associate. This staff member monitored legislation, tracked higher education trends, conferred with Washington-based organizations, and served the membership by creating reading lists and guiding the self-education program. As a membership organization, AAUW worked primarily through local branches.[14] A biennial national convention gathered members to address issues and adopt resolutions that guided the organization, from national policy concerns to local operations.

Whereas AAUW cast its net widely, recruiting female collegians interested in education, NADW targeted education professionals. NADW's primary goals included advocating for a well-trained, competent woman dean in every institution, and supporting the professional confraternity of deans. Originally, NADW had met as a department of the National Education Association (NEA), an origin that encouraged the participation of deans of girls in secondary schools alongside their collegiate counterparts. The deans emphasized "continuity in the guidance and support of women students," whether they were girls or young collegians. Including deans of girls also boosted membership; by 1926, just ten years after its founding, NADW boasted nearly a thousand members.[15]

The 1930s challenged the deans' organization financially; collegiate funding for professional development shrank, and many deans lost their positions entirely. Yet during this period NADW established its own journal, opened a Washington

office, joined a new Council of Guidance and Personnel Associations, and became an associate member of ACE. Although NADW, like AAUW, operated state
branches, its main work occurred in the national office, supported by annual
conventions and an active journal.

Both NADW and AAUW entered the postwar period as sturdy but watchful
organizations, confronting an environment filled with confusion over the purposes and approaches for educating collegiate women. Their first challenge lay
in deciding how to advocate for women's preparation and their futures.

THE FIRST CHALLENGE: PLANNING WOMEN'S EDUCATION
FOR WOMEN'S LIVES

In the postwar world, collegiate women found a variety of possible ways to
use their education, whether professionally or in community activities. Marjorie
Bell Chambers, a longtime AAUW member, exemplifies the influence of membership in "the fellowship of the concerned" on how women considered their
options. Chambers recalled that on the morning of her graduation from Mount
Holyoke College in 1943, she received a membership application for AAUW. A
college official suggested that she tuck the card away "with your jewelry, [for] you
may want it sometime." At that point in her life, Chambers had no specific plans
for the future, but she heeded the suggestion.[16]

In 1950, she described herself as a housewife in Los Alamos, New Mexico,
"going nuts" tending two young children. Looking for something to "keep my
brain going," Chambers attended a local AAUW meeting. Inspired by the group's
mandate to "do something for our community," she became active in AAUW,
and in 1975 was elected to the national presidency.[17] Chambers later pursued
a career in international relations and earned a doctorate in history. However,
in the 1950s and 1960s, she was rare in reaching AAUW national leadership
without a Ph.D., and her election marked a growing shift in the organization's
outreach to nonprofessionals.

AAUW and NADW followed two approaches to translating societal expectations for women into educational plans: self-education and programmatic action.
To educate their members about women's choices, the organizations used journals, conventions, and local study programs, often relying on research promulgated by the ACE Commission on the Education of Women. They also instituted
programs to support women and expand opportunities. Some of these were research-oriented. AAUW, for example, produced studies on collegiate curricula,
the effects of anti-nepotism rules, and the needs of older women graduates.

As advocacy organizations, AAUW and NADW recognized a need to educate their own members. The quarterly journals of both groups became important educational tools, and the postwar volumes read like shorthand versions of the era's educational debates. The economic utilitarians, cultural conformists, and equity-based planners discussed in chapter 2 were all fully represented in these pages, often provoking debate with each other as well as among organization members. The journals became an important way for these practitioners to engage with research.

President Lynn White of Mills College, for instance, addressed the national conventions of both AAUW and NADW, offering his view that current women's curricula led too far from their real feminine strengths, leaving them unprepared for lives in families and community service. Many association members agreed. Dean Margaret Habein supported White in the NADW journal, arguing that educators must be "realistic" in training women for social responsibility and in presenting a more flexible collegiate curriculum. She pleaded for both women students and educators to be "less concerned with their 'equality,' as regards men, [and] more concerned with their own particular and unique gifts."[18]

White's and Habein's approach was challenged, however, by equity-oriented scholars like Mirra Komarovsky, who doubted the suitability of the "yardsticks" White used to measure female achievement. Women looked less successful because they had rarely received a fair chance at the full range of career and avocational options, Komarovsky argued. Noting that psychologists found greater within-sex than between-sex differences in mental ability, Komarovsky asked for deeper training rather than a narrower focus: "Should we not rather face the fact that society today frustrates the legitimate interests of women and has not yet given women a real choice in the matter of their lives?"[19]

In addition to curriculum debates, journal readers also found workforce analyses by prominent economic utilitarians. Findings appeared from both the President's Commission on Higher Education and the *Womanpower* study of the National Manpower Council.[20] In fact, NADW members were so compelled by *Womanpower* that, after hearing a presentation by author Eli Ginzberg, they arranged to distribute the book to all members and to examine it at their next annual meeting.

As professionals in higher education, NADW's deans were more familiar with these issues than the average AAUW member who had, most likely, ended her education at the bachelor's level and not considered the long-term implications of equity debates. AAUW functioned differently than NADW, promoting self-education through its branches and bringing research ideas to local members. The

AAUW study program emanated from national headquarters, with direction and guidance filtered through state and local chairs. The approach was to move "from principle to program." That is, the national convention would pass a resolution advocating an organization-wide position on education; this idea would then be explored by local members through readings, questions, and discussion points recommended by national staff members.[21]

In 1957, for example, the convention passed a resolution on the future of higher education: "We recognize that the coming growth of the college population will impose new problems on our colleges and universities. We therefore resolve to inform ourselves on the implications of these problems and we express our continued concern that higher education be supported and strengthened." To move "from principle to program," branches addressed specific issues: "What problems need study now to prepare well for this student increase?—policy, quality, facilities, finance, scholarships, faculty, curriculum? Is higher education of a whole people desirable? What about admission of women when institutions are crowded? What action can your branch or committee take following study?"[22] The higher education associate created a reading list with study questions, distributing this "study-action material" to state and branch education chairs.

The associates also regularly disseminated reports from branches so that others might copy good ideas. Associate Eleanor Dolan summarized branch work in 1959–60 on scholarships, college guidance, teacher education, and junior colleges. She reported that the Parma, Ohio, branch had discovered—through its own research—that only a small percentage of local female high school graduates pursued college. Members responded by creating a pamphlet about local opportunities, including scholarships, to encourage girls to consider college. The Northern Montana branch sponsored a party for high school girls and appointed four local women to serve as informal "consultants" on college planning. This locally targeted activity fit AAUW's self-image as a large and efficient adult education operation.[23]

Beyond self-education, AAUW and NADW found study of their own membership a useful research opportunity. As the nation's largest group of female college graduates, AAUW offered a particularly fruitful survey population. In 1955, AAUW conducted a membership study with results that surprised some of its leaders. Although quite racially homogeneous, the organization's class and status makeup was beginning to change. Results showed that "the typical Association member was as likely to be an educated housewife as a college dean or lawyer—a vast change from the traditional membership composed almost entirely of professional career women." Although they might have noticed the increased participation of nonprofessionals like Marjorie Chambers, AAUW leadership professed shock from the shift: "We were struck dumb," said survey chair Hallie Farmer of the result that two-thirds of members were married, two-thirds were under age 46, and more than 50 percent were mothers. The press enjoyed reporting the findings, amused that so many college graduates were able to find husbands, teasing that "college and cooking can mix."[24] For those outsiders who viewed AAUW as a group of dissatisfied feminists, the image was a turnabout. It also confirmed the tendency to see women as incidental students, even as their campus numbers grew.

The apparent differences in members' backgrounds fueled a continuing debate within AAUW about the sort of collegiate education best suited to modern women's lives. For several decades, the national leadership had constituted well-trained, career-focused single women; but, as the 1955 survey revealed, ordinary members increasingly represented a new middle-class, college-educated consumer.

The findings reflected the change occurring among American students as college-going became a more widely practiced middle-class endeavor. As the century progressed, colleges served an ever-wider economic group of women and men—like the G.I. Bill veterans—seeking college training for a variety of reasons. No longer did attaining a degree require women to choose between career and family; the two-thirds of married AAUW graduates testified to an easier mix. Acknowledgment of the changes in members' personal choices and professional ambitions sparked a shift in AAUW programming. Recognizing the new opportunities, AAUW supported three prominent programs in the postwar period: extending its longstanding fellowship program, organizing a roster of women holding the Ph.D., and creating a new College Faculty Program. All three demonstrated the potential of a group like AAUW to affect women's opportunities.

The fellowship program was the longest-running and most prominent AAUW effort. Since 1881 AAUW had provided financial support for women's graduate education, an effort that was begun because women were generally ignored by other fellowship sources. Over the decades, fellowships for both undergraduate and graduate training were offered nationally and locally, although branches could set their own criteria.[25] In 1927 the association inaugurated a Million Dollar Campaign for fellowships, and by 1936 had reached more than one-quarter of the goal.[26] In 1955, AAUW took the significant step of creating an Educational Foundation that organized its fellowship fundraising into an endowment, permitting tax-exempt status for such gifts. The Educational Foundation proved an effective organizational means of planning projects, soliciting support, and organizing efforts. The new foundation galvanized the fellowship effort, and by 1960

AAUW provided more than $200,000 annually in fellowship awards, marking it as a key resource for women's education.[27]

Raising fellowship money demonstrated the real grass-roots strength of a membership organization like AAUW. Although the ACE Commission on the Education of Women struggled to find funding for its research efforts, the AAUW's Million Dollar Campaign and Educational Foundation revealed the committed personal and financial involvement of AAUW members. Despite the labor-intensive nature of the fundraising (members frequently ignored the costs of their own time), the fellowship program won ongoing support.[28] It also provided a comfortable way to support other women; many members declined to label the fundraising "feminist," stressing that "the advancement of knowledge was quite as important a motive as the advancement of women."[29]

A 1957 analysis of the fellowships by Ruth Tryon documented both the nature of women's professional opportunities across the century and the particular impact of the AAUW program. Tryon surveyed the 431 women who had won national AAUW fellowships between 1890 and 1956, a group divided fairly evenly among the sciences, social sciences, and humanities. Three-quarters held the Ph.D. (earned either before or after the fellowship), and three-quarters eventually pursued college teaching. Program evaluators were quick to cite quality as their prime criterion in choosing fellows over time. They looked for a sense of purpose and "personal qualities that are likely to produce a true scholar," emphasizing that "fellowships are given to develop people, not to get a piece of work done."[30]

The shift over time in characteristics of AAUW fellows and their careers reflected national changes in women's professional opportunities. Tryon noted that the proportion of fellows over age 35 had risen each decade; by the 1950s, 25 percent of recipients were over age 40. In addition, married women and fellows with children became more common. Before 1929 no fellowship had been awarded to a married woman, but by the 1940s fellows with children were "commonplace."[31]

The program also furthered AAUW's global commitments. After World War II concern for displaced women scholars created fellowships for women in Europe and Latin America. However, the commitment to global diversity rarely extended to the home front. No African American woman won an AAUW fellowship until 1962, when Queen E. Shootes received support for a project on black women home economists.[32]

Although fellowships helped strengthen the growth of women with graduate and professional degrees, a growing concern about the dearth of women on college faculties produced two new AAUW efforts: a roster of women who already

held the Ph.D. and were eligible for faculty roles, and a College Faculty Program
to train women for college teaching. Both programs recognized that women
were adversely affected by the usual operations of the academic labor market.
Neither the numbers nor the prognosis for women as college faculty was strong
in the 1950s. As we have seen, women faculty achieved some progress during
World War II, holding nearly 30 percent of academic posts in 1944. After the
war, however, men and veterans often displaced women faculty. Economic and
cultural influences, combined with the effect of the G.I. Bill, prompted a decline
in women's percentage as graduate students during the 1950s. As the National
Education Association found, women held only 22 percent of full-time faculty
jobs in 1954–55, and a large proportion of institutions rejected women as potential resources for filling gaps.[33]

AAUW began its own examination of faculty data, and, in cooperation with
the National Research Council, organized a roster of women holding doctorates. By 1958 the groups had gathered information on 10,000 women who
had earned the doctorate since 1935; 3,410 of these asked to be included on a
roster "of those who are willing to consider another job even though they may
be already employed."[34] The roster sought to simplify institutional recruiting.
In an era when colleges found little incentive to include women among job
candidates, the ready availability of the roster encouraged seeing women as potential resources. However, in an echo of CEW's experience, the roster suffered
from lack of funding; foundations proved unwilling to support it, even though
AAUW demonstrated that seventy schools consulted it for names in the first
year of operation.[35]

AAUW's appeal to foundations was more successful for a new College Faculty
Program. As early as 1955, through its various committees on standards, development, research, and education, AAUW pursued support for several training
and retraining programs. Some projects concentrated on preparing women for
jobs in science and mathematics, including teaching in secondary school. With
its Educational Foundation in place to coordinate fundraising, AAUW won support from the Rockefeller Brothers Fund in 1961 for a program "to encourage
mature women to return to graduate studies in preparation for careers in college
teaching, administration, and research." Rockefeller gave nearly $300,000 for
a three-year pilot program.[36] The "womanpower" aspects of the proposal apparently matched the foundation's interests.

After assessing both the greatest need and the most sympathetic institutions,
AAUW initiated the program in eleven Southern states.[37] During the three years
of Rockefeller funding (1962–65), 126 tuition awards went to women over age

35 for a year of "refresher" graduate studies to prepare them for collegiate-level positions.[38] The program demonstrated a good success rate. Eighty-nine percent of fellows completed their academic work; two years after the pilot ended, 52 percent held jobs on college faculties, most in liberal arts colleges.[39]

The energy generated through the roster and the College Faculty Program led AAUW into a joint education and fundraising effort that demonstrated the organization's power. In 1959 leaders called for a "crusade" to develop "A High Regard for College Teaching as a Career." With higher priority than a regular organizational resolution, the Crusade pulled together multiple AAUW interests, including its longstanding commitment to "advance the cause of women and raise the standards of education." A fact sheet about the Crusade explained that neither cause "is possible in the future without more and better qualified faculty. Such faculty will not be available until the public realizes their importance." AAUW argued that its membership was "strategically well placed to mold the public opinion and identify the able."[40]

Crusade-related tasks for individual members included providing information to the public, working to change attitudes about college teaching as a career, and encouraging "people of high ability" to qualify themselves for the work. As AAUW leaders approached various foundations for financial support, its branches—especially in the South—worked locally to raise money and awareness. Although Rockefeller declined further support after the initial three years, AAUW did not abandon the program. Using the grass-roots fundraising skills honed in the fellowship program, branches continued the College Faculty Program on a smaller scale, ensuring that the groundwork laid within states and institutions would not be wasted.[41] In this effort, members demonstrated their longstanding willingness to support women on their own.

Although the College Faculty Program dominated AAUW's higher education effort for several years, it did not replace attention either to the fellowship program or research efforts. Both the higher education committee and the research committee generated numerous research studies. One such study investigated how to promote more liberal arts training within burgeoning professional programs in education, nursing, and home economics.[42] Another examined how anti-nepotism rules prohibiting family members from holding academic posts on the same campus usually disadvantaged the female partner in academic marriages.[43]

These ongoing efforts to study the collegiate curriculum, to support women in academic job searches, and to train mature candidates for faculty roles all demonstrate organizational responses to the postwar situation for women, even as they laid the groundwork for collective activity. Women's use of education was shifting, as indicated by the numbers of older and married women using the fellowship program and the roster. Women were finding expanded choices for supplying their "womanpower" to the job market, and professional organizations worked to offer new opportunities. At the same time, however, changes among the college-educated population exerted stresses within women's organizations. AAUW's own survey had revealed increasing differences among members, especially in their marital and economic status. One characteristic that did not significantly change, however, was the racial homogeneity of the membership. As the postwar era progressed, both AAUW and NADW faced challenges in racially integrating the membership of their groups.

THE SECOND CHALLENGE: CONFRONTING RACISM AND EXPANDING THE "FELLOWSHIP"

Althea Hottel was an energetic young dean of women at the University of Pennsylvania when she assumed the presidency of AAUW in 1947. Later she would head the International Federation of University Women and direct the ACE Commission on the Education of Women, but the AAUW presidency was her first national leadership role. Hottel began her four-year term during a particularly difficult moment for AAUW, as members faced the consequences of their longstanding avoidance of racial issues and the toleration of differential practices by local branches.

AAUW had long been racially and socioeconomically uniform. When the organization started in the 1880s, liberal arts education was rare for women, and educational opportunities for African Americans lagged far behind those of whites. Although some black women attended collegiate-level schools such as Oberlin, the Seven Sister colleges, and state universities, many black colleges barely exceeded high school level at the turn of the twentieth century.[44] As the decades progressed, curricular opportunities for African American women only slowly approximated those of whites. Even in the 1950s, African American women were much less likely than white women to hold degrees from four-year liberal arts institutions.

AAUW did not specifically ban African American members. However, its focus on liberal arts graduates, coupled with its insistence on approving institutions, eliminated most black colleges struggling to upgrade curricula, programming, and facilities. Furthermore, although black graduates of AAUW-approved (often white) institutions could join as national members, local custom often found them unwelcome at the branch level.

Even though AAUW worked to expand its membership during the twentieth century, the organization continued to rely on what historian Susan Levine calls "elite egalitarianism"—a belief that professional and public rewards should accrue to people who demonstrate merit, most visibly through their educational achievement.[45] Thus, AAUW worked to upgrade education by certifying college curricula but did not explicitly recognize that many students were excluded from first-rate programs. Similarly, AAUW branches could choose members who matched particular local interests without acknowledging any discriminatory intent.

Throughout the early twentieth century, the national office followed a hands-off approach toward member recruitment, with the consequence that large differences appeared not only among branches but also between headquarters and the locals. These dual operations of AAUW gave it what Levine calls two distinct but not necessarily compatible functions: "a social club and an agent of social change."[46] That is, national efforts focused on change for American women, but local gatherings—even while they pursued national themes—were more socially oriented. In an era witnessing increased conflict around race, an organization as widely dispersed as AAUW inevitably faced varied internal views and practices.

Dissension had been brewing for several years when Hottel assumed her presidency. Throughout the 1930s, AAUW had not encouraged membership from black graduates. In this, it was not alone; other women's groups like the Business and Professional Women's Clubs and the League of Women Voters rarely adopted integrationist agendas. The YWCA, one of the more liberal groups on racial issues, faced its own internal crisis in 1946 after it passed an Interracial Charter calling for wider membership.[47]

Throughout the war years, AAUW Director Kathryn McHale sidestepped racial issues, even while observing an increasing level of concern among her members. By war's end, only seven branches in the country had integrated. Like many AAUW officers, McHale was more comfortable encouraging African American women to become national members than urging branches to change local practices. As a result, AAUW's proud collegiality with the International Federation of University Women (IFUW) was threatened when IFUW compared the American group's racial policies to those leading to the wartime expulsion of IFUW branches in Germany, Austria, and Italy.[48]

Pressure on AAUW's national office for integration was heightened by a confrontation orchestrated by the District of Columbia branch. A clubhouse dining room was available in Washington for the hospitality of all AAUW members. However, since the DC branch provided primary financial support for the dining room, it considered the clubhouse its own. Traditionally, the dining room had served black members, but even small attempts at racial mixing among members had proved awkward. In 1945 one faction of the DC branch pushed for integration of both the clubhouse and the association. The national board remained uncertain, worrying over how members would receive unilateral action they might take on membership policy.

In 1946 nationally prominent African American educator Mary Church Terrell agreed to be a test case for DC branch membership. Born in 1863 to a wealthy Memphis family, Terrell was among the black community's most respected activists. In 1896 she co-founded the National Association of Colored Women to improve conditions for poorer African Americans through the joint efforts of middle-class and educated black women. Over the years, Terrell increasingly applied economic and social analyses to her work.[49] Following World War II she was struck, like many, by the discrepancy between America's espoused values and the persistence of segregation, and she began an active campaign for integration, focusing on the nation's capital.[50]

Terrell had allowed her AAUW affiliation to lapse, so a member of the Washington chapter advanced her for local membership, sharply dividing the branch. AAUW's national board had long been reluctant to legislate practice for local branches, but with Terrell's challenge provoking wide concern, they chose to act. With a rare use of what Levine calls "sovereignty from the center," the board affirmed educational criteria as the sole basis for membership decisions, asserting that "there can be no authorization for any discrimination on racial, religious, or political grounds." They threatened to expel the DC branch for its refusal to accept Terrell or other black applicants for membership.[51]

The issue did not disappear with the board's declaration. Uncomfortable with forced change to their social practice, the DC branch sued the national AAUW in U.S. District Court in 1948, charging that the board had no authority to expel branches for refusing to accept the policy interpretation. To the surprise of AAUW leaders, the DC branch won both the first suit and the 1949 appeal. The federal appellate court, writing five years before the *Brown v. Board of Education* desegregation decision, ruled on the basis of the national organization's provisions for membership. The court found that AAUW's existing eligibility regulations meant only that members *could* be admitted if they met requirements, not that they *must* be. Moreover, the national organization had demonstrated a pattern of not interfering with local branch membership decisions. In effect, the rulings meant that branches could continue operating as they wished, rejecting members not perceived suitable.[52]

Hottel assumed her AAUW presidency just as the court decisions finalized, facing the task of uniting an organization divided by branch challenges, the law-suits, and continuing segregation. She consulted her friend, former Supreme Court Justice Owen J. Roberts, who advised the organization to revise its bylaws to clarify authority over membership decisions and eligibility.[53] Hottel pushed this agenda by visiting branches, giving speeches, writing editorials, and per-suading individuals to support the change. Her work succeeded; at the 1949 AAUW national convention, members overwhelmingly approved a change in the bylaws (by a vote of 2168–65)[54] that the only restriction on membership would be "a college degree from an institution on the organization's approved list."[55]

One of the groups Hottel consulted during the racial controversy was the National Association of College Women, an educational organization—like AAUW—for graduates of approved collegiate institutions. The NACW shared the same acronym as Terrell's own National Association of Colored Women, but the two groups differed in scope. Terrell's larger organization treated social and economic concerns across black society, while the small NACW focused on fe-male African American college graduates. The National Association of College Women (NACW) had been created as a response to AAUW's restrictive member-ship practices. Black college graduates shared the larger group's interest in con-tributing to their local communities but found themselves unwelcome in AAUW. In 1910 ten African American graduates in the Washington, D.C., area (includ-ing Terrell) organized a predecessor group to NACW, the College Alumnae Club (CAC), to sponsor reading groups and work for improvement of educational op-portunities for black students.[56]

In 1923, through the invigorating leadership of Lucy Diggs Slowe, the first dean of women at Howard University, the CAC expanded into a national organi-zation. Comparing their concerns while attending a national educational confer-ence, Slowe and several colleagues reorganized the small CAC into the National Association of College Women. Eighty women, black female graduates from the nation's premier institutions, including Stanford, Chicago, Pennsylvania, Fisk, Howard, and the Seven Sisters colleges, joined the new group.[57]

Like AAUW, NACW restricted membership to approved institutions and to graduates of certain disciplines, seeing this as a way to encourage academic quality. It adopted a constitution resembling the AAUW's in scope and effort, organizing five regional sections and several standing committees, including educational poli-cies, interracial relations, fellowships, finance, membership, nominations, social amenities, publicity, and the most important, standards and recognition.

During the infancy of educational accreditation, organizations like NACW and AAUW used their standards and recognition committees as a rare source of leverage for college women. During the 1910s and 1920s, when many black institutions struggled for financial and curricular stability, NACW's committee surveyed schools and visited college presidents to advocate for women. Mirroring AAUW's standards, NACW reported on schools' curricular requirements and electives, women's representation on trustee boards and the faculty, and salary differentials between men and women. With Slowe as a leading proponent, NACW pushed for a women's dean on each campus, advocating for an official who would be "an educational specialist," rather than a mere disciplinarian.[58] While the standards committee advocated stronger campus opportunities, other NACW committees championed community outreach, libraries, scholarships, and overall stronger collegiate education for black women.

Slowe's unexpected death in 1937 affected NACW's momentum, since her leadership had been so powerful.[59] In addition, the 1949 AAUW vote easing membership for African American graduates threatened NACW's vitality as a separate organization. Founded for the same reasons as AAUW—intellectual fellowship and educational advocacy—NACW worried about retaining its strength once AAUW welcomed black members. Some NACW branches did experience membership decline, and one Tennessee chapter disbanded completely when its members joined AAUW.[60] However, NACW had always encouraged cooperation with AAUW. Hottel's presidential visit to NACW's 1950 meeting provided evidence of mutual respect, and joint programming between AAUW and NACW actually increased in the postwar period.

By 1954, NACW shifted gears. Constitutional changes signaled a new interracial interest, replacing the previous focus on "Negro education." Dissolving the longstanding committee on standards, NACW expanded membership to graduates of less-prestigious schools. The focus also broadened to include a wide array of civic activities and "human relations" programs, including family education, home management, and sex education. NACW retained a commitment to black issues, promoting black culture by distributing reading lists, developing bibliographies, and sponsoring programs on African American life and history.[61]

NACW was a small organization, with only 600 active members and a budget of merely $6000 in 1949. Although it had long raised money to support black women's education, only in 1947 were funds sufficient to grant a national fellowship.[62] However, though modest in size, NACW sustained black women's educational advocacy during a period when white organizations ignored their concerns, thereby asserting black women's place in the "fellowship of the concerned."

NACW was not the only educational organization created in response to discrimination by predominantly white groups. African American deans also felt a need to organize on their own behalf, finding only a lukewarm welcome in the National Association of Deans of Women. Once again, Lucy Diggs Slowe of Howard University proved instrumental in creating a group specifically focused on black concerns.

Slowe was the first African American member of NADW and was deeply committed to its advocacy for deans of women.[63] However, as her leadership in NACW demonstrated, Slowe also promoted attention to African American institutions—an issue finding little hearing within NADW. Seeking an opportunity to meet with colleagues who shared responsibility for advising African American students, Slowe instigated a gathering of such advisers at NADW's annual meeting in 1929. The connection proved helpful to women in this role, and the colleagues met annually at NACW for several years. In 1935 they organized themselves into the Association of Deans of Women and Advisers to Girls in Negro Schools. This specialized group shared with NACW a general interest in black women students, and with NADW a belief in the power of the dean's office. As a separate organization, the association allowed specific attention to the intersection of black women's concerns and the deanship.[64] For twenty-five years, the "Colored Deans of Women" worked to "bolster a spirit of unity and cooperation" among deans, enhance their professional status, increase their knowledge, and help female students develop "physically, mentally, socially, and morally."[65]

Although NADW never excluded black members, African American deans had to fight for acceptance within the organization. Black members stressed the contributions of older black deans who served as mentors, and collegial white members who supported their participation. Bennett College dean Ruth Brett Quarles (later a member of ACE's Commission on the Education of Women) recalled that her first NADW meeting in 1940 was held in a hotel that did not serve blacks. This common occurrence provoked a formal protest to NADW by Hilda Davis, then president of the Association of Deans of Women and Advisers to Girls in Negro Schools; however, it was several years before NADW resolved not to hold its conferences in segregated settings.[66]

Many early black deans expressed surprise that "NADW, a professional organization of educated women, could not effect change in its own organization."[67] Even with good intentions, integration was difficult to accomplish in the 1940s and 1950s. Brett explained that many black members chose to carefully mix their criticism with patience, watching the organization's efforts. She acknowledged the important support of NADW leaders, recalling how her white colleague Irma Voight once walked several black members through the lobby of a segregated hotel to a private lunch with NADW president Sarah Blanding.[68]

A generation after Lucy Slowe, African American scholar Jeanne Noble followed Slowe's strategy of connecting work across various postwar women's organizations, showing the value of networking. Noble, whose work was frequently
cited by the ACE Commission on the Education of Women, studied with CEW
chair Esther Lloyd-Jones at the influential Columbia University Teachers College
program for deans and published frequently with CEW director Opal David.
Noble's thesis, published in 1956 as *The Negro Woman's College Education*, became a key resource on black women collegians' history, efforts, attitudes, and
careers.[69] Throughout the 1950s, Noble published in the NADW journal and
chaired its research committee. Later she served on John F. Kennedy's President's
Commission on the Status of Women.[70]

The two predominantly white organizations—AAUW and NADW—responded differently to postwar racial concerns. NADW approached race more comfortably than AAUW. It was the only guidance organization to openly support the
1954 Brown desegregation decision, whereas AAUW was unable to craft a statement acceptable to members.[71] And although AAUW had supported a program
for international women since the 1920s, only in 1962 did it grant the first fellowship to an American black woman. Even in 1980, women of color constituted
only 3 percent of AAUW members.[72]

AAUW's difficulty in accommodating racial diversity likely stemmed from
its varied purposes. While members felt comfortable working toward common
national goals of advancing women's education, they hesitated when local work
required social mixing across racial groups. As a professional organization with
more easily shared commitments, NADW experienced a smoother transition
to integration. Yet accommodating racial differences also posed difficulties for
NADW; the existence of a separate black organization suggested that racial concerns among deans were not easily solved. Black women themselves seemed
more attuned to the impact of collective activity, simultaneously challenging the
predominantly white organizations and creating their own affinity groups.

Difficult as the racial issues were, the postwar era witnessed even an greater
challenge to the deans from outside their organization, one that threatened their
livelihoods. In a campus environment where women's presence as students, faculty, and professionals seemed increasingly incidental, female educators faced
a major issue in advocating for their own efficacy—and sometimes their very
survival—on collegiate campuses.

THE THIRD CHALLENGE: FACING PERSONAL AND PROFESSIONAL LIMITS

When Ruth Strang retired as editor of the NADW journal in 1960, she had held the job for twenty-two years. During that period, she taught doctoral students in higher education at Columbia University, University of California Berkeley, and University of Arizona. To honor her work, NADW printed research articles by thirty-one of Strang's students, many of whom had pursued academic careers in counseling and student affairs. By proudly featuring the scholarly work of Strang's protégés, NADW was promoting a vision of the model modern dean: a well-educated researcher and prolific teacher, active and knowledgeable about guidance, and dedicated to improving the lives of female collegians.[73]

Strang's experience of postwar higher education had been more satisfying than that of Ruth McCarn, the dean of women fired by Northwestern University. Although McCarn had a particularly difficult tenure at Northwestern, her dismissal illustrated a noticeable postwar pattern of institutions firing or demoting deans of women in favor of a "dean of students." This new configuration often featured a man as head of a larger student affairs office, with little particular attention paid to women's concerns and low visibility for female administrators.

Watching this shift in the first decade after the war, members of NADW and AAUW seemed puzzled by the sudden diminution of women's administrative roles, which left them feeling personally attacked and professionally insufficient. Protesting the changes and assessing their meaning for deans' careers occupied the energies of both groups in the two decades following the war. The two women's organizations faced three significant challenges to their professionalism following the war, each of which pushed them to clarify their roles. First, amid structural changes in deans' offices, women deans had to fight for their continued existence as student affairs professionals dedicated to women students. Second, they had to choose whether to identify with guidance professionals, seeing there a threat to their self-image as educators. Finally, they were pushed to justify their commitment to feminism in an era when such outright identification raised concerns. Each of these posed the challenge of seeing issues from a collective viewpoint.

The years after World War II saw a steep decline in dean of women's positions as well as the remaining deans' access to campus leaders. In 1940, 86 percent of deans of women reported directly to their presidents; by 1962, only 30 percent did so.[74] Most frequently, dean of women positions were eliminated entirely in a new bureaucracy that favored a single dean for all students. Sometimes the new structure created one dean of students with subordinate deans dealing separately with men and women. But most often men assumed the new dean of student jobs, diminishing women's opportunity for influential professional roles on campuses. And as with McCarn, when jobs shrank or disappeared, the women holding them—usually experienced, trained, and older professionals—were often dismissed.

Three forces influenced the dramatic changes in women deans' roles: the tendency to see women as incidental on the postwar campus, the appeal of military men as campus leaders, and the growing shift in the student affairs profession toward a centralized hierarchy. As discussed in chapter 2, women's postwar influence in higher education generally diminished with the impact of the G.I. Bill and the growth of the research university. With so many veterans filling campuses, student affairs professionals saw good sense in placing ex-military men in charge of student life. Men who had proven effective in managing wartime personnel seemed ideal for campuses burgeoning with new students and new needs.

Throughout the 1930s, business influence increasingly permeated higher education. Walter Dill Scott of Northwestern (who was president when Ruth McCarn began her job there) pioneered the application of business ideas to student affairs departments, believing that treating students as "personnel" would permit deans to specialize in particular aspects of student life and tailor their work to student needs. The goal was an efficient, customized student experience.[75] In 1937 the American Council on Education sponsored a study whose very title indicated acceptance of Scott's call for greater centralization and coordination in student affairs. *The Student Personnel Point of View* sought to convince presidents and faculty to treat student affairs colleagues as fellow educators whose focus was different, but complementary. Deans might not teach in college classrooms, but they nonetheless influenced the education of students. The ACE revised the monograph in 1948 to accommodate the postwar recommendations of the President's Commission on Higher Education. That committee highlighted the enhanced role of higher education in preparing global citizens, once again envisioning deans as partners in the academic experience.[76] Both versions of the book recommended a centralized student affairs office under a single leader.

The experience of Indiana University's Kate Hevner Mueller showed Scott's business approach in action. Mueller, a well-known NADW member who had edited its journal and published an influential book on collegiate women, had worked as Indiana's dean of women since 1937.[77] Indiana president Herman B. Wells was influenced by the student personnel approach and had, for several years, recommended a centralization plan for the student affairs division.[78] At Indiana, the postwar veteran influx was enormous, as five thousand new students poured onto an ill-prepared campus within six months of the war's end. To President Wells, the time seemed right to reorganize student affairs, and he turned to Col. Raymond B. Shoemaker, who headed the university's wartime military programs. The reorganization made Shoemaker dean of students, heading a new Division of Student Personnel. In Wells' original plan, the extant dean of men and dean of women's offices were to be retained, but concerns about redundancy—as well as problematic personalities—resulted in a new set of assistant deans, each handling a special aspect of student personnel work. Mueller, who had long functioned as an autonomous dean of women, was demoted to "assistant dean and senior counselor to women." Not only Mueller's title, but most of her duties, disappeared.[79]

Although some concerns had already surfaced about Mueller's administrative abilities (and she later admitted that she brought little expertise to the dean's job), her demotion nonetheless seemed harsh. Mueller was not consulted about the changes and was informed of her new job by a junior male colleague. This pattern of older women deans being replaced by ex-military men appeared across the country. As one of Mueller's colleagues explained: "The ROTC commandant would go into student affairs; he seemed to be a natural choice. . . . He could fit with those veterans very nicely." The same process occurred at Texas A&M, Missouri, Kentucky, Florida, and Michigan universities.[80]

Many of the women demoted or dismissed were, like Mueller, active nationally and well-known in NADW and AAUW. Their stories circulated quickly within the profession, often provoking protest by the organizations. Overall, although NADW members were more immediately and personally affected by the decisions, AAUW took a more combative stance in protesting the diminution of women's campus roles. Some in NADW worried about being seen as "militant" if they complained too vocally.[81] AAUW found the situation worrisome enough that in 1944 it issued a statement criticizing women deans' loss of authority. In 1945 the organization surveyed deans' status, finding that about a third of all institutions lacked a woman dean with faculty status and a significant role in policy making.[82] They used their journal to highlight these concerns. In 1946, AAUW higher education specialist Helen Hosp cautioned that collegiate women were in danger of becoming "our country's first postwar casualty."[83] Dean Alice Lloyd concurred, tying the importance of women's role to their defense of democracy: "The position of women in the educational world of the postwar period must concern all people who are interested in the protection of minority groups and all who are concerned with maintaining the principles of democracy in higher education."[84]

AAUW had an additional tool for exerting pressure: its accreditation program that had long measured quality on collegiate campuses. AAUW's committee on standards and recognition assumed the lead in examining and protesting the position of women on campuses. Before the war, an AAUW standard required schools to have a dean of women to meet the needs of female students. As organizational changes began to reach student affairs divisions, the committee backed away from this requirement, suggesting that the new jobs might actually be sufficient to meet the "spirit of coeducation." In 1947 the committee relinquished its demand for an actual dean of women, stating quite generally that it "expects the institution to commit itself to further the opportunities and advance the interests of women in higher education."[85]

NADW and AAUW shared a commitment to advocating for women's campus needs, and NADW clearly appreciated AAUW's leadership in opposing the demotions. However, considerable tension was generated over the groups' differing views of the dean's job.[86] Although many NADW deans were also active members of AAUW, the latter group emphasized the importance of the liberal arts and often opposed the professionalized student personnel programs that trained most deans. AAUW endorsed the increase of women in all academic posts, and they especially advocated for faculty status for deans, holding to an older practice where deans held degrees in traditional academic disciplines before assuming administrative roles. NADW, on the other hand, was comfortable with the new professional preparation for the deanship.

Early in the history of the field, faculty status had been a common element of the dean's job. In the 1890s, with so few women on campuses, the dean of women often held both administrative and faculty roles. In essence, the deanship became an entry point for academic women who were unlikely to be hired as full-time faculty. Over time, however, the rise of the "student personnel point of view" and the increasing availability of student affairs training subordinated the academic part of deans' work, creating a sharp divide between student affairs and the academic side of campus life.[87]

By the postwar era, deans more readily identified as student affairs professionals than as frustrated academics. NADW particularly advanced the notion of the dean as educator, a partner with faculty in preparing young women and men for the modern world. As Katharine McBride (who herself held the doctorate) explained, deans were teachers, albeit without a particular specialty: the dean's subject, she explained, is "life between seventeen and twenty-two."[88] ACE president Arthur Adams agreed about the importance of the job, especially in the postwar milieu. "The Dean of Women," he noted, "is the one person in our whole educational organization whose particular role it is to be concerned about and do something about dealing with the impact which these [postwar] changes have brought about."[89]

Yet NADW leaders' frequent insistence on the dean's educative importance suggested that their academic influence was actually tenuous. One concern was the mix of duties performed by deans. While some NADW members sat on the president's cabinet as valued contributors to academic planning, others were limited to administering residence hall policies and enforcing parietal rules. NADW's varied membership of college deans and secondary school deans diluted the focus on extracurricular and residential responsibilities that marked the specific concerns of college life.

Striking a balance between supporting deans as educators and as practitioners proved difficult for the organization. The variety of articles in NADW's journal suggested the challenge: theoretical pieces with deep philosophical underpinnings appeared alongside practical suggestions for managing housing, clubs, and student discipline. A 1955 survey soliciting NADW members' preferences for topics to be discussed at their annual meeting showed how the press of daily business usually prevailed over educational philosophy. The top choice of issues was housing and residence hall problems; next, helping students manage extracurricular activities. Last on the list, following student government, student leaders, and counseling, appeared the more sweeping issue of women's education.[90]

The one role that most deans could agree on was that of counselor to women. Even those who preferred to stress the academic focus over student affairs understood the importance of supporting women students on the postwar campus. Work on counseling began to predominate in the journal, at the annual meeting, and in the thinking of NADW leaders. However, as the deans increasingly positioned themselves as counselors, they made some strategic decisions that eventually weakened both NADW and women's influence on campus, even while they clarified the group's commitment to feminism.

NADW's first organizational decision came in the late 1940s over whether to join a new federation of guidance groups, a move that would require abandoning NADW's specific commitment to women. NADW already belonged to one guidance consortium called the American Council of Guidance and Personnel Associations (CGPA); there, NADW was the only member devoted to women. Concerned about the direction of the profession, some constituent members of CGPA had decided to create a new federation, to be called the American Personnel and Guidance Association (APGA). Both NADW, as representative of deans of women, and the National Association of Deans of Men (NADM) were asked to join.[91]

The "unification decision," as it was called, proved troubling and dramatic for NADW. Members feared losing control of their organization and its dedication to women, wondering whether they would be swallowed up by guidance groups focused on clinical psychology and testing.[92] With the increasing loss of women's authority on campuses—exemplified by the demotion of women deans—this fear was real. The worry was exacerbated by the deans' perceptions about the proposed new leadership. Lucile Allen of Cornell (later a NADW president) reported hearing CGPA president Daniel Feder say that "women played a secondary role in culture, and therefore, they should be willing to do so in personnel"—hardly an auspicious sentiment for creating a new partnership.[93]

After three years of discussion, NADW in 1951 voted against the unification proposal. Ruth McCarn explained that NADW would lose too much in the new arrangement, saying, "Women need a framework within which they operate with all the responsibilities, and not just as secretary."[94] NADW leaders framed their choice as demonstrating strength and courage, yet the decision presented long-term dilemmas. Lynn Gangone, NADW's last director before it closed in 2000, suggested that this and other postwar decisions isolated the organization and countered its previous pattern of collaboration with other groups.[95] The unification vote also exacerbated financial concerns. NADW was freed from the rather hefty CGPA membership fee, but it became the nation's smallest and most specialized personnel and guidance group, operating independently and relying on a shrinking membership base for financial support.

Following the unification decision, NADW took steps to strengthen its new independence, including a membership drive that netted a 10 percent gain.[96] It also explored two new approaches: changing its name to indicate a tighter connection with counseling, and reconsidering its role in producing research. Although NADW's goals had long included research sponsorship, fitting that task into regular operations posed continuing difficulties. Severing ties with CGPA—where most of the field's scholars resided—highlighted NADW's own unsophisticated approach to research.[97] The NADW journal regularly published theoretical research on guidance and counseling, usually gleaned from other outlets. Its own members often revealed a quite unrefined view of what constituted research, defending everything from experimental studies to quick surveys of members.[98] NADW maintained a committee on research, but it operated sporadically. In 1956 the committee experienced rejuvenation when Jeanne Noble became its chair, an appointment signaling new attention not only to research but also to racial equity within the organization. Noble increased the prominence of research articles in the journal, even publishing her own bibliographic summaries of recent work. Subsequent NADW presidents and committee chairs devoted less attention to research, however, and once again the organization's support of research waned.

In 1956 NADW faced another identity issue. Five years after declaring independence from the guidance consortium, NADW changed its name from National Association of Deans of Women to National Association of Women Deans and Counselors (NAWDC). Although members had always held a variety of titles, the specific addition of "counselors" was designed to draw new participants. Leaders were sensitive to current members' reluctance to "break with a long and honorable tradition" of supporting the title of dean, but they also urged "a healthy sense of reality" about the changing roles of women on campuses.[99] Ultimately, the name change signaled both an increasingly diffuse sense of organizational mission and a recognition of women's diminishing campus presence.[100]

While undergoing this organizational change, NADW faced a new challenge from within the field that highlighted continuing ambiguities around women's issues as well as the discomfort provoked by a feminist stance in the late-1950s. In 1957 two researchers studying collegiate guidance harshly criticized NADW as narrow, overly specialized, and disconnected from important issues. In *Modern Issues of Guidance-Personnel Work,* scholars Ruth Barry and Beverly Wolf cited NADW's female-only focus as especially detrimental to its impact, calling the organization "severely limited in the scope of its influence and leadership." The problem, Barry and Wolf argued, was NADW's outmoded approach: "As might be expected of an association founded in 1916, when votes and education for women were controversial topics, it has distinctly feministic aims."[101]

Three problems resulted, in their view. First, NADW members did not think widely enough, focusing on women at the expense of all students. Second, the "exclusive concentration has led other guidance-personnel workers and educators to view the Association as a group of specialists and consider its suggestions limited in application." In other words, NADW was irrelevant. Third, a woman-only approach retarded growth of the field: "How can the Association further both the cause of women and that of guidance-personnel work without having one negate the other?"[102] In an era uncomfortable with explicit feminism and uncertain about women's professionalism, NADW's choice of separatism seemed incongruous and puzzling to mainstream observers.[103] Although organizations like AAUW and YWCA also focused on women, they commonly treated women's educational and career concerns as one aspect of their commitments to family and community. With its attention to women professionals and its specific interest in educating women for varied futures, NADW offered a more complex approach that seemed out of sync with cultural preferences. Barry and Wolf's argument echoed widely heard language and sentiments; even the ACE Commission on the Education of Women had frequently claimed that women should seek no special privileges.

Many NADW members resented the Barry and Wolf critique and challenged its analysis. As CEW commissioner Margaret Habein told her colleagues, "I sometimes wonder if women like you and me, who have been able to achieve our professional goal with a minimum of difficulty, tend to become unaware that there are still problems in the field."[104] Yet NADW members also had long experience in downplaying or disavowing the explicit feminist implications of their activities and interests. Keuka College president Katherine Blyley (also a CEW commissioner) resembled many in disclaiming that her commitment to women deans constituted "a feminist point of view." Even while she advocated an expansion of women's policy-making influence, Blyley rejected feminist impulses.[105] The connotations of feminism were still too risky for most of the deans.

Although the outside critique pained many deans, they accepted the challenge to reexamine their organization and its commitments. NADW created a committee on evaluation to study their approach to women's professionalism, asking whether their feminist perspective "stemmed from insecurity" about the role women could play in higher education and in society.[106] Ultimately, the organization reaffirmed its commitment both to guidance and to a woman-centered focus, asserting that their attention to counseling women fostered a wide understanding of higher education and rejecting the critique of narrowness.

Yet some NADW leaders argued that women deans bore responsibility for the situation, suggesting they had been too passive in responding to undesirable changes. Sarah Gibson Blanding, president of Vassar College, past president of NADW, and member of the Truman Commission on Higher Education, took a self-described "hard line": "I think the movement toward men deans of students has gained headway because we have not lived up to our responsibility as molders of educational thought and policy." Women deans—and too often women faculty—have "forgotten to step up and offer opinions on matters of academics and policy."[107] Eunice Roberts agreed that women had too readily assumed a back seat in academic discussions. She pushed women to earn doctorates and conduct research, saying, "It is time women quit pleading lack of recognition and concentrated on earning it."[108]

This viewpoint that women themselves had not tried hard enough to warrant a secure place in academe typified other postwar sentiment. Sociologist Jessie Bernard echoed this view in her influential book *Academic Women*, arguing that women preferred to be conservators rather than originators of knowledge and that they valued serving students over conducting research.[109]

But discussion of the issue began a subtle shift in the early 1960s. Women continued to fault themselves for lack of professional progress, but they now blamed their own lack of protest rather than their insufficient preparation or poor training. Perhaps the growth of the civil rights movement as well as incipient feminism encouraged 1960s women deans to see their situation as one to be challenged rather than accommodated. Outgoing NADW president Helen Schleman was particularly troubled in 1965 by an American Association of University Professors (AAUP) report urging faculty to assume a stronger role in guiding students, especially outside the classroom. Where others might simply see a call for expanded roles by professors, Schleman saw a negation of deans' work and philosophy, especially their long-sought partnership with faculty. What's more, she noted, "I attribute responsibility for the present unhappy state of affairs as much to us as personnel workers, unaccountably suffering from timidity, self-effacing meekness, and virtuous silence."[110]

Betty Friedan's provocative *Feminine Mystique*, with its language of inequity and frustration, further sparked the deans' self-analysis. Eunice Hilton noted that many deans agreed with Friedan, citing instances of discrimination they had witnessed against female students, deans, and faculty. Yet, having watched this treatment over time, Hilton charged that "we, the counselors and the older, wiser generation, have protested little. Instead we have been seeking to adapt our own thinking to the new circumstances, rather than to stand against them."[111]

A dean who analyzed NADW's history a few years later characterized it as a "feminist organization with a ladylike emphasis."[112] She acknowledged that Barry and Wolf were correct in ascribing "feministic" aims to this women's group but recognized that deans active in the 1960s had built careers during a time when feminism was downplayed and society held ambivalent views about women's professional roles. Although these deans inherited an organization founded during the suffrage movement and dedicated to the advancement of women professionals, they also operated in an environment increasingly equivocal about women's place on campus. As counselors to women, the deans understood the complexities of female choices in the postwar era and tried to address the variety of opportunities. Yet as a new language and way of analyzing women's decisions developed, they questioned past approaches and choices. In the case of their own professional development, the deans remained committed to individual efforts, only turning to collective analysis when threats to the profession grew precipitously.

CONCLUSION

Although some 1960s deans judged their past work harshly, they were wrong in labeling themselves passive or unconcerned. Rather, in choosing to work within extant structures, these women stayed attuned to the demands and approaches of their era. Although stymied by postwar challenges in curriculum, racial integration, and professional growth, the AAUW and NADW addressed these concerns through the language, approaches, and philosophies of the postwar era. In a time of "womanpower," they pushed higher education to serve a wider array of national needs, even as they defended the liberal base of collegiate education. In an era of civil rights, they argued for expanded student populations, even as they faced awkward challenges in integrating their own organizations. And in an era uncertain about its commitment to women's professionalism, they developed programs to expand women's careers, even as they witnessed the diminution of their own jobs and influence.

At times the groups turned to systemic understandings and collective approaches, for example, using their influence to affect accreditation or surveying the dean of women population. But often they were overwhelmed by the variety of choices facing women students and professionals, preferring to let individuals make decisions and accept the consequences. Only when the profession itself was threatened did women begin to find value in tackling their concerns systemically. When they did respond, these educated women found support in the professional networks that their organizations had provided across the decades.

Even with mixed success, organizations like AAUW and NADW played vital roles in keeping attention on women's educational concerns throughout two postwar decades of collegiate change and uncertainty. Building on their long histories of service to women, the two groups helped connect earlier periods of educational growth with the difficult developments of the postwar era. The "fellowship of the concerned" provided an important network among scholars, researchers, and other advocates who actively promoted inquiry into women's educational needs. Their postwar efforts—supported by their networking capabilities—helped position women to respond to the changes of the later 1960s.

CHAPTER FIVE

Policy

The President's Commission on the Status of Women

Agnes Meyer was an intriguing choice for service on the President's Commission on the Status of Women (PCSW) created by John F. Kennedy in 1961. In many ways, Meyer's life personified the challenges and ambiguities the commission confronted in assessing American women's status. At age 75, this self-described "author, social worker, and humanitarian" had led a flamboyant life packed with travel, work, philanthropy, and public service, all the while asserting that a woman's first duty was to husband and family.[1]

Graduating from Barnard College in 1907, Meyer (then Agnes Ernst) had pursued a love of art and writing as a rare female reporter for the *New York Sun*. Studying in Paris, she befriended artists Auguste Rodin, Constantin Brancusi, Thomas Mann, and Leo and Gertrude Stein, and had advised Charles Freer on his unparalleled collection of Asian art. At age 23 she married 34-year-old multimillionaire financier Eugene Meyer, who in 1933 purchased the *Washington Post*. The Meyers had five children in eleven years; the fourth was Katharine, who in 1963 succeeded her husband, Philip Graham, as publisher of the *Washington Post*.[2]

Despite her statements about the primacy of motherhood, Meyer remained emotionally and physically distant from her family; she lived alone for significant periods of time and frequently traveled without either husband or children. Katharine recalled her surprise when reading an interview in which her mother asserted that "a woman could have her own work but always had to take care of her husband first," countering that "motherhood was not exactly Mother's first priority."[3] Yet Meyer accomplished much that home-oriented mothers could not. She wrote for the *Washington Post*; published several books; lectured widely on public affairs; became influential in Democratic party politics; advocated for creating the Department of Health, Education, and Welfare; and dispensed considerable philanthropy. Meyer's interest in education grew after World War II. She encouraged educational volunteerism, helping to create both the Urban Service Corps and the National Committee for Support of Public Schools. In the 1950s she tangled publicly with Catholic church leaders—as did Eleanor Roosevelt—over federal aid to public schools. *Newsweek* magazine called Meyer "a one-woman reform movement."[4]

With her political connections and her involvement in education, Agnes Meyer represented a reasonable choice for a seat on the Education Committee of the President's Commission on the Status of Women. Less obviously, the balancing act that marked her colorful life highlighted the complications facing commission members. Kennedy had created the two-year, twenty-six-member panel to "review progress and make recommendations" regarding American women's employment, their civil and political rights, and the services—including education—necessary for women's full participation as modern citizens.[5] Working during an era that valorized women's family role, yet increasingly aware of potential "womanpower" and women's movement into the workforce, the President's Commission accepted the task of addressing—if not reconciling—expectations for women like Agnes Meyer. How could women follow their talents yet maintain a commitment to home, family, and community?

Ultimately, the commission found an answer in the notion of individual choice. A woman like Meyer might choose to vary her commitments over time, sometimes favoring family roles and other times more public pursuits. Alternatively, a woman might happily choose to commit herself to family and community, while her neighbor might prefer full-time employment. The commission saw its role as clarifying the choices confronting modern American women and challenging the barriers to their effectiveness, but also demonstrating how each choice could fulfill women's obligations to community and family.

The President's Commission on the Status of Women serves as a useful benchmark of thinking about women in the early 1960s as well as an indicator of developments since the ACE Commission on the Education of Women (CEW) began its work a decade earlier. Some concerns about women had stayed the same: How could they balance home and career? How could they meet their duties as citizens? What role could education play? Yet the PCSW also captured a moment in postwar women's history when several ideas about change came into the national spotlight. One was the potential of a constitutional Equal Rights Amendment (ERA), a measure that, if passed, would forcefully proclaim gender equality in legal, employment, and social realms. A second was the increasingly vigorous national challenge around civil rights, with growing calls for equitable treatment of African Americans and other "minority" citizens. Third was a new awareness of education as potential a lever for social change.

Within a few years, all these areas saw important legislative action that signaled new national attention and commitment. The Civil Rights Act of 1964, followed by the 1965 Voting Rights Act, codified (although hardly solved) responses to civil rights demands. In 1965 the two largest educational bills ever created passed after decades of stalemate: the Elementary and Secondary Education Act, and the Higher Education Act, which poured more than a billion dollars into educational activities. Although the Equal Rights Amendment did not come to fruition, an Equal Pay Act passed in 1963.

These ideas for change were in the air while the President's Commission met from 1961 to 1963. Ultimately, however, the commission sidestepped strong recommendations on all of them. The ERA proved too controversial, and the Kennedy administration did not favor that particular route to enhancing women's opportunities. Concern for civil rights was visible in the commission's deliberations; for example, they organized a special "consultation" of important black leaders to advise them. But ultimately, the commission's recommendations about poverty, civil rights, and class issues were muted. Only on education did the commission take a somewhat stronger stand, opening its final report with education and calling it a key factor in the lives of girls and women. Although the commission backed away from the implications of claiming education as a potent lever for change, it did use it as a safe way to discuss issues of women's personal choices.

Scholars have generally overlooked the PCSW's consideration of education. Its battles over the ERA seemed more compelling, and its treatment of social security, tax provisions, and social insurance have provided evidence of growing political commitment to economic issues. Others have attached symbolic value to the commission's 1963 report, *American Women* (published in the same year as Betty Friedan's *Feminine Mystique*), as an early marker of the revivified women's movement of the 1960s, even if little feminism appears in the report. But reading the commission's work through the lens of education demonstrates a significant step toward feminist arguments on behalf of women that appeared more forcefully in the later-1960s and 1970s. In some ways, these discussions replicated the work of the equity-based educational analysts presented in chapter 2. And although the commission ultimately stepped back from a strong statement, its tentative recognition of the potential of education to change women's lives and to prepare them for choices nonetheless merits attention.

ORGANIZING THE PRESIDENT'S COMMISSION

The President's Commission on the Status of Women was the brainchild of Esther Peterson, Kennedy's director of the Women's Bureau and Assistant Secretary of Labor, along with women's groups that had long tried to promote federal interest in women. Housed in the Department of Labor, the commission always had a stronger focus on labor and wage-earning than on social concerns. Originally, five subcommittees treated economic issues, and only one handled social matters; education was added only after the initial meeting.

Peterson brought to Kennedy's team impressive credentials in the labor movement, having lobbied for the Amalgamated Clothing Workers of America and the Industrial Union Department of the AFL-CIO. She had also strongly supported Kennedy's presidential bid among women and blue-collar workers. Peterson had worked well with Kennedy during his Senate years and made a good choice for the Women's Bureau position—the most visible executive post dedicated to women's concerns.[6] Peterson hoped to advance Kennedy's agenda on several fronts. She supported government intervention in labor issues, drawing a thread from New Deal activism to the New Frontier. She advocated for poor and black constituents, recognizing their disadvantages in a segmented labor market. And she believed that a robust economy offered the best solution for labor market discrimination: individual liabilities would disappear when labor was needed across a variety of settings. Throughout PCSW deliberations, Peterson often articulated the needs of the poor.

During the Eisenhower years, the Women's Bureau had eased away from a focus on labor. Republican Alice Leopold directed the Bureau from 1953 to 1961, bringing closer connections to professional and suburban interests than to the unionism of her predecessor, Frieda Miller, or her successor, Peterson. Leopold supported the "womanpower" notion by encouraging workforce participation of women with technical and specialized skills. She pushed advanced training, leadership opportunities, and public service projects for the Women's Bureau, fostering alliances with the Business and Professional Women's Clubs and AAUW. Succeeding Leopold, Peterson reconnected the Women's Bureau with earlier allies, including the National Council of Jewish Women, the National Council of Negro Women, the YWCA, and the National Council of Catholic Women.

One group without friends in the Women's Bureau was the National Women's Party (NWP), headed by activist Emma Guffey Miller. The NWP provided a link to early twentieth-century suffragism and the Nineteenth Amendment. When the label "feminist" was used in the 1950s and early 1960s, it usually connoted actual NWP supporters who forcefully supported the Equal Rights Amendment. Peterson opposed the ERA's blanket approach to protecting women's interests, preferring the more tailored "specific bills for specific ills."[7] She and her colleagues brought strong experience to the effort to secure women's political, economic, and civil rights. They had worked for decades on protective labor legislation, securing opportunities in fields that had excluded women but adding safeguards where women might be open to abuse.

By the 1960s, protective labor legislation and social insurance constituted a complicated patchwork of provisions, some with national coverage and others statewide only. For instance, some laws supported women's right to compete for lucrative jobs in automotive and other heavy industries, emphasizing their ability to perform the work. Earlier arguments about women's weakness had kept them in lower-paying jobs off the high-earning assembly lines. Yet other legislation applied the opposite argument: women needed special treatment to protect them as mothers and wives. For instance, to avoid exploitation, regulations existed concerning women's work hours and the amount of weight they could be required to lift on the job. The longstanding debate over whether women should be treated equally or differently played out in protective labor laws.[8]

The Equal Rights Amendment, however, would force clarification of the same/ different debate: "Equality of rights under the law shall not be denied or abridged by the United States or any state on account of sex." To Peterson and anti-ERA forces, the amendment threatened gains they had won over many years. Their careful calculus of laws would be wiped out by a blanket provision. Kennedy himself was wary of the ERA, and in naming Peterson as Women's Bureau director, he chose an ally who shared his views. Certainly, supporting an alternative to the ERA was not the sole reason to create the PCSW. The commission also signaled Kennedy's support for women. Like the last two presidents, Kennedy faced increased demands to appoint women to policymaking roles. AAUW and other women's organizations plied the White House with rosters of women who could fill important posts; the commission could help buy time on these demands, even as it generated support among women voters.[9] With women's workforce presence increasing, a high-level examination of women's status seemed useful.

As a model for the PCSW, Peterson and Secretary of Labor Arthur Goldberg turned to the President's Commission on Equal Employment Opportunity. A similar presidential directive—Executive Order 10980 of December 1961—made the Commission on Women a presidential-level group rather than simply a Labor Department delegation. The preamble of the executive order signaled the PCSW's wide agenda, emphasizing women's "basic rights" as part of the country's commitment to "human dignity, freedom, and democracy." Echoing "womanpower" language, it explained that the national interest was served when all citizens could develop their capacities, use their skills, and meet their aspirations. Since women had proven themselves repeatedly during crises, their needs deserved attention "irrespective of national exigencies."[10] Kennedy sought a report that would accentuate American progress in social, economic, and civil matters related to women. He welcomed the commission's recommendations for improvements, but true to the Cold War spirit, he wished to highlight America's achievements regarding its female citizens.

A strong labor influence appeared in the areas designated as the commission's purview. The PCSW was to investigate employment policies and practices affecting women in federal contracts, whether held by private employers or by the government itself. The federal government should be a "showcase" for enlightened employment policies. Social insurance and tax laws should be scrutinized for their effect on women. Likewise, federal and state labor laws should be measured against "changing technological, economic, and social conditions." Laws related to property rights, civil rights, and family relations should be examined. And, turning to social concerns, the commission was to recommend any "new and expanded services" deemed necessary for women to fulfill their roles, including education, counseling, training, day care, or home services.

For chair of the President's Commission, Peterson and Goldberg recruited the nation's most noted advocate for women: Eleanor Roosevelt. Relations were strained between Roosevelt and Kennedy, stemming from her campaign preferences for Adlai Stevenson. But with Peterson's intervention, Roosevelt agreed to take the post, chairing the group's first year before her death in 1962. Twenty-six commissioners handled the group's agenda. Some represented government agencies or political roles, including the secretaries of Agriculture, Commerce, Labor, and HEW, the attorney general, and the chair of the Civil Service Commission, as well as two senators and two congresspersons (three of them women). Nongovernmental appointments represented various interest groups: Mary Callahan of the electricians' union, William Schnitzler of the AFL-CIO, Norman Nicholson of Kaiser Industries, Dorothy Height of the National Council of Negro Women, Viola Hymes of the National Council of Jewish Women, and Margaret Mealey of the National Council of Catholic Women. Several represented general constituencies: Margaret Hickey of the *Ladies Home Journal;* Henry David, president of the New School for Social Research and former National Manpower Council chair; and Mary I. Bunting, president of Radcliffe College. In all, fifteen women and eleven men were recruited, with Peterson noting of the gender mix: "I did not want a women's commission. I wanted people who were in a position to act."[11]

THE WORK OF THE COMMISSION

The President's Commission faced a wide agenda, ranging from the ERA, to economic concerns, to social supports. To pursue its work over two years, the commission divided into seven subcommittees, each supported by a staff person, chaired by a member of the larger commission, and expanded with new members from around the country who represented various interests and constituencies. Adding additional participants not only brought expertise to committee deliberations but also helped create a larger group to invest in the commission's work and its recommendations.

The commission as a whole met eight times, beginning at the White House with a February 12–13, 1962, meeting where the main agenda item was subdividing the work. The five committees on economic concerns were federal employment, government contracts, federal tax and social insurance, protective labor legislation, and civil and political rights. During that first meeting, the group agreed to expand social concerns into two committees: one on home and community, the other on education. The committees arranged their own schedules, knowing that their job was to deliberate on a series of questions, bring recommendations to the entire commission, and contribute to the final report, which was planned for April 1963.

Although the committees produced an array of discussions and recommendations, their most significant efforts fell into three areas: the ERA; economic concerns, including the poor and minorities; and social matters, including education.

THE EQUAL RIGHTS AMENDMENT

The PCSW took a twofold approach to handling the Equal Rights Amendment, arguably the most controversial item on its agenda. First, Peterson generally chose as commissioners people who opposed the amendment. Second, the commission channeled work on the ERA into one subgroup: the committee on civil and political rights, which agreed to bring a mediated recommendation to the entire group. In the end, limiting the ERA discussion to one subgroup freed other committees to examine wider issues.

Most of the members Peterson recruited to the commission either actively opposed or simply did not support the blanket provisions of the ERA. They preferred the more moderate, although more complicated approach of individually tailored protective labor legislation. Of all commission members, only lawyer Marguerite Rawalt (past president of the Federation of Business and Professional Women's Clubs) was a known ERA supporter. Even so, Peterson liked her conciliatory style. Agitation by the feminist National Women's Party to win a seat for their president Emma Guffey Miller was rebuffed.

Even with so few ERA supporters on hand, the PCSW's work could easily have been derailed by debates over the amendment. Instead, the group agreed that the committee on civil and political rights would sort out the commission's position on the amendment. As an early spokesperson for that committee, Margaret Hickey promised that they would approach the ERA "factually and objectively with no preconceived opinion."[12]

Ultimately, the committee took what one historian called an "exceedingly civilized" approach to considering the amendment.[13] Aware that strong opinions existed, members gathered and heard from interested parties. Soon, however, they received an interesting alternative proposal from one of the new members recruited specifically for that committee. Pauli Murray, an African American attorney with considerable civil rights experience, focused the committee's attention on the possibility that the Fourteenth Amendment of the Constitution might already contain provisions for dealing with sex discrimination. Convincing the Supreme Court to hear cases based on a Fourteenth Amendment argument would obviate the need for a blanket ERA, while also eliminating state-by-state litigation on specific matters. Murray's idea offered the committee and the commission an alternative stand on this contentious issue. Peterson immediately favored the idea, seeing it less as a compromise than as a hopeful new approach. She and Murray campaigned to convince both the commission and its allies of the promise of a Fourteenth Amendment challenge. Although they did not gain complete agreement, the entire commission ultimately supported Murray's strategy as the preferred way to achieve clarity on women's legal rights.

Recognizing that months of debate had occurred within the committee, the PCSW proceeded carefully when deciding how to phrase its formal statement about the ERA. In the final report, it first presented the legal issue at hand, offering nicely balanced discussions of three possible ways to secure "greater recognition" for women—the ERA, state-level legislation, and national test litigation based on the Fourteenth Amendment—ultimately recommending the third approach.

Although many of the commission's final recommendations were approved in spirit by the assembled members and later subjected to revision by wordsmiths, the ERA resolution was considered word for word by the entire group. In the end, the statement suited Peterson's supporters, while also allowing ERA sympathizer Marguerite Rawalt to insert a small opening for future consideration. The final statement read: "Since the Commission is convinced that the United States Constitution now embodies equality of rights for men and women, we conclude that a constitutional amendment need not *now* be sought in order to establish the principle" (emphasis added).[14] Rawalt had successfully pushed for the one-word addition "now." Having left this door open, the commission called for "early and definitive court pronouncement" around the Fourteenth Amendment challenge but did not quash ERA advocacy.

ECONOMIC CONCERNS

With the ERA sequestered into one subgroup, the other committees turned to the PCSW's labor-oriented agenda: women's economic concerns, tax and insurance measures, federal contracts, and other labor regulations. As committees considered these economic issues, their deliberations fell into three categories: differential treatment for women, racial and class differences, and the role of individual choice. The theme that connected deliberations across committees was the debate over differential treatment for women; that is, should women be treated the same as men to equalize opportunities and outcomes, or did their differences argue for variable treatment to protect them in certain situations? Clearly, this issue lay at the heart of the disagreement over the ERA and protective labor legislation.

While the civil and political rights committee examined this issue via the ERA, other committees focused on more specific matters. One early breakthrough came in the committee on federal employment. President Kennedy and Labor Secretary Goldberg wished to portray the federal government as a model employer of women. Yet a longstanding prejudice against considering women for a full range of jobs had calcified into policy, so that certain jobs were designated (sometimes formally, sometimes by practice) for men or for women.

The notion that women were neither long-term nor serious employees—examined so thoroughly by Dael Wolfle and *Womanpower*—had, over time, disadvantaged federally employed women.[15] According to a 1959 survey of federal employment, the median salary grade for men was rising, while women's median salary, already much lower, was stagnating. Women constituted a quarter of the federal workforce but overwhelmingly served in low-level posts. Only 1 percent of the 1,500 employees in high grades were women.[16]

Previous attempts to eliminate a rule allowing agencies to determine whether a job was "male" or "female" had proven unsuccessful; even the Civil Service Commission resisted the revision. Yet Kennedy and Goldberg supported change. When the federal employment committee raised the issue early in its deliberations, commission staff forwarded their comment directly to the president. With PCSW advocacy in hand, along with support from the president and the attorney general, Civil Service Commissioner Macy changed the rule. Some improvements in female hiring resulted, although the new order contained few penalties or enforcement measures.[17]

The committee on federal contracts for private employers moved carefully, aware that its recommendations would widely affect business and industry. Although hardly sanguine about sex discrimination in private employment, members debated their authority to recommend changes with far-reaching implications. They invited an outside consultation on private employment, allowing additional business, union, and organization leaders to offer viewpoints on this touchy subject. Ultimately, the committee offered a strong statement advocating "equal opportunity for women in hiring, training, and promotion [as] the governing principle in private employment," and urged the president to sign an executive order to this effect. However, having recently created an order prohibiting aspects of racial discrimination in employment, Kennedy proved less eager to add one on sex discrimination. In the end, the commission pushed for educating employers and pressuring them to support women but advocated few enforcement provisions. Nevertheless, by pre–War on Poverty standards, the commission had made a firm statement on equal opportunity in its final report.[18]

With the ERA under consideration elsewhere, the committee handling protective labor legislation proceeded without worry over inconsistencies in the differential treatment debate. It dove into the task of reviewing national- and state-level protective laws, trying to determine which ones actually helped women. For instance, the committee supported changing the minimum wage and equal pay legislation to treat women more equitably, but it also supported differential treatment via laws on weight restrictions and maternity benefits. Legislation on special hours highlighted the conundrum within differential treatment. While rules limiting forced overtime generally helped working mothers, similar laws restricting professional women's hours negatively affected their income (54–59). The committee also disagreed over whether laws limiting hours—crafted for women—could be extended to men. A compromise reached by the committee demonstrated the case-by-case approach of most protective labor laws: the commission encouraged hours limitations where they provided useful protection, but pushed to exempt professional women (128–38).

The committees considered another difficulty in the differential treatment debate. To secure certain economic benefits for women, wives had to be treated as secondary earners to their husbands. The committee on social insurance and taxes, for instance, argued that women merited the Social Security benefits they earned themselves and that they deserved their husbands' full benefits if widowed. Because the woman was a secondary earner, however, a widowed husband could not recoup on his wife's earnings (137–41). Similarly, the committee supported women's choice about work and homemaking decisions, but advocated their protection through alimony, child support, and guardianship. The committee on civil and political rights took the same approach, arguing that "the husband should continue to have primary responsibility for support of his wife and minor children"; this would entitle a non-wage-earning wife 's legal claim on family income and property (69). Recognizing the inconsistencies inherent in differential treatment, the group explained its guiding principle: "In suggesting remedies, the Commission balanced a desire to find and eliminate discrimination with an equivalent interest in encouraging women to assume appropriate responsibility" (152).

The question of how to approach discussions of race and class—increasingly prominent issues in the early-1960s—confounded the PCSW. Had the group devoted a subcommittee to issues of the poor or to civil rights, as it had with the ERA, its ultimate treatment of these concerns might have been stronger. However, consideration of class and race remained scattered throughout a variety of commission discussions and recommendations on economic concerns.

An early indication that balancing class and race concerns would be difficult for a group charged with emphasizing progress appeared in a background paper prepared for the commission by historian Caroline Ware. In addition to regular staffers and commission members, the PCSW had hired a few consultants like Ware for special reports. Ware wrote a long paper that was eventually printed in somewhat revised form as the "American Women Today" section of the commission's final report.

Knowing that Kennedy had asked for a report stressing American progress relative to the rest of the world, Ware emphasized the vast, positive differences between the lives of women in the 1960s and those of their grandmothers. Just since 1900, Ware noted, women's life expectancy had risen by twenty-one years; they could expect to see more of their babies survive, and they enjoyed a much improved standard of living. In measuring women's advances, Ware focused on what she termed "the suburban norm," calling it an unarguable American success. Her laudatory comments about middle-class women's advantages echoed Richard Nixon's "kitchen debate" with Nikita Khrushchev, where the American vice president argued that suburban women's use of labor-saving machinery, their increased leisure time, and their freedom not to hold wage-earning positions marked the superior quality of American life.[19]

While highlighting these advances, Ware acknowledged that the good life eluded some women, notably "Negroes and other minority groups." But like many instances where the commission briefly treated race and class issues, she quickly returned to noting the increased professional possibilities, enhanced educational options, and "special measure of opportunity" available to modern American women, without offering any particular recommendations for the poor (78–95).

Although the PCSW did not devote a committee to civil rights issues, it invited a special consultation on "the problems of Negro women" to provide expert opinion to its committees. Peterson later explained that the staff decided in advance not to create a specific committee on race, but rather to spread the work on racial issues across the various topics.[20] She had also ensured some representation by African American participants. In addition to Dorothy Height, president of the National Council on Negro Women, who served on the commission itself, black women served on several committees: Pauli Murray on civil and political rights, Lillian Harvey on education, Rosa Gragg on home and community, and Jeanne Noble on federal employment.

Unlike the other three consultations, which all had at least twenty-nine guests (including one on the media's portrayal of women), the more focused group on Negro women invited eleven participants from education, Congress, state government, unions, business, and advocacy groups. The group began by considering the "matriarchal nature of black society"—a prominent issue of the era. They cited Jeanne Noble's work on how black women used college, noting how the strong need for vocational preparation stymied both black women's achievement and the growth of black institutions. They agreed that discrimination and personal responses to prejudice inhibited the development of African American educational, community, and volunteer options. In addition, the concentration of black women in lower paid, poorly secured jobs limited long-term advancement. Height summarized their conclusions by noting that, although most of these issues affected women regardless of race, black women experienced additional complications. Without a concomitant rise in the status of black men, they cautioned, black women would find it hard to expand their achievements.

Peterson hailed the work of the consultative group as "one of the best documents" produced for the PCSW.[21] Although their report appeared as an appendix in *American Women*, the ideas and contributions of the group were dispersed throughout the commission's work, never resulting in a focused argument about race or civil rights. The disadvantage of decentralizing the issue meant that no one committee forcefully advocated for such concerns.

In an era when discussions of civil rights remained difficult and considerations of women's dual responsibilities at home and work remained controversial, a smoother way to account for the variety of outcomes was to assert that each woman made her own calculus of family need. Thus, by emphasizing the issue of individual and familial choice, the commission could simultaneously hold visions of a prosperous America and yet acknowledge that some still suffered discrimination and disadvantage. Society's responsibility was to provide the supports women required for any particular choice. The role of the President's Commission was to assess whether women could find such supports, and point out areas where improvements were needed.

While most committees dealt with employment and legal rights, the subgroups on home and community and on education focused on social concerns such as the need for day care, the value of volunteers, the nature of women's home life, and preparation for female adulthood. Commission members recognized the value of focusing energy on these issues. Viola Hymes, chair of the home and community committee, joked when presenting her final report to the commission that "this report ought to go very fast because we are all for Home and Community and Mother Love."[22] In considering social concerns, the two committees confronted a dilemma inherent in much of the PCSW's thinking: could they advocate for women's increased potency as wage earners while still supporting their primary commitment to home and family? Even though the commission was very focused on wage-earning (in fact, some members worried that their final report would be seen as too one-sided), it respected society's emphasis on women as nurturers of family and home.

Ultimately, both committees—and the commission as a whole—advocated that women's roles as mothers and homemakers were "fundamental." But since women played the larger role in sustaining the family, society must provide new and expanded services, including education, to support them. The committees thus advocated for more extensive child care with stricter standards; larger tax deductions for child care expenses of working families; and stronger, more coordinated community programming for health, rehabilitation, and family services. The education committee pushed for better adult and basic education, supported by federal funding; more sophisticated guidance and counseling; flexibility and support for "mature women" to continue schooling; and programming to support women at home.[23]

Both committees relied on the notion of familial choice to highlight women's needs. If the family chose for the mother to work, society must provide creative day care opportunities that would also educate the children, teach and support the mother, and expand learning options for child care workers. If the family chose for the mother to stay home, educational opportunities and volunteer options must allow her to feel engaged in intellectual growth. What this approach did not admit, however, was that most poor women could not afford such a "choice." The closest the committees came to acknowledging their dilemma was to say that "culturally deprived" women needing extra help to raise their families must not be forced into working but should be recognized as valuable supports within their homes. They stopped short of recommending specific welfare or other government subsidies.

EDUCATION

Even though placing education in a separate committee was an afterthought in the commission's original planning, the theme of education eventually took center stage in the PCSW's presentation to the public. When *American Women* was published, the recommendations of the education committee preceded all others; when committee reports were appended to the final document, education again led the way. Education was heralded throughout the report as a key to providing options for women.

Education, in fact, became a convenient means for the President's Commission to discuss more difficult issues. Although the commission eased away from the potent issues of the Equal Rights Amendment and civil rights, it was more successful in recognizing education as a third new area of change in the early 1960s. Through the education committee, as well as through discussions within the larger group, the commission treated education in three ways: as a potential lever for social change, as a means to raise thornier issues, and as advocacy for middle-class women.

Ultimately, education became the answer for how women would enact and benefit from their individual choices. The education committee laid out this thinking in its final report to the commission: women should have wider opportunities to exercise choice; however, these decisions should not displace women's traditional responsibilities within home and community; nonetheless, an expanded economy would provide room for a full range of personal choices.[24] But reaching that level of consensus took eighteen months of careful deliberation.

Organizing the Committee

The education committee was an eclectic group, with most members based in educational practice. Although they represented a variety of interests, from informal educational programs to state-level school policy, the committee recognized itself as "top heavy" with people focused on college women and their lives after graduation.[25] Chairing the committee was Mary "Polly" Bunting, who had also chaired the ACE Commission on the Education of Women in 1958–59, just before she assumed the presidency of Radcliffe College. A microbiologist entering her third year at Radcliffe, Bunting was steadily gaining national prominence.

Bunting and Esther Peterson strategized about the committee's membership, balancing educational experts with those who could strengthen practical alliances. The fifteen committee members included two of Bunting's friends who, like her, had won support from the Carnegie Corporation for experimental programs on behalf of women. Esther Raushenbush and Virginia Senders had created innovative programs at Sarah Lawrence College and the University of Minnesota, respectively, that eased the return of female drop-outs to college. Raushenbush, a senior educator who became president of Sarah Lawrence in 1965, and Senders often joined Bunting as a Carnegie-supported traveling trio, promoting a new conception of continuing education for women.

Three other members came from collegiate administration. Helen Schleman had survived the postwar challenges to deans of women, holding that post at Purdue University since 1947. Schleman's background included one of the features that allowed many male administrators to succeed as deans: she had performed military service, participating in the Women's Coast Guard Reserve during World War II. As president-elect of NAWDC, Schleman hoped that commission membership would expand the visibility of the deans' group. Lillian Holland Harvey, a nurse educator and dean of nursing at historically black Tuskegee University, was the sole African American committee member. Like many black educators who felt a deep responsibility to the community, Harvey was an active clubwoman, notably in the National Negro Business and Professional Women's Club, a Women's Bureau ally. Seymour Farber, assistant dean of continuing education at the University of California San Francisco, was one of three men on the committee. A physician specializing in diseases of the lungs and chest, Farber enjoyed playing committee provocateur, frequently citing his dissatisfied female patients as examples of educated women facing unsupportive environments.

The committee's two other men were chosen for their complementary knowledge of education. Superintendent of schools for Denver, Colorado, Kenneth Oberholtzer had served as an Army education officer during the war. Like Agnes Meyer, he brought experience with a previous presidential board, the 1958 Eisenhower Commission on Education Beyond the High School. Lawrence Rogin advocated for nontraditional education from his post as education director for the AFL-CIO, which was a keen supporter of Peterson. Rogin was a longtime labor educator, having worked at the socialist Brookwood Labor College in 1935.[26] Elizabeth Drews, the committee's only full-time scholar, was recruited for her expertise on psychological differences between boys and girls. Education professor at Michigan State University, Drews had taught at every level from kindergarten to college. Gifted children were the focus of her research agenda—specifically, ways in which talented girls might challenge traditional role identifications. Her earlier work had influenced ACE CEW thinking.

Two other women brought national perspective and personified the interconnections among women's organizations. Pauline Tompkins was AAUW General Director, closely connected to the policymakers on the PCSW and in Congress. With its full-time legislative lobbyist and 143,000 members, AAUW was one of Peterson's most important non-labor allies.[27] Opal David brought connections to the powerful ACE: she had directed its Commission on the Education of Women during Bunting's chairmanship and helped organize its final activity at the 1962 Itasca conference on continuing education. At least fourteen members of the President's Commission or its committees attended the invitational Itasca conference.

Bunting also recruited Edna Amidon, director of the Home Economics Education Branch, to represent the federal Office of Education. With more than twenty years experience in home economics, Amidon understood the government's capacity to respond to educational concerns. The backgrounds of the final members, Algie Ballif and Martha Briscoe, most closely resembled those of humanitarian Agnes Meyer. They represented traditional—if notably successful—women who had alternated between paid employment and volunteer leadership. Ballif, a former teacher and now an active clubwoman, had served the Provo, Utah, school board for twenty-three years, following two terms in the Utah state legislature. Briscoe, who held a Radcliffe master's degree in economics, was former state president of Connecticut's League of Women Voters and now served on the national board of the League, which was another Women's Bureau ally.

The organizational work for the committee's four meetings and most of the report writing were handled by staff. Antonia Chayes, well connected with the White House and later Under Secretary of the Air Force under President Jimmy Carter, served as technical secretary and organizer of the draft reports. At most meetings, staff from other committees sat in to help connect discussions across commission topics. Katherine Ellickson, the PCSW's executive secretary, often facilitated these connections, while Esther Peterson and Caroline Ware visited occasionally.

The Committee's Early Thinking

Early discussions by the education committee revealed the continuity of many postwar women's issues: how women could balance their dual roles, how they might respond to "womanpower" challenges, and how education should respond to the differential treatment debate. However, other points indicated substantial progress on women's concerns since the start of the ACE Commission on the Education of Women in 1953. The volume of material about women had expanded, and scholarship about their concerns had become more sophisticated. Discussion of new opportunities such as counseling and guidance, community colleges, continuing education, and volunteerism indicated an enlivened connection between educational opportunities and women's needs.

At the committee's initial meeting in May 1962, Bunting's invitation for each member to outline his or her particular concerns produced a range of issues. Bunting noted two beliefs that had guided her own work with the ACE CEW. First, asserting her view on differential treatment, she argued that women had outgrown their quest to match men in terms of education and could now afford to look at differences; and second, revealing her own scientific bent, she recommended experimentation as the best way to generate a variety of answers to educational questions.[28] The other members offered particular concerns, although the value of guidance for women's flexible lives surfaced as a strong theme. Agnes Meyer, the senior member, emphasized that women must realize how long life is and how many options they could pursue over time. Marriage, she noted, was never an endpoint. AAUW's Tompkins agreed, raising the importance of guidance to help women plan for diverse lives. Lillian Harvey of Tuskegee raised a specific interest in improving urban settings, echoing John Kennedy's call for a "domestic peace corps." As she did throughout committee discussions, Harvey advocated pushing the African American community to support its own needs. Generally, the group followed Harvey's lead on racial issues, although Meyer proved the most comfortable in raising concerns about class and race. NAWDC president Schleman emphasized the connections between school and college, noting that guidance helped women resist too-early marriage and persist in their studies.

Bunting and Chayes had sent advance questions to help organize the meeting, outlining an agenda not outwardly different from what ACE CEW might have discussed.[29] The first question probed the extant research base: "Do women have special educational needs arising from inherent differences?" Unlike CEW discussions, however, the conversation revealed how widespread knowledge about women had become. Even though Drews was their acknowledged expert, other members easily discussed how biological and physiological differences might affect women's educational needs and recognized researchers' growing awareness of a subtle array of differences.

The phrasing of their second question revealed readiness to examine the problematic mix of women's roles: "Do women have special educational needs to prepare them for their unique roles as women in our society today?" For many, the answer rested in making education available in different configurations. Certainly, the experiments at Radcliffe, Sarah Lawrence, and Minnesota responded to these challenges. But the committee also raised its first concerns about class differences, suggesting that "different social and economic groups may not have the same educational requirements for a future homemaking role."[30] Harvey and Meyer cited non-college-bound women, emphasizing their need for basic skills and—raising a point that would later bedevil the commission—for sex education and family planning information.

"Womanpower" appeared in the third question: "What social needs exist in our country which can be met by the skills of women properly trained and educated?" The group generally agreed with Bunting's notion that women need not compete with men but should emphasize their particular strengths in fields like recreation, mental health, social work, nursing, and education. In fact, they suggested, an array of women could lead the way in communities' responses to special needs, from the older woman returning to the workforce, to the homemaker with extra time to volunteer, to the teenager needing to integrate into the community.

The last question provoked little discussion at this early stage: "How can these special needs of women and the training for society's needs mesh with the present education now offered?" Yet the question became a springboard for the group's deep concerns about proper educational guidance and counseling for women at all levels and of all backgrounds.

In this first meeting, the committee generated a list of additional concerns: continuing education, the role of the community college, better models for guidance and counseling, special needs of the suburbs, responses to the teacher shortage. They decided to solicit background papers on as many of these topics as possible. One of the most striking background documents, the very size of which indicated the change in knowledge about women, was a bibliography on women's education prepared by psychologist Evelyn Perloff of Purdue University. In 1953, when the ACE CEW began, the work on women was minimal; however, Perloff now included 284 items in an initial bibliography, supplemented by 124 others in a 1961–62 addendum.[31]

Committee members used the background projects to influence deliberations around their particular interests. Home economist Edna Amidon, for example, presented the home as a "place of respite" that required women to be educated for this important role. Amidon revealed a good understanding of how age and life circumstances affected women's developmental concerns. She worried about early adulthood, for example, which she called "the fullest of 'teachable moments,' and the emptiest of efforts to teach."[32]

Elizabeth Drews' contribution replicated much of what she had presented to ACE. She stressed that women's lack of preparation for their lives and the absence of monetary reward for family work made it hard for them to achieve their potential. Looking at places where women actually outperformed men, she encouraged their efforts in areas related to "survival, the human condition, [and] basic needs (educational, mental health, and physical health)." Rather than focusing on the usual calls for scientific "womanpower," Drews felt women could serve best by moving into these fields.[33]

Raushenbush and Senders offered papers explicating their work with mature women, presenting case histories of older women who, with family support, had successfully returned to college. By adding the viewpoints of husbands and children, Raushenbush stressed that women's choices need not disadvantage their families. She quoted the husband of "Mrs. Furness," who, when their daughter decided to marry, told her firmly that she could not expect her mother to assume responsibility for wedding planning, explaining, "Your mother has committed herself to an academic program." Senders continued the issue from the other side, showing how educational counselors could help women manage the "choice points" related to return-to-school decisions. Senders counseled working with husbands, explaining that "a woman's problem is often a problem man."[34]

The issue of guidance became a mutual focus of the education and the home and community committees. They sponsored two papers, one outlining the public services available to women through the U.S. Employment Service, and the other a detailed review by Columbia University's Esther Westervelt of the recruitment and training of educational counselors. Unusual for its time, Westervelt's paper cautioned that counselors were conspicuously unprepared for dealing with women's needs, sometimes allowing their prejudices to limit recommendations for female clients. She recommended two new requirements for counselor training: a course focusing on psychological and physiological differences, and a practicum working with women's concerns. Both recommendations found their way into *American Women*.[35]

Another background paper demonstrated the committee's good intentions but also indicated the middle-class inclinations of its members. Commission staffer Ruth Prokop prepared a discussion of community colleges as a growing new opportunity for women.[36] The fact that a staff member rather than a specialist prepared the paper signified committee members' lack of deep knowledge or connections with community colleges. In 1962 community colleges were a rapidly growing force in higher education. With their flexible admissions requirements, favorable scheduling, affordable costs, and geographic accessibility, these institutions were quickly expanding the reach of higher education. These factors also promised increasing receptivity to women.

Over time, community colleges fulfilled this promise, proving to be an important entry point for both women and nontraditional students. In the early 1960s, community colleges witnessed an upward trend in female participation, with fully 38 percent of their student body female (see Table 2.3). More experienced with traditional educational institutions, members of the education committee highlighted the potential of community colleges, especially for women who were "geographically trapped," but ultimately, they offered little specificity in either their discussions or their recommendations.

Organizing the Committee's Work

Recognizing that the committee had only four meetings in which to prepare recommendations for the entire commission, Chayes and Bunting worked to organize the group's thinking. Although the members' initial interests spanned an array of issues, Chayes used an October 1962 progress report to focus thinking on how different groups of post-high-school women might use education. Keeping women apprized of their options was a key recommendation applied to women in various situations. Women who had not finished high school or who had stopped after high school graduation must be encouraged not to be "placid" about further education. To keep women from falling into this category, the committee urged stronger early training and guidance. A second group of "unfocused" college graduates must be encouraged to use their talents, whether at home or later in the job market. Finally, "highly motivated" women pursuing graduate or professional training must receive help in balancing career demands with family, even as they focused on meeting society's needs. Noticeably absent from consideration were women who had very little education; however, Chayes reminded the group not to forget the concerns of "special economic and social groups . . . [being] Negroes, Puerto Ricans, farm women."[37] Even with such encouragement, the college-oriented committee often neglected certain areas of educational needs.

As the committee moved toward its April deadline for a report to the commission, discussions in the October and December meetings[38] stayed within the bounds of middle-class collegiate concerns. However, at times, committee members or staff pushed the group to consider more controversial issues, notably sex education and family planning, federal aid to the schools, and the new feminist ideas of Betty Friedan. As before, considerations of civil rights, racial issues, and the poor received only scattered attention.

To help the committee move toward specific recommendations, Chayes started with a twenty-page set of worksheets that organized the group's thinking by levels of education: the elementary and high school years, the college years, and post-college. But with the over-representation of collegiate educators, the latter two received the bulk of attention. In fact, when Bunting broke the committee into subgroups to focus on the three areas, she found it hard to generate much interest or expertise for the elementary and high school discussion.[39] Considering elementary school, the committee raised concern over two issues: providing girls "early mental stimulus [and] a secure environment," and teacher quality. They argued that girls needed strong education in their early years as a base for later choices. Here the committee also highlighted the needs of the poor, noting that education "cannot take place under conditions of privation and want."[40] Their thinking on child care recognized that good centers not only provided care for children but also educated needy mothers; this focus on parental education carried forward an early-twentieth-century progressive idea of educating the community through the school.

In recommending support for federal aid to education, the committee (and eventually the commission) took a stand on a contentious contemporary debate. Discussion leading to the 1965 Elementary and Secondary Education Act, with its $1 billion in federal aid to schools, was fraught with disagreement over how aid should be distributed. Many states wanted federal money but worried about federal oversight; Southern locales still struggling with desegregation were especially concerned. Furthermore, the question of whether federal aid should go to Catholic schools remained divisive, and the courts had offered only narrow decisions describing the "wall between church and state" in educational settings. Both Agnes Meyer and Eleanor Roosevelt had argued publicly with Catholic officials over federal education aid.[41]

In its recommendations, the committee avoided the particulars of this fight, generally focusing on using federal money to support teacher training. Since teaching remained a feminized profession, their push for enhanced professional development supported not only girls as students but also women as professionals. The committee recognized that not all high school girls would go to college but that, regardless of eventual career plans, all needed training in hygiene, health, and nutrition. The committee argued that high school girls should be shown many ways "to be a good American wife." They chided the limited imagery of many textbooks, suggesting that seeing women performing unusual roles might expand girls' early view of their choices.

Turning to the college years, the group stayed with themes they had earlier agreed upon. They encouraged better counseling for women students. And, echoing ideas long encouraged by NADW, they demanded campus professionals who possessed a wide understanding of women's life patterns and who could stimulate students' aspirations. Discussion of the years after college attracted most of the committee's energy, bespeaking the influence of continuing education advocates Senders, Raushenbush, Farber, and Bunting. The recommendations here were quite specific, centering around flexibility, support, adaptability, and accommodation for women in their young adult years. They advocated making it easier to transfer credits among schools, to qualify for fellowship aid as part-time students, to skip irrelevant requirements when returning for a degree, and to find courses particular to women's needs. The committee also highlighted the potential of community colleges, adult education, and extension education for serving women.

For her progress report in December 1962, Chayes presented four recommendations for the committee's consideration and offered another nine possibilities, all based on conversations the group had generated. The four areas where she anticipated strong committee support included expansion of nursery schools and day care facilities, federal aid to education (with a particular focus on teachers), federal seed money to state universities for guidance centers, and federal money to the Office of Education for research on women. Although worried about a tight-fisted Congress, the committee believed they could successfully argue that these four ideas met clear needs. Less certain, but clearly of interest, were calls for better information to counselors in training; provisions for continuing education, including proficiency testing and part-time scholarships; and some still-vague recommendations about the teacher shortage, homemaking education, and family planning.[42]

The issues of family planning and sex education were commission-wide concerns that, although attracting less attention than the ERA or equal pay, posed potential public relations problems for the PCSW. Planned Parenthood had provided the commission with a statement about family planning explicitly calling for dissemination of birth control information, saying that "family planning information should be available to all women for reasons of physical and mental health and of personal and public responsibility." Women worn out by overwhelming family demands could not give their children the "affection and wisdom" they required. Thus, Planned Parenthood argued, careful family planning benefited both the individual and society.[43]

The education committee was interested in this issue for two reasons: without some control over family size, women would find it even harder to plan their lives; and as "the agency most directly touching the greatest number of people," the school was identified as the best place to offer such information. Committee members strongly supported the distribution of material on family planning and sex education. The idea of individual women balancing their responsibilities with choice fit the approach they were developing. However, the larger commission found this a touchy subject, requiring behind-the-scenes compromise to reach a statement that all could support. In fact, the very last item treated in full commission deliberations was Bunting's request that stronger language about sex education be added to *American Women*.[44]

As the education committee finalized its report, disagreements arose that demonstrated the complications facing early 1960s women's advocates. One point about which Bunting differed strongly from the majority, was whether to suggest that women's difficulties resulted from ill-treatment by men or outright discrimination. Bunting resisted Drews' view—derived from her research—that boys often "diminished" girls and their opportunities. When other members responded favorably to Drews' idea, wanting to stress a boys vs. girls approach, Bunting firmly steered the conversation away, saying that, in her experience, this behavior was not widespread among boys.[45]

Bunting's objection to painting women as victims also appeared in her discomfort with recommending separate options for them. During her term on the ACE CEW, Bunting had balked at seeking special privileges for women, always asking whether men could benefit from any particular recommendation. In the education committee, she cautioned that "you always have got this problem when you do things for a special group. It seems to me that you set it up and you protect and you emphasize it. And if it works, then you have the problem of getting out of the box."[46] Her view of equity was compensatory. She fully supported programming that repaired problems for women, such as options for part-time fellowships or programs to ease their reentry to schooling, but she objected to separate, supplementary efforts favoring them. In many ways, this discussion replicated the protective labor legislation argument, and it showed the variety of thinking about how to solve women's problems.

A related disagreement was whether girls and young women had special needs due simply to their gender or whether such concerns arose as mature women faced the family/career balancing act. All committee members recognized adult women's special challenges trying to plan their choices around education, marriage, motherhood, and work. Yet they disagreed about whether school-age girls and young women differed enough from boys that their education should proceed differently at younger ages. Ultimately, the committee avoided a statement about whether education for homemaking should replace either training for work or a more liberal education that could suit any potential future—a prominent issue among contemporary educators. Their recommendation became a more generic call for good preparation for the home at all stages of girls' lives; they did not recommend similar training for boys. When one member suggested adding a strong statement urging that women be educated to be more than wives and mothers, Bunting countered that "it is also good for them to be educated *as* women and mothers" (emphasis added).[47]

These disagreements demonstrated the committee's—and the commission's—ongoing concern not to be seen as favoring work at the expense of women's other roles. In a milieu that valued family, even a labor-oriented group like the PCSW needed to tread carefully in advocating for women across all circumstances. Like the ACE Commission on the Education of Women a decade earlier, the PCSW recognized how complicated women's roles and choices had become. Committee member Farber became impatient with such distinctions, arguing that all women were working women. Presaging later feminist arguments, he asserted that housewives indeed contributed to the "economic unit" of family and community. For him the real "demarcation" was between women with intellectual aspirations and those without. The committee's challenge, in Farber's thinking, was figuring out how to provide education appropriate to women's varied situations.[48] Senders supported Farber, comparing his thinking to her recent reading of *The Feminine Mystique*. Although few on the committee shared their enthusiasm for

Betty Friedan, Senders and Farber appreciated not only Friedan's analysis but also the boldness of her delivery.[49] They argued that the commission should similarly seize its potential to reach a national audience. At one point, after several hours of careful deliberation of their draft report, Farber burst out with the challenge, "But who the devil is going to read this?" urging his colleagues to make bolder statements and to reach out to people who needed to shake their thinking.[50]

The committee took a bold stance in focusing on the needs of mature women who were, in fact, often overlooked in contemporary educational planning. Bunting noted that their attention to adults—whether well-educated women who needed a career boost or under-educated adults needing flexible, affordable basic education—was noteworthy and unusual. By doing so, she explained, they were taking "as axiomatic" a position not currently popular among collegiate administrators. Their assertion that "the worth of the student, [and] his rank in the list of educational priorities is independent of his age" challenged higher education to recognize both the strength and the "pay-off" that such students brought.[51]

THE FINAL EDUCATION COMMITTEE REPORT

The report that the education committee submitted to the entire commission took some political and intellectual risks. In its attention to older women, its call for sex education, its support for federal education aid, and its request for a federal office of research on women, the committee advocated innovative positions. But the committee's argument reached farthest in its call to recognize education as a potential lever for social change.

John Kennedy's administration was laying groundwork for social legislation that reached fruition during Lyndon Johnson's Great Society. Within a few years, scholars and politicians would advocate for education as the most effective means to equalize opportunity for Americans. During World War II, Gunnar Myrdal's *American Dilemma* had highlighted issues of racial inequality. As the postwar period progressed, the prominence of urban concerns led to new questions about poverty, race relations, and inequality. Michael Harrington's *The Other America: Poverty in the United States* (1962) raised the issues for both scholars and the public. Daniel Patrick Moynihan's controversial 1965 report on the black family deepened concern over how to effect change. By 1966, James Coleman had studied the impact of education on families. His report on *Equality of Educational Opportunity* advocated for equalizing educational benefits. Instead of blaming the victims of poverty, he argued, the government should commit to evening out opportunity, which would eventually lead to more equitable results.[52]

This idea of using education to effect social change was in the air as the education committee considered women's needs. In presenting its case to the PCSW, the committee opened with a ringing call that recognized the potential of education for equalizing opportunity: "The education a woman gets will have a deeper effect on her life and status than anything else within the range of immediate social action."[53] Such a sentiment, carried to its conclusions by policymakers, could recommend the overhaul of American education, not just for women but for all those disadvantaged by differences in opportunity.

Accompanying this powerful opening statement were potent data demonstrating both women's educational achievements and the gaps remaining. Beginning with the greatest need, the figures showed that 20 percent of American women (and 24% of men) had acquired less than eight years of formal education; the committee used this figure to call for adult basic education. Once in high school, however, women performed very well. Confirming a trend evident since the turn of the twentieth century, more women than men attended and completed high school (48% of women vs. 40% of men). At college, however, came what the committee identified as another major gap. Calling this "the great divide," the committee noted that women constituted only 41 percent of college enrollees and merely one-third of B.A. graduates.[54] Thus, women's needs occurred at all levels, but particularly at the lowest and highest ends of the educational spectrum.

The committee organized its report around adult women's educational needs, asking for "immediate attention" to mature women and arguing for a different type of "womanpower": "Their neglect is a negation of our values. Their influence on the interests and aspirations of the next generation is inescapable." Although they might have devoted time to school-age and adolescent girls, committee members reasoned that solving problems for older women and mothers would trickle down to their daughters. They recognized that mature women could be found in a variety of circumstances, each dictating different educational provisions. The woman in school, for instance, "challenges our assumptions about the time dimensions of an education." The woman on the job ("often a lesser one than her abilities warrant") "contradicts the conventional wisdom about the place of a woman." If at home, trying to keep alive earlier interests and skills, the woman's needs "provide clues to inadequacies at earlier stages in the educational process."[55]

The most prominent idea guiding the report was that women's lives were discontinuous and differed from men's because of family responsibilities. Bearing in mind their audience and their provenance as a federal commission, the committee called on both the community and the federal government to accept an obligation to smooth the shifts among the various phases of women's lives. The committee offered nine recommendations, and the commission accepted all of them, although several members asked for more attention to poor and under-educated women, correctly perceiving the committee's strong focus on collegians. Bunting presented the education report at the whole commission's April 1–2 meeting, a session devoted to considering as many recommendations as possible. After a full day's work, extending into the evening, the education committee reported toward the end of the second day.

The first four recommendations related to education for adults, including support for *adult basic education,* especially as it affected women; *continuing education for mature women,* with more flexibility in admissions, testing, scheduling, curriculum, and guidance in post-high-school settings; *federal financial support* for adult programming, including fellowship and loan programs for part-time students; and *community methods to help homemakers* "maintain and develop interests and skills," including educational television. Although the commission accepted all four suggestions, members worried about insufficient attention to those women who had not finished high school or who needed technical training. In these commission-wide discussions, Esther Peterson was a notable advocate for the needs of the poor.

The fifth recommendation addressed the federal aid question, seeking *expanded federal support for education* "from kindergarten through graduate school." The committee called for funding nursery schools and day care; teacher training and salaries; graduate, professional, and technical training; and community colleges. Here the commission warned against encouraging advanced education where it was not appropriate. But this recommendation also highlighted the controversy surrounding federal aid; one member asked to have her opposition registered "on principle."

Three of the remaining four suggestions were accepted quite easily. Requests for more attention to *vocational guidance,* including materials and courses relating to women's needs, and expansion of the NDEA training institutes, found easy agreement. So too did a statement favoring the *use of volunteers* for home and community needs. The recommendation asking for a special federal *research program on women* matched ideas that other committees had advocated.

The committee tried to keep vague its final recommendation around family planning, with Bunting noting their wish not to be too "directive." It called for sponsoring experimental programs to help women prepare for *health, homemaking, and family life.* But tucked within this suggestion was a call for students to "learn about human reproduction and sexual activity in the context of education for family responsibility." The committee purposely substituted the term "family responsibility" for "family planning" but still felt strongly about the message. Fortunately, the commission as a whole had tackled this touchy issue the previous day, compromising on language allowing for differences in "religious philosophies" about family planning. They worried aloud about public relations damage if they openly advocated birth control. In approving the education committee's ideas, the group settled on quiet language: "Women should have the opportunity for education about human reproduction." In the final published report, the idea of "education for family responsibility" was fully covered in the relative safety of the education section, emphasizing the deleterious effects on women's health and opportunities that would result from poor family planning.

After a year and a half of work, the education committee's recommendations met with easy acceptance by the PCSW even though their report far outweighed the other subgroups' reports in both length and specificity. Some of the committee's ideas, such as expanded use of volunteers and better training for homemakers were noncontroversial. Other suggestions highlighted women's particular needs, such as better guidance training, teacher preparation, basic adult education, and continuing education opportunities. And a few recommendations challenged mainstream ideas, especially the encouragement of family planning and federal aid that could target women.

As it weighed the committee's ideas, the PCSW saw ways to use educational arguments to advocate for women more generally. In presenting the committee's report, chairman Bunting acknowledged their assumptions that women should have more opportunities to exercise choice but argued that these decisions should sustain women's traditional responsibilities within home and community.[56] For the committee—and eventually for the commission—education became the way that women could best exercise their choices. That is, some women might *choose* to give primary attention to education and career; others might *choose* to forego career focus, devoting themselves to family. Or, individual women might create their own calculus of when to focus on various parts of their lives, perhaps leaving school to raise a family but returning to college or work after children were grown. By steadfastly holding that women could choose how to balance their lives, the commission offered recommendations that provided the greatest flexibility. But ensuring that all women had equal educational opportunity was a necessary first step to exercising such choice.

THE COMMISSION REPORTS TO THE PUBLIC

In the two decades following the President's Commission, "status of women reports" from the government, professional organizations, and educational institutions became commonplace. But *American Women*, published in 1963 as a set of governmental reports and reprinted in 1965 as a trade book edited by Margaret Mead and Frances B. Kaplan, was the first such report from a high-level governmental body. Circumscribed by the needs of its political sponsors and by the limited gender analyses available in 1963, the report mixed recommendations, pronouncements, and somewhat disjointed messages. Nevertheless, *American Women* stands as a useful benchmark in thinking about women's concerns just before the 1960s renewal of the feminist movement.[57]

Although the report did not promote a single strong theme, "freedom of choice" came closest to an organizing idea. The commission asserted freedom and equality as the "great levers for constructive social change" in American democracy, calling freedom to choose among different life patterns one of the most important opportunities (17). By emphasizing choice, the commission explored a whole range of opportunities open to women without having to recommend any particular model of a female life. According to the commission, the keys to using freedom were, first, a recognition that all choices were acceptable, and then, the removal of barriers. This approach allowed the commission to treat protective labor laws, social security, child care, and other issues as obstacles standing in the way of choice. Flexibility around education promised the widest and most significant choice of all, since by preparing for a variety of life options, a woman kept herself free for subsequent decisions.

The report itself was rather disconnected, presenting its work in four sections plus appendices. The commission's editors decided that rather than present findings and recommendations from the various committees separately, the report should offer one conjoined statement. (More detailed commentary from each committee appeared as appendices.) The opening section of *American Women*—its "Invitation to Action"—presented this solidified view, calling on Americans to acknowledge women's contributions over time and the necessity of addressing their new options. This section highlighted demographic issues as well as outlining the legal, economic, and social concerns that the commission addressed.

Caroline Ware's background paper analyzing changes and accomplishments for American women appeared as the second section. In effect, her presentation became the "progress report" Kennedy had demanded. Ware took readers through changes across the previous century, emphasizing women's increasing movement into the labor force, politics, and education. She stressed that changes in family life had definitely occurred, but she analyzed these within the context of women's ongoing commitment to the home. Although her section focused on change, it assured readers that women continued to respect their family responsibilities.

After these two sections, the PCSW outlined its thinking and recommendations. Education provided the opening wedge, notwithstanding the fact that economic and legal issues had prompted the formation of the commission and had dominated its deliberations. Presenting education as an uncontroversial core American value provided a smooth beginning for subsequent recommendations. Once education was seen as key to expanding women's choices, attention to the Equal Rights Amendment, tax laws, job discrimination, and social security seemed to follow logically as ways for women to exercise their needs—always with the understanding that the family had made a joint decision.

In taking this approach, the commission used education as a safe way to introduce other concerns. However, this obviated the education committee's idea to paint educational opportunity as a means for dramatic social change. In the final report, the earlier clarion statement about education as the most effective social action was replaced by a milder claim that nothing could better meet the special needs of women than "improvement in the quality of education available to all the nation's youth" (25).[58] The idea was laudatory, allowing the commission to advocate for basic educational aid and better teacher training, but it hardly matched the notion of using education to reallocate social benefits.

A second result of using education this way was directing the recommendations at middle-class women who had actual choices in education and jobs. That is, by asserting that women's circumstances were a matter of choice, the commission skirted the fact that poorer women had limited educational opportunities leading, in turn, to circumscribed economic and personal choices. As with the committee reports, the overall document addressed the situations of poor and "minority" women but without a focused agenda on their behalf.

In addressing education, American Women adopted the committee's focus on older women. Although the sentiment had been nowhere evident in the larger deliberations, the commission now asserted that, "[a]s our work progressed, we became convinced that greater public understanding of the value of continuing education for all mature Americans is perhaps the highest priority item on the American agenda" (23). Here it explained that education no longer existed just for the young, nor should it be considered complete at any stage. Rather, people should seize the chance to upgrade their skills, "follow the frontiers of learn-ing," and refresh their ability to reenter the labor market. By focusing on "ma-ture women," the report introduced the idea of basic adult education and better preparation for homemaking. Here the commission did not focus solely on colle-giate women, but stressed the overall number of females in the workforce, many of them ill-prepared. A few points about collegiate training appeared, but the overall recommendation supported flexible continuing education in a variety of settings and urged particular attention to the needs of African American women and poor families.

The main part of the report featured particular elements from each committee, cohering into an overall set of recommendations. From the civil and political rights committee, for example, came the discussion about the ERA, with its strong em-phasis on the Fourteenth Amendment solution. From the home and community committee came suggestions for expanding day care. Recognizing that such ed-iting left out valuable expert analyses from the subgroups, the report presented shortened, edited versions of each committee report at the back of the book.

The condensed education committee section cobbled together pieces from the original report, leaving a series of suggestions without any particular theme. In an introductory page, the writers emphasized that three considerations had appeared concerning education. The first, that "the culturally deprived must be motivated," had never actually appeared in the reports, although the commit-tee had urged sensitivity to poorer women. The second consideration, support-ing expanded guidance and counseling, was certainly a mainstay of committee discussions; while the third, focusing on part-time study, seemed a small slice of the committee's ideas about continuing education. Nothing in the section contravened the committee's work; in fact, whole portions of its report were re-printed, including very prominent attention to the programs at Sarah Lawrence, Radcliffe, and Minnesota. Overall, the section covered education for a large range of women and girls; discussion of college was minimized, and graduate/profes-sional schooling was nearly absent.

PUBLIC RECEPTION OF *American Women*

The 1963 versions of the President's Commission report were the original, government-issue copies. No editorial comment was included. However, interest in the work resulted in commercial publication by Scribner's with an introduc-tion and a 24-page epilogue by Margaret Mead, one of the most prominent wom-en in America and a noted commentator on women's issues. Mead could always be counted on for a unique perspective on women, and her epilogue (181–204) constituted a quite independent analysis of the report. Although she commended the commission for conducting its work "responsibly and with clarity," she challenged its focus on paid employment and the treatment of family life as an "episode" that women should finish quickly. She also faulted the commission for assuming that conditions existing at one time would continue without change, and its resultant approach of fitting women's needs into current possibilities.

Mead did not present herself as a critic, but she outlined how the commission's assumptions led into questionable territory. The first assumption—which she saw as implicit—was that "in the modern world anything peculiarly feminine is a handicap"—or, as she rephrased it, "all roles and status should be equalized toward those of the American, white, Protestant, well-educated, adult male." A second assumption, she argued, was that "both males and females attain full biological humanity only through marriage and the presence of children in the home." In this, the commission "overwhelmingly deals with the typical woman," who marries early, bears several children, and then finds many years of life ahead once the children are grown. Here, Mead acknowledged the commission's worry that it would be seen as advocating against home and family. Finally, Mead explained, the commission assumed that "the right to work at a paid job is an intrinsic condition of human dignity." Accordingly, barriers to women's full economic participation should be eliminated; and, in addition, exercising the right to work should never adversely affect home life (183–86). These three assumptions, Mead argued, grew naturally from postwar life in America and the world, where concern over "economic and social deprivation" as well as "the cult of sexuality" had dictated American thinking about the family as the bulwark of defense.

Mead outlined two other assumptions she found in the report, calling them "conflicting values." First was that "the individual should be able to make choices," clearly the mainstay of commission thinking. Yet Mead castigated the report both for not recognizing that poor women lacked real choices and for not speaking more strongly on behalf of talented, educated women who encountered barriers to full participation. She recognized the lack of attention to women as leaders. Finally, Mead noted the commission's frequent equating of "job" with "career," without recognizing the commitment, privilege, hard work, and education necessary for the latter.

Analyzing these assumptions allowed Mead to expound on one of her long-standing themes: life in the home deserved greater dignity and recognition. By over-valuing the male approach to career, she cautioned, Americans disregarded the special contribution that home life offered men, women, and children. It was no surprise, she reasoned, that the present situation developed. After war's end, "a generation that feared there would be no future grasped at all of life at once"; now they found instead a "feeling of anticlimax" (199). Rather than swinging the pendulum in the opposite direction, which she perceived to be the commission's approach, Mead urged Americans to consider different options than they saw around them. If the focus on big families and full employment were scaled down, women who enjoyed the home could stay there without suffering a waste of their talents. If women preferring a long-term career were encouraged and supported, higher satisfaction would result. Homemaking and volunteer work should be equal to paid employment, with no hierarchy valorizing paid work.

In the two years between release of the commission's report in 1963 and Mead's commentary in 1965, a shift in thinking about women had begun. Betty Friedan's work (which Mead did not explicitly acknowledge) had captured a wave of feeling about the limits on women's options. Members of the President's Commission—as evidenced by Senders, Farber, and Bunting in the education committee—had different reactions to Friedan's analysis. Mead recognized this new way of thinking but argued for what she perceived as a middle ground between valuing home and work: "In 1964, women were promised the same rewards for working that previously had been offered them for staying home. They would be more attractive to men, more vital and interesting to their husbands, better mothers to their children, and they would stay young longer" (191). This tendency to promise all good things through education and work bothered Mead, who worried that the home suffered through the revaluing of work. The fact that few women were openly welcomed into the professions did not alleviate her concern. Ultimately, although the commission had tried to navigate the postwar confusion about women's balancing of home and career, it failed to satisfy Mead, who preferred a different calculus altogether.

In fact, perhaps because the commission tried to address the whole range of women's situations, readers judged success based on their own angle of vision. Mead worried that the home was devalued. Likewise, reviewer Edward Eddy, president of the all-women Chatham College, lamented the PCSW's "startling denial of the right of women to be female." He sided with Mead, suggesting that the commission capitulated to society's materialism, valuing the "almighty dollar" over every other female contribution. Echoing educators like David Riesman and Harold Taylor, Eddy wondered about the costs of focusing education on vocationalism; he especially decried the loss of "the power of women to shape ideas, to force the making of sound decisions, to act as conscience for the world."[59] Yet a reader looking for the report's guidance as to how women could enact this influence, particularly as leaders in the professions, would have found only a few vague references.

AFTER THE REPORT: CONTINUING THE COMMISSION'S IDEAS

Taking advantage of the two-year hiatus between completion of the PCSW's work and the publication of *American Women*, the editors added to the book nine pages of federal and congressional accomplishments on women's issues that had occurred since 1963. The report highlighted passage of the Higher Education Facilities Act, the Nurse Training Act, and the Library Services and Construction Act, all passed in 1964. Likewise, improvements to counseling and fellowship programs and the Job Corps now benefited female applicants. Although several of these efforts had been underway independently, the report attributed at least part of their success to the "continuing leadership" prompted by the report's recommendations.[60]

After completing its report, the President's Commission disbanded. Peterson said she had always intended to turn implementation over to "women's groups and the Women's Bureau [who] could get in and get busy."[61] Two groups were created to extend commission efforts both inside and outside the government. An Interdepartmental Committee, composed of various cabinet secretaries and the Women's Bureau, was organized to monitor and encourage federal efforts on the commission's ideas. A similar Citizens' Advisory Council on the Status of Women assembled representatives from private organizations. Ultimately, neither of these committees fulfilled its promise. Peterson called the interdepartmental effort "kind of a flop" because it didn't "ride herd" or sufficiently follow up the President's Commission ideas. And the advisory council, she argued, never achieved the level of independence it needed.[62] But in many ways Peterson herself did not push an extended agenda for women's rights, and her views clashed with the more expansive approach of Lyndon Johnson's new Women's Bureau director Mary Keyserling and Secretary of Labor Willard Wirtz, who moved the department away from the protective legislation approach favored by Peterson and her allies.

After Kennedy's assassination, Johnson supported the PCSW recommendations. He exceeded his predecessors in appointing women to prominent roles, adding sixteen new women to his administration.[63] In addition, Johnson promoted passage of the Civil Rights Act of 1964, which contained, in Title VII, the provision prohibiting employment discrimination based on race or sex. Ironically, proponents of women's rights had differed over including the sex provision in Title VII, replicating many of the same divisions caused by the ERA.

Over time, organized work on behalf of women came less from federal instigation than from the private sector, particularly women's advocacy groups and the newly formed National Organization for Women (NOW). However, the President's Commission prompted a new network of agencies that addressed women's concerns: state commissions on the status of women. The PCSW had encouraged creation of such groups within each state; by 1965, thirty-six had been organized. These state-level organizations provided a framework that responded to the growing women's movement, often with a more activist approach than the President's Commission had taken.[64]

As the feminist movement grew in the late 1960s, the contributions of postwar groups like the President's Commission and the ACE CEW began to seem rather conservative. For those drawn to NOW's militancy, the earlier groups seemed hesitant and too accepting of limitations on women. However, some who had straddled both eras, trying to think their way through advocacy for women when surrounded by postwar thinking, were more measured in their judgment. Kathryn Clarenbach, chair of the 1960s Wisconsin Commission on the Status of Women and a founder of NOW, stressed the importance of national and state commissions for laying groundwork. Although few of the more radical groups ever commended the contributions of the President's Commission or the subsequent Citizens Advisory Council, Clarenbach explained their significance as necessary first steps: "Doing the public education, fishing up of information about what the life of American women really is, what the facts are, the circumstances and what public policy exacerbates these circumstances and what public policy needs to be changed in order to make things better. . . . This laid the groundwork that was absolutely necessary." "This is all educational work," she stressed. Asked to choose between the Wisconsin commission and her role in NOW as her most significant accomplishment, Clarenbach demurred, noting that the second could never have occurred without the first.[65]

The President's Commission on the Status of Women did not argue for radical social change. It was a product of its era in trying to balance women's commitments to home and family with opportunities to stretch themselves economically and culturally. Its 1963 report captured a time in women's history when individual choice, rather than collective action, marked women's decision making. Even two years later, when the popular version of the report was published, greater discrepancies in thinking about women were already obvious in cultural analyses like *The Feminine Mystique*, in organizations like NOW, and in legislative accomplishments like the Great Society. Yet the PCSW's effort to understand women's circumstances and to advocate for change, and its quiet recognition of the potential power of education, drew attention to approaches that could ultimately affect women's lives.

PART THREE

Responses

CHAPTER SIX

Women's Continuing Education as an Institutional Response

Mary "Polly" Bunting traveled a long road to the prominence of her member-ship on the President's Commission on the Status of Women in 1961 and chair of the ACE's Commission on the Education of Women. Her experiences as a female scientist, widowed mother of four, and president of Radcliffe College marked her as unusual during the postwar era. Yet in trying to establish herself profession-ally, Bunting encountered the same challenges faced by most women academics, and her history offers clues as to how some women managed professional suc-cess in an often unwelcoming postwar milieu.

Born in 1910 in Brooklyn, New York, Bunting and three siblings found sup-port and high expectations from their lawyer father and activist mother. Bunting's mother, Mary Ingraham, who served as national president of the YWCA during its challenges in the 1940s over integration, set a model for involved leadership. In her teen years, Bunting developed an interest in science, earning her M.A. and Ph.D. (1934) from the University of Wisconsin in agricultural bacteriology.[1] At Wisconsin, Bunting met her husband, Henry, whose father taught their class in pathology. After graduation, Henry pursued two years of medical training at Harvard, while Polly remained at Wisconsin conducting postdoctoral research. When Polly received a teaching offer at Bennington College, she took it for one year, followed by another year teaching physiology at Goucher College. The cou-ple delayed marriage until 1937, while Henry completed an internship at the Johns Hopkins Medical School (he was required to sign a pledge not to marry during his time there). When Henry settled at Yale, Polly took a job as a laboratory technician because the director gave her free use of the lab facilities, permitting her continued genetics investigation into the bacterium *Serratia marcescens*.

The Buntings had four children between 1940 and 1947. Polly stayed at home with the children, characterizing herself as having "dropped out," although she actively pursued civic affairs, including public health nursing and the school board. Family life shifted, however, when Henry died unexpectedly from a brain tumor in 1954. With four children to support, Polly returned to work full-time, as dean of Douglass College at Rutgers University. There she established credentials as a creative educator, tapped for highly visible positions on national committees, particularly those related to scientific manpower. In 1960 she accepted the presidency of Radcliffe. In later years, Bunting cited her five years of postdoctoral experience as key to her ability to reenter academe after her husband's death. Cognizant of both the difficulty and the importance of returning skilled women to the job market, Bunting created several programs—first at Douglass and then at Radcliffe—marking her as a founder of a new movement in continuing education that "reclaimed" women for educational and professional contributions.

Bunting and other educators recognized the nascent labor market potential in women who had left school or the labor force to raise families but now wished to return. They also understood the psychological benefits that would accrue to both women and their families from active, personally fulfilled motherhood. Their ideas for specialized continuing education programs for women wove together patriotic, economic, cultural, and psychological ideologies by providing ways for women to resume schooling while still fulfilling their roles as wives and mothers.

The women's continuing education movement of the early 1960s created a structural response to the educational challenges facing women in the early postwar period. Such programs, designed to return women to the college class-room and the academic profession, built on the work of the ACE Commission on the Education of Women (CEW), the President's Commission on the Status of Women (PCSW), the American Association of University Women (AAUW), and the National Association of Deans of Women (NADW). Because of those previous efforts, educators had significant professional networks and a firm research base on which to build the continuing education movement. As a structural answer for women's concerns—particularly for middle-class, college-oriented women—continuing education demonstrated a slow movement away from individualized answers and toward a collective response on behalf of women. As such—even as its founders resisted the feminist label—the programs became a small-scale harbinger of more openly feminist activity, particularly in education, in the later 1960s.

ORIGINS OF THE CONTINUING EDUCATION IDEA

Adult and continuing education had existed for decades on college campuses, growing out of earlier efforts to provide vocational and humanistic training for adults in local schools and community agencies.[2] The movement of such programs into land grant universities was spurred by the 1887 Hatch Act, which provided funding for agricultural extension programs for adults. Expanding from the original focus on agriculture, land grant universities began offering workshops and classes in varied community settings as well as television and radio programming that eventually brought home economics and liberal arts programming to taxpayers.[3]

Adult education programs grew on college campuses throughout the twentieth century, receiving a boost from the expanding post–World War II collegiate populations and the growth of community colleges. However, such offerings usually supplemented the regular daytime college program and seldom led to degrees. It was much more difficult for those beyond the usual college age—later known as "nontraditional students"—to earn degrees through part-time attendance. At some institutions it was possible to pursue courses part-time and even work toward a degree through extension, but this required special permission, and different parts of the university often applied their own regulations. Throughout the 1950s, students unable to attend traditional daytime classes were less likely to earn sufficient credits for degrees and were rarely treated as seriously as those pursuing full-time programs.

When adults did return to college, they frequently experienced problems transferring or claiming credits for past work. Many institutions were reluctant to accept credit for courses completed elsewhere, especially if much time had passed. Requirements could differ from school to school or from program to program. Arranging full credit for work done elsewhere could be time-consuming and difficult. Although college reached a much wider and older middle-class population following the war, particularly through the influence of World War II veterans, the curriculum and the schedule were planned around traditional students—young high school graduates. The arrival of veterans had encouraged institutions to be more flexible in terms of curriculum, but they less commonly adjusted schedules to help people with family responsibilities take classes at unconventional times.

In such circumstances adult women trying to resume schooling were particularly disadvantaged. Since married women tended to relocate as their husbands' job demanded, their transcripts often included credits from a wide variety of institutions. Curricular requirements often asked them to duplicate work done elsewhere or simply seemed less suitable for adult women; physical education classes, for example, could feel very different to a 30-year-old mother than to her 18-year-old classmate. Women with children might be less able to attend regular daytime classes. Those who had been away from school for some time frequently felt "rusty" in their reading, writing, and study skills.[4]

The women's continuing education movement of the early 1960s envisioned all these concerns as manageable. Its advocates believed that institutions could create accommodations allowing women to return to school, thereby reclaiming their intellectual strength, their economic contribution, and their psychological health. Continuing education encompassed a wide range of programs; its early proponents consciously planned innovations that differed from setting to setting. Many programs provided a parallel curriculum through which women "dropouts" could return to school, filling gaps in their transcripts and eventually completing their degrees. Others emphasized transitional coursework, helping women dust off skills before they entered traditional college classrooms. Still others focused on women who had achieved the bachelor's degree earlier but who needed refresher work or a professional boost to resume career paths. Finally, many programs targeted traditional female students while still in school, hoping to convince them to plan ahead for complicated lives.

Later in the century, "continuing education" connoted a commonplace approach to serving nontraditional students in alternative ways, but in the early 1960s such programming for women was both innovative and specific. As one advocate explained, the term "women's continuing education" was a deliberate choice with "clear and specific meaning: that of a return to curricular discipline designed by authoritative faculty to expand skills and to introduce newly discovered knowledge to those with previous experience in higher education at varying levels."[5] These students—so easy to dismiss as incidental—were being consciously reclaimed for higher education and prepared for subsequent creative contributions to their communities.

THE FIRST PROGRAMS

The first program deliberately designed around women's continuing educational needs appeared at the University of Minnesota through the joint efforts of psychologist Virginia Senders and extension specialist Elizabeth Cless. The Minnesota Plan for the Continuing Education of Women won a $110,000 grant from the Carnegie Corporation in 1960. Within two years, Carnegie funded similar programs at Sarah Lawrence College and Radcliffe College. This trio of innovations—given prominence through Carnegie's visibility—inaugurated the women's continuing education movement, created a model for dozens of other institutions, and sparked a small but effective women-focused philanthropic agenda at Carnegie, the Rockefeller Foundation, and other private funders.

Virginia Senders had long been interested in nontraditional programming for women. A 1947 Ph.D. graduate of Radcliffe, Senders worked during the mid-1950s at Ohio's Antioch College, a school known for its nontraditional approach to education. In Antioch's small town, she met many educated women staying at home with families whom she viewed as surprisingly complacent about not directly using their educations.[6] Writing later about the genesis of her continuing education ideas, Senders recalled an incident in which a plane had crashed near Antioch. As a group of local women discussed the newspaper's speculation on causes for the accident, she noted their unscientific explanations. "I thought that these women hadn't always been like that," she observed. "When they were students, most had applied what they knew of natural science and had understood what they read. I wondered what had happened to them." She worried that, because they rarely had cause to use their scientific background, these college graduates were letting their knowledge stagnate.[7]

Such thinking prompted Senders to consider whether educational programming could be designed to stimulate women who found themselves in such circumstances. She proposed a nine-point plan for Antioch that would allow women to continue working with faculty after they finished college, purchase academic journals, conduct independent research, and attend "keep-in-touch seminars" on campus. Placing both psychological and monetary value on this independent work, Senders suggested a competition to award prize money for exemplary work. Such stipends could support women's time, including babysitting costs. She envisioned the growth of such programs around the country, believing that society would thereby gain productivity and women would gain happiness.[8]

Colleagues at Antioch expressed only mild support for Senders' idea but encouraged her to seek outside funding. Senders sent her proposal to ACE's Commission on the Education of Women. CEW communicated considerable interest but explained that—under financial pressure of their own—they were unable to provide financial support.[9] She then sent her proposal to John Gardner, president of the Carnegie Corporation, who, in his earlier faculty role at Mount Holyoke College, had sponsored her undergraduate independent study on women's motivation. Although Gardner liked Senders' idea, he encouraged her to send it to ACE. Frustrated by the circular correspondence, Senders set her plan aside.[10]

The Gardner connection proved propitious a few years later when Senders moved to the University of Minnesota as a lecturer in the psychology department. Even in such a large institution in a bustling city, Senders saw many of the same issues surrounding women students and dropouts that she had observed in small town Antioch. As she inquired about curricular, counseling, and financial opportunities for women on the Minnesota campus, Senders was repeatedly referred to Elizabeth Cless. As assistant to the dean and a lecturer in the university's busy Extension Division, Cless had experimented with courses for community women seeking to reinvigorate their skills. Using the extension model of short-term programming, Cless had created a course in 1958 called "New Worlds of Knowledge" to update women's understanding of the interplay between liberal arts and science disciplines. Finding significant enthusiasm among women in the community, she recruited as teachers regular university faculty who appreciated adult students.[11]

Senders and Cless brought different perspectives to their concerns about women's education. Senders was especially focused on young women who were still students, hoping that a sort of early warning system about the intellectual challenges ahead could redirect their educational plans while they were still in school. Cless focused on women who had already left the university or had given up on collegiate education, envisioning ways to reconnect them. Working together, they created the Minnesota Plan for the Continuing Education of Women, a multifaceted program to serve both traditional college students and women of the community. Its three-pronged approach offered a residential program, an extension program, and a variety of other opportunities to strengthen and reinvigorate women's educational options.

For the first group, traditional-aged undergraduate women already on campus, the residential element of the Plan provided "orientation to the multiple roles of later life so that realistic preparation can be made for them." Through special courses, individual counseling sessions, and group discussions (sometimes with students' boyfriends present), the planners aimed at what they called "intellectual rust-proofing": helping young women understand early the dangers of dropping out or "rusting out" might prompt them to attend more seriously to opportunities at hand. The extension element targeted a second audience made up of young mothers already raising families. For them, special courses and counseling offered throughout the day and evening would allow more consistent attendance. The third group consisted of "the mature woman whose formal education is already far behind her," who could pursue career retraining or personal enrichment through special courses and guidance about the university's resources.[12]

As Senders and Cless prepared a proposal seeking funding for their plan, they turned to the era's familiar "womanpower" language to emphasize national need:

> It is widely recognized that the United States urgently needs to develop and utilize all possible resources of trained or trainable manpower, and particularly needs to make use of its gifted and high-ability individuals. Manpower wastage occurs when able people do not obtain or use education to the limit of their abilities. . . . This wastage is particularly common among women.[13]

But their programmatic goal included more than enhancing "womanpower":

> Its objectives are twofold: first, to return to the nation's (paid or unpaid) manpower pool at appropriate levels a group of intelligent, educated women whose abilities would otherwise be underused during their mature years; and, second, to increase the personal happiness of many women by exposing them to new interests, by helping them find new objectives, and by making the goals of the more distant future an integral part of their present lives.[14]

Structurally, the Minnesota Plan was neither a curriculum nor a degree. Its creators called it "a program to mobilize all the resources of the University in an attempt to meet flexibly and individually the diverse time-tables, interests, and questions of individual women." Tailored specifically to the University of Minnesota, the Plan coordinated functions across disparate areas on behalf of women—a new focus for the institution. As Senders and Cless explained, "we are building into, rather than onto, existing agencies. . . . We are 'infiltrating' the university."[15]

The thinking behind the Minnesota Plan relied on ideas advanced and popularized throughout the decade by the ACE CEW, the AAUW, NADW, and other groups. Such organizations had stressed the nation's under-utilized "womanpower," resulting both from some women's avoidance of the workforce and from the treatment of others as incidental workers. These groups had also examined various curricular options, hoping to find the ideal educational balance between vocationalism and liberal studies to prepare women for modern life. The organizations had also examined psychological assertions that women's own lack of motivation for advanced training and careers might be not only the cause for their limited success but also a sensible response to a milieu that valued men's professionalism.

Research on women's psychology increasingly stressed the notion that women must fill multiple roles. Psychologist Elizabeth Douvan emphasized the difficult choices facing young girls who worried about the incompatibility of college and family. Since the culture most often prized career achievement for men and family contributions for women, only the most dedicated women were likely to choose advanced training and professionalism.[16] Douvan and others argued that women used college differently from men. Since young men knew early on that they would be following a vocation for life, they used college to plan and test possible work roles. Young women, however, focused on marriage as their likely future. Thus, their collegiate planning was often "insubstantial, contradictory, and stereotyped," lacking the "coherence and realism" of young men. For women, college either became an end in itself, divorced from vocational aspects, or an opportunity to find a husband.[17]

Sociologists Viola Klein and Alva Myrdal had considered these same issues, popularizing the notion of choice in their 1956 book, *Women's Two Roles: Home and Work*. They challenged the prevailing assumption of role incompatibility, arguing that a more holistic approach to women's lives would allow them to shift back and forth among their tasks. Wider community support for day care would allow women needed flexibility. Likewise, other structural changes could permit women to manage their responsibilities successfully. Klein and Myrdal were clear in their message that children—as long as they were loved and tended by caring adults—could prosper without full-time attention from their mothers.[18]

Cless and Senders combined ideas from *Women's Two Roles* with statistics from labor force analyses like *Womanpower* and *Work in the Lives of Married Women*.[19] Viewing women's educational challenges from a lifelong perspective showed that, within just a few years, the same young women who were abandoning college for home and family would be sending their own children to school. With the age of marriage decreasing, mothers faced an "empty nest" quite early in their lives. This long-term perspective led Senders and Cless to a striking image:

> By the time they reach twenty, half the women in the country are married. Their last child is born by the time they are twenty-six years old. So, it's a thirty-two year old mother who takes her youngest child off to first grade. When this same last child graduates from high school, twelve years later, his mother is forty-four years old. Seventeen years later, when the woman is sixty-one years old, her husband dies. And fifteen years later, at age 76, the woman herself dies.[20]

Looking at women in this way, the Minnesota educators saw both wasted womanpower and wasted womanhood. Young mothers—so ready to focus on family—would ultimately have many decades of life when they might return to school, pursue a career, or challenge themselves with volunteer work. If women could be convinced to see education as the solution to long-term needs, they could plan differently as college students and rejoin the educational milieu when older.

A particular strength of the Minnesota Plan was its simultaneous service to both undergraduates and community women. Another was the recognition that it belonged to no one division of the university, but rather coordinated efforts across areas. This notion of combining the resources of a large organization caught the attention of the Carnegie Corporation and won Minnesota an important start-up grant.

Carnegie had entertained other requests to support women's education since World War II. The ACE CEW had long sought its support, as we have seen, but Carnegie had responded with only $9,900 for the 1957 Rye research conference. Other philanthropies had supported education for adults but without a specific focus on women. The Ford Foundation, for instance, sustained a special fund for adult education.[21] But in 1960 several factors combined to enhance Carnegie's attraction to the Minnesota program. First, recognizing the ongoing national interest in manpower, Carnegie was developing a funding stream in "better use of human resources." The foundation targeted a range of programs to enhance America's technological and labor force capacities. One such opportunity, well recognized via the numerous "womanpower" studies, resided in women. The 1960 Carnegie annual report, which explored the human resources goal, indicated its intention to include women: "Many studies indicate that, numerically at least, the greatest wastage of human resources in the United States today is the under-utilization of intelligent women. Part—and perhaps a major part—of this waste is unnecessary."[22]

A second reason for Carnegie's interest was the involvement of corporation secretary Florence Anderson, whose personal concern for women's education affected foundation decision making throughout the 1950s and 1960s. Anderson was an unusual participant in Carnegie affairs. She joined the corporation as a clerical secretary immediately following her graduation from Mount Holyoke. After serving several years in a variety of posts, she was named corporation secretary in 1954.[23] By 1955 her interest in women's education led her to visit the ACE Commission on the Education of Women, and she was influential in providing Carnegie money for the commission's work. In later years, Cless singled out Anderson as a key force supporting women's continuing education, calling her "practical and tenacious" in her grant-making. Cless explained that Anderson "returned academic proposals in this field over and over again, until they were rewritten in such a way that they could stand on their own, not as imitations of other new CEW programs."[24]

A third reason explains why the Minnesota Plan caught Carnegie's eye. Senders knew Gardner from their earlier association at Mount Holyoke, and she had renewed the acquaintance by sending him her ideas about Antioch. In the Minnesota proposal, Senders and Cless had expanded those earlier ideas into a plan reaching more women, demonstrating the involvement of the larger university administration, and carefully matching its womanpower language to Carnegie's human resource goals. Senders' connections, along with the proposal's strategic targeting and its widely based university support, convinced Carnegie to award a three-year grant of $110,000.

"THE WIFE WE SAVE MAY BE YOUR OWN"

The Carnegie Corporation interpreted the Minnesota Plan's range of support around the university as a sign that the program would indeed "infiltrate" the campus. As Anderson indicated after a visit, "I was particularly pleased to note the many ways in which this program has been made an integral part of the University rather than a tangential activity."[25] Carnegie awarded the grant in April 1960; programs were running by September. In the two weeks following a single announcement about the Plan, 213 women requested applications.[26]

Work proceeded in all three of the Minnesota Plan's areas. For current students, the program provided group discussions in a variety of extracurricular settings, including dormitories, sororities, and honorary societies. The goal was to change the attitudes of young women about their need for education and planning for the future. Senders realized the drawbacks of traditional pedagogical approaches, noting that "originally the lecture method was used. . . . For the most part, the result of this intellectual approach was an intellectual response." The students listened dutifully but left unconvinced. Senders began to target the young men in students' lives, reminding them that "the wife we save may be your own."[27] She combined group discussions with individual counseling and special seminars such as "The Educated Woman in the United States," designed to inform women about life-cycle patterns. To reach more candidates, counselors even wrote letters to Minnesota students who announced their engagements, alerting them to the Plan before they left school. Although it produced few applications, the technique signified the Plan's creative approach.[28]

The second element, counseling and programming for young mothers, drew considerably more women than the planners had imagined. Women found the flexible schedules and the supportive style of plan counselors and teachers especially appealing. Young mothers pushed the university to create a child care center to facilitate their daytime class attendance—something no one had envisioned. The third phase, programming for mature women of the community, was presented through the Extension Division with special courses, credit by examination, home study tutorials, and weekend seminars. Students from the community received scholarships through the Plan, funded by the Carnegie grant. Although the stipends provided only $75 per student, the amount covered courses or child care, making a real difference in many women's ability to attend.

Senders and Cless recognized that previous experience with adult students across the university, especially in the counseling and extension divisions, supported the new focus on women. They also valued faculty volunteers who especially enjoyed the challenge of teaching adults. And, in the days before consciousness-raising, they organized an informal advisory group of women faculty members, hoping to "create a climate of acceptance in their minds." Ultimately, the two founders judged their first year a success, although they were surprised at the balance of students drawn to the Plan: they were "almost swamped by older women," including many with preschool-aged children, but found little interest within the traditional undergraduate population.[29]

THE IDEA SPREADS

While Cless and Senders were organizing the Minnesota Plan, a similar idea for easing women's return to college developed at Sarah Lawrence College in suburban New York City. Esther Raushenbush, professor of English, dean of the college (1946–57), and later president (1965–69), raised many of the same concerns about reaching women who had dropped off the educational track. Initially, Raushenbush was not aware of Minnesota's work, but learning about Carnegie's grant to Minnesota spurred her interest in the continuing education idea, connected her with Cless and Senders, and ultimately won Carnegie support for her program as well as giving her national prominence as a continuing education pioneer.

As dean, Raushenbush met many women—especially mothers of her students—who had devoted their early lives to family and who now wished to reconnect intellectually, either through completing college degrees or by reentering the workforce. In 1957 Raushenbush prepared a paper called "Women of Forty" for her faculty colleagues, emphasizing how often women found themselves at loose ends once their children left home. In just the first month of the academic year, Raushenbush noted, a dozen adult women had visited her office, hoping to find ways to "do something with themselves." She described them as leading "an adjunct kind of life,"[30] and asked the Sarah Lawrence faculty, "Have we any interest in these women?"[31]

Sarah Lawrence was a reasonable place to ask such a question. A small, prestigious women's college founded in 1926, Sarah Lawrence in the 1950s sat at the opposite end of the collegiate scale from the large, variegated University of Minnesota. The college prided itself on individualized attention to a select student body. Centering its curriculum in humanities and liberal arts, Sarah Lawrence offered several distinctive features: classes of fifteen students conducted as discussion groups, coupled with individualized student-teacher tutorials and personalized faculty "donning" modeled on the British practice.[32]

Since the 1940s, Sarah Lawrence had made small efforts to help its own students who had dropped out of college, usually referring them to classes at other schools in the New York City area. In 1960 Raushenbush created two special alumnae courses—similar to Cless's extension classes at Minnesota—for Sarah Lawrence dropouts wishing to complete their degrees. But she hoped to do more for former students as well as for the large numbers of women in suburban Westchester now hoping to reinvigorate their collegiate work.

In an article called "What Now?" for the alumnae magazine, Raushenbush discussed the frustration, anxiety, and lack of fulfillment women often felt as they entered adulthood. Hoping to generate ideas from the alumnae audience, she included a questionnaire asking what sorts of educational opportunities might appeal to them.[33] Raushenbush's article came to the attention of Arthur Adams and Opal David at the ACE Commission on the Education of Women, who invited her to present her paper to their group. By 1960 the commission was becoming increasingly interested in both the life-span notion of women's education and the possibility of continuing education directed to adult women. In conversations with Raushenbush, CEW director Opal David noted the recent Carnegie grant to Minnesota, and encouraged Raushenbush to contact Cless and Senders.[34]

Raushenbush used the evidence of ACE's and Carnegie's support for continuing education, as well as encouraging replies from her alumnae questionnaire, to boost campus interest for her idea of special programming for returning adult women. Working with college president Paul Ward, Raushenbush prepared a proposal for a Sarah Lawrence College center to provide upper-level work for women with disrupted educational careers. The center would apply the same admissions requirements used at the college; students would be serious scholars committed either to earning a degree or progressing toward a specific intellectual goal. In a school like Sarah Lawrence, which emphasized individualized student learning, the goals of the center seemed a good fit. The overall aim was to remove obstacles of scheduling, timing, and comfort, allowing women an easier road back to college.[35]

Raushenbush and Ward first considered the Ford Foundation as a possible funder, given its long interest in adult education. They soon learned, however, that its Fund for Adult Education was closing its doors. With encouragement from an alumna, they appealed to Ford's Fund for the Advancement of Education, but that group declined support, saying that although it sympathized with the issue, it found the proposal too reliant on "the conventional apparatus of courses, credits, and degrees," and not "sufficiently different from the usual college program."[36]

Raushenbush bristled at this assessment of her idea as conventional. She responded to Ford, noting how little educators knew about these learners. Emphasizing that mature women students represented a new kind of adult education population, she stressed the importance of meeting their needs in unique ways. "In short," she argued, "this program is 'experimental' in at least three ways":

> (1) It is experimenting with the intellectual potential of a part of the population to whose education no particular thought has yet been given, although they, the individuals, are intellectually superior people; (2) It is experimenting with the problem of discovering what this population can profitably do with the mature years by setting up a research and planning program for them; and (3) It extends to this public, for their new needs, the experimenting with highly flexible curriculum planning, courses, class organization, tutorials, independent study, and individual planning generally that has given the present undergraduate college its character.[37]

The Ford Foundation was not persuaded; nor was the Carnegie Corporation convinced by Sarah Lawrence's first appeal. In early 1961, a year after supporting the Minnesota program, Carnegie claimed insufficient funds for a project not considered "central" to its "major program interests." However, in a letter to President Ward, Carnegie Secretary Florence Anderson noted that she had "personal interest" in the area and would "enjoy discussing the plan with Mrs. Raushenbush."[38]

Anderson's interest made all the difference for Sarah Lawrence, as Raushenbush reworked her proposal to meet Carnegie's specifications. In December 1961, Sarah Lawrence received a three-year grant of $76,000 from Carnegie for a center "(1) to learn more about the educational needs and goals of the college women in Westchester; (2) to provide a rather substantial counseling service for them; and (3) to help them find the kind of education or training which they and the counselor believe they need."[39] Combining the Carnegie money with an anonymous alumnae gift of $15,000 allowed the college to open its Center for the Continuing Education of Women in spring of 1962.

Just as Minnesota's first announcement had generated hundreds of inquiries, Sarah Lawrence fielded one hundred calls in one day following an article about the center in the *New York Times*. Within two-and-a-half weeks, 250 letters of inquiry arrived.[40] In the first academic year (1962–63), the center served 33 students in continuing education courses and conducted individual counseling interviews with 418 clients. As at Minnesota, courses—including American Social Thought, Greek Philosophy, and English Romantic Poetry—were taught by college faculty with a strong interest in mature students. Students followed the Sarah Lawrence tradition of creating independent study projects under faculty supervision, and as director, Raushenbush served as faculty don to all.[41]

Faculty were pleased with the students' effort and accomplishments. One professor explained the differences between center students and traditional undergraduates, noting that for older students, the teacher "is unlikely to be a formative intellectual influence" since they more easily integrated new intellectual ideas into their own understandings. At the end of the first year, six of the thirty-three students matriculated to the regular degree program, and none left the program.[42]

The counseling component attracted many more women than the campus courses. Although Raushenbush had imagined the purpose of counseling as placing women into Sarah Lawrence courses, she quickly found that nearly half the clients already held the B.A., and some had pursued graduate work. Most were women over the age of 30 who wanted a quick way to return to school or the work force. And in many cases, students' job market interest related less to financial need than to women's desire to utilize their skills. As Raushenbush summarized her work with these women, she noted the absence of "the image familiar in recent popular literature of the 'frustrated' woman, beating her fists against the imprisonment of domesticity. She probably exists, but we have encountered few of her."[43]

A DIFFERENT APPROACH TO
CONTINUING EDUCATION

Although the counselors at Sarah Lawrence tried to guide women clients interested in graduate training or professional jobs, their program was best suited to the small numbers of women needing to finish the bachelor's degree. Yet, as the wide interest at both Sarah Lawrence and Minnesota indicated, many women with advanced skills sought ways to reenter the professional world. A third program supported and publicized by Carnegie targeted this more experienced group through a center aimed at reconnecting Ph.D.-level women with intellectual and employment opportunities. Through the efforts of Radcliffe's new president, Mary Bunting, the Radcliffe Institute for Independent Study opened in 1960, offering year-long, part-time, funded fellowships for women professionals wishing to pursue independent scholarly or creative projects in the Harvard/ Radcliffe setting.

Bunting's interest in highly trained women was neither circumstantial nor new. She and Raushenbush had discussed the wide variety of needs among educated women, recognizing the different capacities of their institutions. The two women were joint members of an accrediting team visiting Swarthmore College in 1959, after Bunting had accepted the Radcliffe presidency. As Raushenbush recalled, "One night we stood in our hotel room doors discussing the business of educating women whose education had been interrupted. . . . In the course of our conversation we decided that Radcliffe College would be a marvelous place to have such a program for women who had completed college and who were far advanced in their intellectual lives and wanted to undertake intellectual work again, and that Sarah Lawrence would be an equally good place for undergraduate women who had broken off their undergraduate lives."[44]

Bunting's interest in doctorate-level women might have stemmed from her own experience reentering academe after the death of her husband. In addition, her background as a scientist drew her to populations of women with technical and scientific skills, a group less often targeted by the general programs at Minnesota and Sarah Lawrence. During her deanship at Douglass College, Bunting had experimented with several continuing education opportunities, although her initial ideas pertained, not to women specifically, but to any student seeking to reenter academe.[45] Long concerned about the effect on women and men alike of requiring full-time study for degrees, Bunting successfully encouraged a program at Douglass for easier admission of part-timers. The effort focused more on helping those students leading complicated lives than on reclaiming dropouts, but Bunting recognized how family duties often inhibited students' ability to attend school uninterrupted.

A less successful idea at Douglass was Bunting's plan for an "underclass degree" that would award credit for the first two years of college. Recognizing that "stopping out" of school often caused students to lose both credits and momentum as they changed institutions, Bunting tried to formalize the early years of college work into a two-year degree. Rutgers University and Douglass College both resisted the idea,[46] which Bunting later pursued during her 1958–1960 tenure with the ACE Commission on the Education of Women. The commission was only mildly interested, and eventually Bunting shifted toward achievement testing. Her thinking was better received at the Educational Testing Service, which created the College Level Examination Program (CLEP), a program allowing students to establish nationally recognized college credit for past work, in 1964.

Bunting's third effort at Douglass to address educational losses resembled continuing education for women but with a particular technical focus. In 1958 she won support from the Ford Foundation for a program to retrain women in mathematics. Alert to the Sputnik-era dearth of science and mathematics teachers, Bunting surveyed local women with backgrounds in mathematics to see if they wanted a teaching career and then canvassed local employers to investigate potential job opportunities. When results on both sides proved positive, Ford offered support for a program to refresh women's background in mathematics and then aid in job placement. The effort continued for several years, gaining Bunting national attention within the continuing education movement.[47]

BUNTING THEORIZES WOMEN'S CHOICES

As she became nationally known in the late 1950s, particularly through her work with ACE, Bunting received an appointment that she later credited with "awakening" both her deeper understanding about women's needs and her commitment to helping the highly skilled. Shortly after the launch of Sputnik, Bunting joined the National Science Foundation Committee for Scientific Personnel and Education, a group charged with strengthening the nation's corps of engineers, scientists, technical personnel, and teachers. "It was a single statistic that sparked my interest in women as such," she explained later:

> It seemed important as we checked over the flow of talent into science to know, along with many other inquiries, how many able high school graduates did not continue to college. Foundation staff analyses of data from three sources indicated that of all high school graduates scoring in the top ten percent of ability tests, at least 97 percent and perhaps 99 percent of those who did *not* go on to college were female. This statistic surprised me. I expected girls to be in the majority, but not by such a margin. How sad, I thought. What a waste. Who were they? What had stopped them?

What galvanized Bunting was not merely seeing the data, but noticing the committee's lack of interest in pursuing it. She guessed that "the Foundation staff believed that if America knew that all the bright boys were going to college, no one would think there was a problem in the schools." The absence of girls and women was much less likely to generate concern.[48]

Bunting hypothesized that what she called a "climate of unexpectation" faced women throughout their educational and professional lives.[49] Low expectations for women's productivity, along with an educational system poorly geared to their life circumstances, conjoined to frustrate women at various decision points. While young, girls experienced an anti-intellectualism that encouraged marriage and motherhood more than education and profession. Thus, as the NSF statistics indicated, high school graduation often became the endpoint for talented girls who might otherwise have profited from college. Even those who continued often found the draw of marriage stronger than the push for intellectual accomplishment.

Educational structures also complicated a woman's ability to combine marriage with study, since few part-time opportunities existed in either colleges or professions. Even professionally oriented women who entered graduate school found a "subtle environmental effect" working against their success. Although most graduate students found their first year of advanced training difficult, Bunting suggested that a discouraged man was often bolstered by an advisor, but that a hesitant woman seldom received similar encouragement. "All too often, academic advisors do not believe that the loss of a young female scholar is of any real significance. 'She is bright, but not important.'" Thinking about available research on academe and motivation, Bunting suggested that both internal and external forces worked against women, frustrating both their ambition and their opportunities.[50]

Bunting believed that an answer lay in creating educational and career options that responded to women's needs. Employing a favorite metaphor, she encouraged educators to see students, not on a racetrack where everyone runs the same course and the fastest wins, but rather in a garden where each could grow at his or her own pace, responding to whatever stimulus best fostered growth.[51] Borrowing ideas from the growing continuing education movement, Bunting was identifying flexibility as a key element in women's success. She also adapted the era's manpower language, prompted by her work with scientific and technical labor shortages. Bunting denounced the "waste of trained brainpower" represented by under-utilized women, calling it "undemocratic" to deny people the opportunity to develop their full potential. And, acknowledging the impact of women's domestic responsibilities, she argued that unfulfilled mothers would "stifle the curiosity and ambition of the son as well as the daughter," a poor approach in an era promoting national defense.[52]

Approaching an issue that later feminists framed as a "same/different" debate—that is, should women be recognized and compensated for their differences or prove their abilities through identical treatment to men—Bunting comfortably chose differentiated treatment. She never doubted women's equal abilities, but rather she worried that personal and environmental inhibitors (she called them "hidden dissuaders," echoing the era's marketing language) would jeopardize women's progress.[53] In recommending different treatment, however, Bunting came close to lowering her own expectations for what women might accomplish. In explaining why women need not compete with men, she suggested that "women, because they are not generally the principal bread winners, can perhaps be most useful as the trail breakers, working along the by-paths, doing the unusual job that men cannot afford to gamble on. There is always room on the fringes even when competition in the intellectual marketplaces is keen."[54]

Such an analysis was politically astute by suggesting success for women in uncontested intellectual territory. On the other hand, it confirmed the conclusions in Caplow and McGee's *Academic Marketplace* that women resided "outside the prestige system entirely" in academic hiring, and it supported data in Cronkhite's study that found women Ph.D.s most frequently in less-prestigious institutions.[55]

CREATING A NEW PROGRAM

The program created by Bunting at Radcliffe targeted women who had faced the "climate of unexpectation" throughout their careers. Her goal was to help women who had fallen off the traditional career track renew their intellectual and research capabilities in a setting better designed for women's needs. At Radcliffe, Bunting created a postdoctoral program that took advantage of the Harvard environment, offering its fellows "time that is free of personal pressures and obligations; a place to work; the facilities of a great university, from libraries to laboratories, from museums to computers; and the companionship and guidance of authorities in a hundred fields."[56]

Although the Radcliffe Institute was frequently hailed as an important continuing education option, Bunting initially resisted that label. Since the Institute offered no courses or degrees, and because it served women already holding the Ph.D., Bunting felt that it was too different from other continuing education programs to be called by that name.[57] However, the Institute shared many of the same goals: reclaiming the intellectual potential of women whose lives were challenged by family demands, promising an economic and intellectual return on the investment in "womanpower," and pushing educational institutions to loosen their expectations for women's participation as students and faculty. Radcliffe's program seemed to fit Elizabeth Cless's capacious definition of women's continuing education that emphasized the expansion of skills and knowledge among women with previous higher education experience.[58] Bunting expanded the definition by adding highly educated women and investigating ways to sustain their scholarly productivity. She also contributed a new conceptual explanation to women's concerns by identifying how a "climate of unexpectation" affected women from childhood onward, incrementally discouraging their intellectual contributions. Thus, when women dropped out of college or failed to pursue straightforward scholarly careers, they were viewed as fulfilling predictions rather than as disappointing expectations.

CREATION OF THE RADCLIFFE INSTITUTE

Although she had enjoyed experimenting with programs at Douglass, Bunting was drawn to the prominence of Radcliffe College as well as to its national platform for her ideas. In March 1960, new to her presidential post, she introduced her ideas to the Radcliffe executive board, emphasizing the opportunity for Radcliffe to assume leadership in supporting women's talent. She suggested a range of possibilities for an institute, including providing fellowships, creating resident scholar appointments, sponsoring conferences, and fostering research on behalf of women. However, she had not cleared her plan in advance and received only mild encouragement from the board. The trustees approved announcement of the Institute only if the president raised $150,000 from sources that would not directly compete with the college's current fundraising campaign.[59]

Bunting set out to raise funding from a variety of familiar and new sources. Unlike the Minnesota and Sarah Lawrence programs, which drew their main support from Carnegie, Bunting's Radcliffe Institute was supported by more than one foundation and by individual donors.[60] The biggest individual contribution came from Agnes Meyer, the *Washington Post* philanthropist and supporter of women's education. Bunting had little personal connection to Meyer, but persuaded her to commit $50,000 to the new project. Just one year later, Meyer became Bunting's colleague on the education committee of Kennedy's President's Commission on the Status of Women.[61]

Bunting approached Carnegie through her own channels, separate from the appeals by Minnesota and Sarah Lawrence. One connection she enjoyed was a previous acquaintance with Florence Anderson; the two had shared an interest in horseback riding during their teen years in New York.[62] Bunting's focus on women's issues matched Anderson's growing interest in the field. In addition, Bunting saw a good fit between her ideas and those that Carnegie president John Gardner had discussed in his 1958 report for the Rockefeller Brothers Fund, *The Pursuit of Excellence,* and his subsequent popular book, *Excellence.*[63] Gardner was a strong believer that, as Bunting paraphrased, "a society gets the excellence it values," calling on education to meet national needs and on women to see themselves as significant human resources. In writing to Gardner for support, Bunting connected needs and opportunities: "There is something about the education of women in this country that reminds one of plants cultivated under conditions permitting excellent early vegetative growth but few flowers and less fruit. There is a marked discrepancy between the abilities demonstrated by female students in our schools and colleges and their later intellectual achievements."[64] The argument proved successful; in November 1960, Carnegie offered $150,000 for five years of Radcliffe Institute support.

Bunting's national connections won her idea even greater financial backing than Minnesota and Sarah Lawrence. Laurance Rockefeller, of the Rockefeller Brothers Fund, had developed interests in women's issues, sometimes turning to Bunting for advice. When he heard of her plans for the new Institute, Rockefeller invited a proposal from the Radcliffe president. Bunting's appeal was likely helped by the fact that while a student at Vassar, she had roomed with Laurance's sister-in-law, Blanchette.[65] The Rockefeller Brothers Fund gave $250,000 seed money, and Laurance Rockefeller served on the Radcliffe Institute's advisory board for several years. As her work with Agnes Meyer, Florence Anderson, and Laurance Rockefeller indicates, Bunting was a key player in women's philanthropic networks.

PLANNING AND PUBLICITY

Just as the Minnesota Plan targeted three separate audiences, and Sarah Lawrence offered both courses and counseling, the Radcliffe Institute comprised several efforts. Counseling was offered to hundreds of women in the Boston area who, like those in metropolitan New York, presented a wide array of educational and professional needs. Psychologist Martha White conducted individual appointments and group meetings with these clients and subsequently published a guide to Boston's part-time educational opportunities.[66]

The Institute's main focus was the fellowship program for Associate Scholars and Resident Fellows. Associates were part-time researchers living in the Boston area who could benefit from an annual stipend of $500–$3000, office space, the libraries and other academic facilities of Harvard University, and connections with Harvard faculty. The program sought "women who hold an advanced degree or its equivalent in achievement and status, but the selection of scholars is not dependent on rigid academic requirements. They may be concerned with any realm of scholarship or creative art. . . . What is essential is that they be able to show evidence of past accomplishment and the promise of purposeful activity in a specific plan of work which they will be required to detail as a condition of their selection for the institute." Although the Institute never restricted applications to married women with children, it noted that the associates program was "directed primarily to the talented woman who, after marriage, finds it difficult, if not impossible, to continue to be intellectually creative without assistance."[67]

The Resident Fellows were envisioned as professionals who, unlike the associates, "have been able to maintain continuous careers" but who nonetheless would benefit from time and support in the Harvard community. Planners imagined these successful professionals as role models for the associates. However, although selection committees generated names for resident fellowships over the first few years, this category never attracted many applicants, and it was soon overshadowed by tremendous interest in the part-time associate opportunities. Like Minnesota and Sarah Lawrence, which both drew hundreds of applicants as soon as advertising appeared, Radcliffe quickly received calls and letters of inquiry resulting in 200 completed applications for the first cohort of twenty-one scholars.[68]

THE FIRST COHORT

With such a surfeit of candidates, Bunting and new Institute director Constance Smith chose an impressive group for the initial Institute cohort.[69] Ursula Niebuhr, wife of theologian Reinhold Niebuhr "and a noted theologian in her own right," was appointed the sole research fellow.[70] But as they reviewed applications from women seeking support as associate scholars, Bunting and Smith adjusted their expectations for who could benefit from the time, funding, and facilities of the Institute. Although not initially intending to fund women needing further education, they decided to support three women seeking further medical training in the Boston area. These included a doctor specializing in child psychiatry, a pediatric physician, and a dental surgeon from New Zealand seeking work in radiation research. They chose eighteen additional women as associate scholars, including several with college teaching backgrounds, ten pursuing independent research or creative projects, and a few looking for new directions. Their educational backgrounds ranged from the Ph.D. to no college at all, such as poet Anne Sexton.[71]

Although the first cohort showed large differences in age, academic background, level of accomplishment, and future plans, they shared certain similarities. As associate scholar and manuscript curator Lillian Randall noted, "The fact that we came from different backgrounds and pursued different goals mattered less than the ties that bound us: a strong sense of commitment and a need for time. We were all seasoned veterans of the battle for time."[72] Historian Emiliana Noether presented an all-too-common story of what she called being "relegated to the professional dustbin." As she explained, "through a number of personal circumstances and deliberate choices," she found herself in Boston with an eight-year-old daughter, piecing together a career as an "under-used, under-appreciated, and underpaid" lecturer, dependent on last-minute enrollments and without the benefits of an ongoing institutional affiliation.[73] Painter Lois Swirnoff, while teaching at Wellesley College, was forced to cede her appointment when she married a fellow professor. "In those days marriage to my colleague mandated the removal of one of us," she recounted. "Obviously, I was 'it,' since the other option was untenable, if not unthinkable."[74]

PUBLICITY BENEFITS THE EFFORT

The New York Times proved especially supportive of the continuing education programs, particularly through the efforts of education editor Fred Hechinger; the newspaper highlighted plans for the Sarah Lawrence center and covered its early progress.[75] Due partly to Bunting's prominence, the Radcliffe Institute too received considerable publicity in the *Times*: Hechinger featured Bunting's plans in a front-page story in the newspaper's education section, noting Radcliffe's attention to "intellectually displaced women" and liberally quoting Bunting's enthusiasm for helping women across a range of situations. Other newspapers picked up Hechinger's report, attaching their own headlines to his story of a fellowship program for educated women. *Newsday* proclaimed, "Radcliffe Launching Plan to Get Brainy Women Out of Kitchen"; the *Omaha World Herald*, "Female Brain Outlet Sought: College Beckons to Unused Talents"; and the *Christian Science Monitor*, "Radcliffe to Rescue Careers."[76]

During its first year, Hechinger also wrote a follow-up on the Radcliffe Institute, and Bunting was featured in *Life* magazine, in the *New York Times Magazine*, and, most notably, in a November 1961 cover story in *Time* magazine. In these pieces,

Bunting drew attention to women's educational needs and honed her message about "the climate of unexpectation," emphasizing the waste of womanpower and the frustration of unfulfilled women.[77] Her articles also addressed criticism that the Institute would harm families by drawing women away from the home. In an era that valued mothers' physical presence, Bunting challenged those "who attempt to correlate a high divorce rate, juvenile delinquency, even a deterioration in domestic cuisine, with the increase of working mothers." Echoing Alva Myrdal and Viola Klein's call to support rather than criticize such mothers, Bunting emphasized two messages: first, that frustrated women would be poor mothers, and second, that critics seemed to focus only on paid work, rather than on mothers who might be away from home for "bridge-playing" or other activities. In the end, Bunting emphasized, intellectual women's contribution to the nation could override such critique.[78]

In the educational realm, Bunting, Raushenbush, Senders, and Cless became well-known advocates for women's concerns. Because of the notoriety generated by their connection to Carnegie, the founders were frequently sought out for advice and for speaking engagements on women's issues. All three programs were featured at ACE's 1962 Itasca conference on continuing education; the prominence of Minnesota's work prompted ACE to ask that university to host the meeting, and Cless to serve as conference organizer.[79] Bunting held a seat on the President's Commission on the Status of Women; and when chosen as chairperson of its education committee, she invited both Esther Raushenbush and Virginia Senders to join the subgroup, assuring that continuing education ideas would be well represented in the commission's deliberations. ACE featured the three programs in a special issue of *Educational Record* (October 1961) devoted to continuing education. There Raushenbush, Bunting, and Senders were able to outline their thinking about women's educational needs and to describe how their three diverse programs were responding. Women's continuing education was off to a strong and publicly acknowledged start.

MICHIGAN DEVELOPS A SECOND-PHASE PROGRAM

Because—as Carnegie intended—the programs at Minnesota, Sarah Lawrence, and Radcliffe represented three different approaches across a variety of institutional settings, those efforts attracted interest from others seeking their own ways to meet local needs. As the continuing education idea caught hold, however, foundations proved less quick to offer funding. The large philanthropies' level of support for continuing education had never been great when compared to their overall funding priorities;[80] thus, programs launched in the later phase of the continuing education movement had the advantage of extant models but the disadvantage of decreased sources of support.

The Center for the Education of Women created at the University of Michigan in 1964 represents a "second-phase" continuing education program that used the pioneers as models but, partly through necessity and partly through tradition, developed a new funding approach that relied on support from local women rather than on national foundations.[81] As such, Michigan connected itself to a long educational tradition of women advocating for their own needs, helping each other financially, and building parallel institutions within larger settings. Michigan's approach to continuing education added another element of collective action to early 1960s educational efforts for women. Its three-pronged program of research, advocacy, and service in a large Midwestern institution built on and extended the continuing education models.

Whereas the three pioneer centers were founded by professional educators, the program at Michigan resulted from the efforts of a group of women, some holding university jobs and others wives of prominent university faculty members. Although the women's movement later decried the term "faculty wife" for its assignment of status through a husband's role, in the postwar era, with fewer opportunities for professional women, the connection to a husband's situation proved significant and propitious, particularly in less-urban environments.

The advocacy of local women connected by family or civic ties to a university carried a respectable and important tradition in the history of higher education. Before women became numerous as faculty or deans, the few women connected to a campus often played significant roles in supporting female students. Around the turn of the twentieth century, wives of faculty members at many campuses joined with local advocates and alumnae to raise money, provide housing, advocate for women, and otherwise support female educational interests.[82] At Michigan, women donors had built the women's student union and had raised money for a professorship to be held by a woman.[83]

With the higher education boom of the early 1960s, Ann Arbor attracted hundreds of ambitious academics to its sprawling research campus. But, as a Midwestern university town outside a major city, Ann Arbor offered less professional opportunity for women who settled there to support their husbands' careers. The founders of Michigan's center were educated women married to especially influential men on campus. Louise Cain, who crafted the initial proposal for the center, worked in the university's Extension Division; her husband chaired the School of Natural Resources. Her colleagues Jean Campbell and Jane

Likert had husbands who directed programs at the Institute for Social Research and the Survey Research Center, both prominent centers leading the way in Michigan's move into the top tier of research universities.

The creation of Michigan's center reveals a more communal effort than the programs at Minnesota, Sarah Lawrence, and Radcliffe, and demonstrates a connection between community and university. Founders Cain, Campbell, and Likert were all engaged in community activity. Cain had served as statewide president of the League of Women Voters, and all three participated in programming with the AAUW, the Business and Professional Women's Clubs, and the Michigan alumnae association. With other friends, they frequently discussed the dilemmas of women whose children were growing, leaving them curious about how to pursue their own interests and careers.[84]

As a part-time program planner in Michigan's Extension Division, Cain had as one of her responsibilities addressing issues related to women. Pulling together ideas she and her colleagues had discussed, Cain in 1962 presented a memorandum detailing some continuing education options to Roger Heyns, the university's vice president for academic affairs. Although sending her memo directly to Heyns likely skirted proper channels, Heyns was a family friend and was clearly in a position to enact academic decisions. Intrigued with Cain's ideas, he hired her as a special assistant to investigate possibilities in women's continuing education.[85]

Cain's initial proposal indicated how widespread knowledge about women's conditions and the pioneer programs to address them had become. In outlining problems facing women, Cain relied on material from the ACE CEW and from Raushenbush to stress how ill-suited current educational contours were to the discontinuous nature of women's lives. She highlighted efforts on behalf of women around the country, outlining the programs at Minnesota, Sarah Lawrence, and Radcliffe as well as earlier efforts at Douglass. Noting that many local women had already approached her with hopes that Michigan could create a program, Cain presented six steps that the university could undertake, including a survey of local needs and opportunities that could lead to what she called an "advisory, coordinating office" to support women's continuing education. She assured vice president Heyns that outside funding should be readily available for such an effort.[86]

Initially, Cain was not certain whether a separate curriculum or program would be a wise choice for Michigan; she needed to learn what already existed for women across the large university. Under Heyns' supervision, she began a five-month examination of needs and possibilities. With help from an extension school librarian, Cain prepared a bibliography on women's issues that covered significant popular and specialized material, including works by scholars Mirra Komarovsky and Kate Hevner Mueller along with general pieces like *Womanpower, Women's Two Roles,* and Betty Friedan's newly-published *Feminine Mystique.*[87] Cain enhanced her planning with visits to the programs at Sarah Lawrence, Minnesota, and Radcliffe as well as to several Washington-based organizations, including the Department of Labor Women's Bureau, the President's Commission on the Status of Women, ACE's CEW, and the AAUW. Closer to home, she worked with Irene Murphy, the sole woman on the university's Board of Regents, who supported her idea.[88]

Within the university, Cain recognized a potential and important ally in the Michigan Alumnae Association. Even before Heyns had appointed Cain, the Alumnae Council had begun investigating continuing education possibilities for the university.[89] With Cain's involvement, the alumnae created a committee to study programming ideas for Michigan, and they began to educate themselves about the field. The group conducted a day-long meeting on continuing education, including research presentations from Michigan sociologist Robert Blood and psychologist Elizabeth Douvan, whose work had been so influential with the ACE CEW and the President's Commission.[90]

Cain worked with the committee to survey the educational interests and needs of Michigan alumnae, raising the idea of a campus center for women's concerns. Their survey questions introduced the life-span approach to women's roles, suggesting that the dichotomy of career women vs. homemakers was outmoded, and soliciting alumnae's interest as clients or students for a new program.[91] Sixty-one percent of women who responded indicated a wish to pursue additional education, most preferring a degree program. When asked about barriers to their participation, only 2 percent cited their own age as a problem, but more than one-third noted that the age of their children and difficulties with class scheduling might prohibit their classroom attendance.[92]

The data proved useful, especially in providing evidence of a local market for a continuing education center at Michigan. Cain combined the survey results with information she had gathered about the wide variety of women on campus. She had discovered that more than one thousand women over age 30 were already studying at Michigan, the majority attending part-time.[93] Cain redrafted her proposal, now arguing for a center that would facilitate women's needs across campus. Although she envisioned a program tailored to older students, she imagined that the needs of younger women could easily be incorporated.

Cain focused on establishing "a visible, facilitating center" that would assist the university in three ways. First, it would provide information about the university's programs and requirements to the adult woman wishing "to resume her interrupted education," bearing in mind "her continuing home responsibilities and her objectives." Second, the center would advocate for additional flexibility for women across the institution, recognizing both "the resources and needs of this special section of returning students." Finally, the center would sponsor programs "to motivate the young woman undergraduate and to assist the young home-bound mother to continue developing their talents and educational training for future productive use."[94] Like Minnesota—a similarly large public university—Michigan imagined a varied program appealing both to current students and to women in the community. Also like the other institutions, it kept the primacy of women's home and family responsibilities firmly in mind.

Cain's proposal outlined the new center's service function, especially counseling tailored to each woman's need. At the pioneer centers, counseling had been identified as a key ingredient; Michigan expected it to be the most prominent service. Cain also argued for a "visible" office to organize services for women, noting that "there is no single, existing facility in the University to consider the total situation of this adult woman, for whose needs the University program was not designed." In this way, the center would become an advocate within the university. Rather than creating a separate curriculum like Sarah Lawrence, Michigan looked to Minnesota's approach, advocating for women's needs across widespread schools and programs. In a statement that became a guiding principle, she explained that the center would "act as agent and stimulator of adaptations and changes" within the institution. Finally, Cain highlighted the importance of conducting research on this student group and the new services.[95]

With an eye toward possible outside funding, Cain argued that the Michigan plan was unique in four ways: it would serve women planning to work; it embraced a "total counseling concept," which treated home and school together; it targeted undergraduate students along with home-bound mothers and mature women; and it anticipated the importance of research projects over time. In fact, only the emphasis on preparing women specifically for work was unique from previous programs. However, Michigan differed from the pioneers in three ways.

First, as Cain suggested, Michigan focused more strongly on helping women seeking degrees, or at least intending to use their education for professional purposes. Minnesota and Sarah Lawrence rarely differentiated between career-minded women and those simply exploring educational options. Even Radcliffe, although serving Ph.D. holders, did not insist on a particular career goal for its fellows. Michigan's advisory committee of deans—a key group for supporting the center—had expressed a clear preference for training women for professional positions rather than for the personal enrichment or general education goals they saw in other institutions.[96]

Second, Michigan was noteworthy in a way that Cain did not highlight. More explicitly than others, her proposal defined her center as an "agent and stimulator" of change. Although the other programs articulated this position over time, Michigan envisioned itself from the start as working to influence and change the university. Third, Michigan was unique in marshaling the resources—personal and financial—of local women to support and sustain the new center. Whereas the pioneers had garnered large individual donations to supplement their foundation grants, Michigan turned to individual supporters from the beginning.

Raising money through individual gifts was hardly Michigan's first choice; both Cain and Heyns had high initial hopes for foundation support. But by 1964, Carnegie and Rockefeller had shifted their support away from continuing education, although both continued to fund women's issues and Florence Anderson's influence sustained a funding stream at Carnegie. Carnegie supported both the AAUW and the University of Wisconsin in programs to move women into collegiate faculty posts: at AAUW, Carnegie launched the pilot phase of the College Faculty Program in eleven southern states, and at Wisconsin, it supported the E. B. Fred Fellowships for mature women graduate students.[97]

Michigan's early planning explored possible philanthropic sources, including Carnegie, the Fund for Advancement of Education, the Rockefeller Brothers Fund (which had supported Bunting), and the Rockefeller Foundation; they also appraised the likelihood of help from the U.S. Office of Education or from industry, particularly Avon and Revlon in cosmetics, IBM, and various textbook publishers.[98] Cain approached the Kellogg Foundation, a Michigan-based philanthropy.[99] But as the inquiries proved fruitless, Michigan's planners decided to combine their own university resources with local donor support.

The Michigan alumnae were still financially obligated for annual contributions to the women's professorship created in the 1950s, but the university forgave that debt when the Alumnae Association agreed to a three-year fundraising campaign on behalf of the new women's center.[100] The association named local alumna Jean Cobb to head the fundraising effort, a task that she assumed with enormous energy. Over three years, Cobb generated support for the center, clarified its mission to dubious alumnae, shepherded a group of volunteers through the fundraising process, and monitored financial progress.[101]

One of Cobb's most noteworthy efforts was preparing volunteer fundraisers to answer questions from skeptical donors. Working with Cain, she prepared a memorandum that would help committee members counter possible challenges. Their question-and-answer page, although designed to be lighthearted, nevertheless reveals concerns that early 1960s advocates for women needed to rebut:

1. Q. As woman's place is properly in the home raising her children, why should we promote a project which will help them leave home? Won't this increase juvenile delinquency?

   A. Agreed that woman's place is in the home—as long as her children need her. However, current statistics show that most women have their last child at 26, have a life expectancy of over 70 years and, therefore, have at least 20 years of life to live after their duties as mother and full-time housekeeper have diminished. The Center is designed to help these women make this period of their life useful and satisfying.

2. Q. I'm 109 years old. Why should I contribute to a program which is intended to help women in the 30s to 50's?

   A. Ladies of 109 years of age undoubtedly have many daughters, grand-daughters, nieces, grand-nieces, etc. who would be direct beneficiaries of their contributions to C.E.W.

3. Why do we need a 3-year Pilot Program? Why not start a full fledged Center right now?

   A. C.E.W. is a very, very new idea. It has never been tried as a full scale project at an institution as large and complex as U. of M. Like every really new idea, it needs a period of trial, of refinement and reassessment before a concrete program and procedure is developed.

4. Q. The University has a multi-million dollar budget, why can't it finance this 3-year period without money from the alumnae?

   A. Despite the size of the University budget, there is never enough for all the wonderful, worthy projects necessary to educational advancement. University money is budgeted to cover EXISTING programs. Other sources must be found to finance new programs. As the Center will benefit women, the University logically turns to its alumnae for help in financing it.[102]

Although the fundraising challenge had a slow beginning, the alumnae succeeded in their goal of raising $45,000 over three years.[103] The university matched the alumnae contribution through the discretionary fund of Michigan's president Harlan Hatcher. In Hatcher, as with Roger Heyns, the women's center had a strong supporter; Hatcher was a longstanding advocate for women, including lengthy service on ACE's Commission on the Education of Women.[104] The Michigan center opened with an operating budget of $30,000 per year—about the same as at Minnesota and Sarah Lawrence.

During the first year, the program counseled 563 women. To enhance visibility, the center mounted a conference and workshop in March 1965, only seven months after opening. "Opportunities for Women Through Education" focused on job opportunities in social work and education, attracting 238 attendees from across the state, along with 38 university faculty and staff. Esther Raushenbush, newly appointed president of Sarah Lawrence College, delivered the keynote address.[105] The center also supported courses; one on preparing to be a "paraprofessional" social worker, sponsored jointly with the School of Social Work and United Community Services of Metropolitan Detroit, served 106 women. Another 53 people completed a training program as volunteer museum aides.

After the first year, a clear sense of the typical client emerged, one not dissimilar to the profile at Minnesota or Sarah Lawrence: a married woman in her late thirties, "with a professional or student husband, two or three children, some college, or more likely than not a bachelor's degree," seeking help with career planning and with the challenges of fitting into an educational program.[106]

ASSESSING THE MOVEMENT'S ORIGINS

Starting in 1960, the women's continuing education movement homed in on a set of women whose educational and professional careers had been stymied by the competing patriotic, economic, cultural, and psychological ideologies of the postwar period. A variety of campus-based programs created flexibility around educational timing, scheduling, pacing, curricular choices, and funding that accommodated women's multiple roles and changing life circumstances. Programs that facilitated women's return to college or reentry into careers, supported by national foundations and tailored to local needs, created one particular solution to women's needs.

Yet continuing education planners recognized that their programs neither suited nor served all women. Some women, like the resident scholars targeted by the Radcliffe Institute, had managed to forge professional and academic careers even in the face of difficulties; such women were seen as models for those with less-focused career paths. The programs also assumed a target clientele with prior interest in education as well as the financial and personal capabilities to attend school. As such, the programming primarily benefited middle-class women who had already tried college or attempted a career. And in relying on the life-cycle model, the movement demonstrated a firm commitment to the primacy of women's home responsibilities, suggesting that—for many women—the best way to pursue education and career was after marriage and motherhood had already been attempted and their obligations satisfied.

Although the continuing education programs reached a somewhat narrow group of collegians, they nonetheless represented an innovative approach to reclaiming students often treated as incidental. In their early incarnations, they aspired to reach women across a range of situations; Minnesota and Michigan targeted traditional-aged students, mature women, young mothers, and graduate students, all in the same effort. As the programs developed and as continuing education proliferated, the programs became more realistic in their goals. But at the same time, the feminist movement that appeared in the later 1960s raised new ways of thinking about women that challenged both the life-span approach favored by continuing education and its preference for adjusting rather than questioning the educational structure. Feminist challenges, along with the programs' own analyses, prompted difficult decisions and self-critique by continuing education pioneers over the next decade. The growth of the programs paralleled other changes occurring in higher education, changes that eventually diminished the role continuing education played.

CHAPTER SEVEN

The Contributions and Limitations of Women's Continuing Education

Even women committed to academic careers found themselves affected by postwar cultural and psychological ideologies and confounded by the complicated reality of sustaining careers, maintaining homes, and raising families. Several founders of the 1960s continuing education centers interrupted their careers to accommodate family needs and husbands' jobs; in many ways, their own experiences embodied the life-span approach to education, family, and work. Just a few years after organizing the Minnesota Plan, Virginia Senders moved to Massachusetts with her scientist husband, working as a consultant from her new base.[1] At Michigan, both Louise Cain and Jean Campbell joined their husbands on out-of-state sabbaticals while the continuing education program was still forming.[2]

Women did not make such decisions lightly or without consideration of how their programs would be affected. When Cain's husband, Stanley, was offered a federal post as Assistant Secretary of the Interior for Fish and Wildlife during his sabbatical, Louise realized that accepting the appealing offer would mean at least a temporary family move to Washington, D.C. With the continuing education center about to be launched, she raised concerns about leaving to her boss, Michigan's vice president, Roger Heyns. Heyns assured both Cain and Jean Campbell that the university would support the fledgling center, even without Cain's physical presence. He named Cain "director in absentia" during the center's first year, allowing her to remain attached to the program she had envisioned. This arrangement gave Campbell the chance to launch the program as acting director, along with her first paid job at the institution. When Stanley Cain decided to keep the governmental post for three more years, Campbell became the center's sole director. Then, just one year after the center opened, Campbell also followed her husband on sabbatical. Heyns once again ensured that the center would prosper, a testament to his flexibility and support as an academic manager.[3] When Louise Cain returned to Michigan after her husband's four years in public service, the center employed her as a program specialist and conference planner.[4] By that time, Jean Campbell was established as director, a post she then held for twenty years.

Married middle-class women were accustomed to juggling jobs and family, often needing to craft opportunities that supported a delicate balance. With its $15,000 inaugural budget, Michigan covered three women's salaries—including director Campbell's—with part-time wages; Louise Cain had received $4 per hour to organize the program.[5] The founders' own experiences sensitized them to choices facing the women who used their centers. Thus, the continuing education centers, whether geared toward traditional undergraduates planning for the future or toward mature women trying to renew their training, focused on removing institutional barriers and expanding opportunities that would allow women to follow their interests even if the pace of their education and their degrees was less than ideal.

The programs proved most successful in drawing attention to women's needs and in changing policies that had discouraged their educational participation: institutions eased requirements, altered schedules, coordinated programming, and changed financial aid arrangements. However, three of the movement's wider goals proved less tractable. First, conducting research that analyzed women's efforts theoretically eluded busy educators who instead produced simple program evaluations. Second, extending their reach beyond middle-class populations who best fit the continuing education models became another challenge unmet over time. Finally, the continuing limitations of the job market frustrated graduates who, with new degrees or renewed experience in hand, still found balancing their needs a difficult task. And as the new women's movement appeared on campuses in the mid-1960s, programs that had looked innovative by stretching the structures of colleges and universities began to seem outmoded compared to the more radical demands made by feminist educators for women's equality. Even though the programs marked a first step toward the collective action valued by feminists, they nonetheless lacked a deep and wide challenge to academic treatment of women.

PROGRAMMATIC SUCCESSES

As different as the programs at Minnesota, Sarah Lawrence, Radcliffe, and Michigan were, they tackled—and to some extent solved—many structural issues that frustrated women's ability to continue their education. Since Radcliffe focused on Ph.D.-level women reentering the academic work force, its problems and solutions often differed from the other three programs. But Minnesota and Michigan, as large public universities, and Sarah Lawrence, as a small private college, all served both traditional-aged undergraduates and mature women of the community wishing to reinvigorate their collegiate and graduate educations.

Since many of the structural problems were internal to the campuses, different responses appeared across the three undergraduate sites. But many efforts proved replicable. Improvements such as liberalizing admissions expectations, customizing curricula, managing disparate credits, providing financial aid, and offering child care all helped to open opportunities for a student population that had been virtually ignored. The schools developed similar approaches to issues, cutting across differences in their size, locale, and scope.

Most bothersome were problems with course credits, residency requirements, part-time study, financial aid, special course status, and child care. Continuing education counselors spent considerable energy helping students clarify and reclaim past collegiate credits, whether the student wished to enroll in the new programs or to complete a degree from a previous institution. Assessing students' actual class standing could be difficult with a population that had transferred among institutions and dropped in and out of higher education. Not uncommonly, women might need only a few courses to finish a degree, yet their "home" institution rejected past credits or insisted on the same residency requirements that were applied to traditional-aged undergraduates. Continuing education counselors intervened, sometimes persuading another school to allow students to complete work from a distance, other times convincing their own institution to provide advanced standing that would allow a student to progress without penalty.[6]

Cost presented another barrier. In the early 1960s few schools or fellowship programs awarded financial aid to part-time students, and even the three undergraduate program sites originally hesitated to support their continuing education students with regular scholarship funds. The Carnegie grants at Minnesota and Sarah Lawrence provided small scholarships for women whose families could not—or would not—contribute money for their tuition. Although Minnesota successfully managed to certify Plan students for university-level aid, the center at Sarah Lawrence negotiated for nearly a decade before the college designated its continuing education students eligible for regular financial aid funds.[7] At the University of Michigan, support for financial aid increased over time. There, the center helped arrange favorable tuition benefits for wives of male graduate students who returned to the classroom; earlier, they had received no discount or particular financial consideration. As director Campbell reported, "There seems to be a gradual shift in attitude concerning financial aid for part time students. It is increasingly recognized that there is a legitimate new need, and that part time schedules do not mean second-class commitments."[8] However, recognizing that the university's financial aid options remained limited for these students, Michigan's center also inaugurated a plan to raise money to provide its own scholarships.[9]

Child care represented a hidden cost for mothers of young children, one that at first went unrecognized by the continuing education planners. In an early article, Raushenbush had lauded an "imaginative insurance company" in Des Moines, Iowa, for providing a babysitting service for female employees, commenting, "I assume we are not ready to suggest that universities provide baby sitters for all women who want to prepare for a college degree."[10] But in fact, Minnesota's women pushed the Plan to provide child care in a nearby church building, a program the university supported and the women students managed for a number of years.[11]

Women's continuing education programs legitimized pursuit of a degree one or two courses at a time. Minnesota worked to create a new designation for the Plan's part-time students that would not carry the disadvantages of the "adult special student" label usually applied to peripatetic students. Treating Plan students separately gave them the attention they needed as degree-seeking students and allowed university offices to skirt regulations that normally affected part-timers.[12]

At Sarah Lawrence, Raushenbush handpicked students whom she felt were likely to succeed, and she supported the center's students after they matriculated to the main campus. Even though the regular campus dean approved the center's goals, she reminded Raushenbush that "the Center is to some extent responsible for planning the education of those they recommend to us for matriculation."[13] Raushenbush understood the pressure for accountability, emphasizing that she chose "positive" students, "not those who were frustrated women hunting for a way out."[14] Her center targeted applicants already holding some college credits who were committed to earning the bachelors degree. In an era valuing family roles, candidates were also required to demonstrate, through both application and interview, that they had their husbands' support.

Family support could be critical to a continuing education student's success and her ability to persist, and the schools realized that this population needed flexibility. Sarah Lawrence developed a "leave without prejudice" policy that allowed center students to drop in and out of the program as necessary. Ultimately, the program considered the cumulative nature of students' work rather than its continuity, a recognition that marked a definite shift in thinking.

PROGRAMMATIC DIFFERENCES IN APPROACH

The centers at Minnesota, Michigan, and Sarah Lawrence did not completely agree on the best ways to support continuing women students. In fact, early on, the Carnegie Corporation grantors had appreciated that different approaches might prove useful. One of the biggest programmatic differences appeared around whether to create a separate curriculum for the programs or to mainstream continuing education students into regular classes as soon as possible. The curricular choices represented a continuum, with Sarah Lawrence's center-based separate program on one end, Michigan's general advocacy on the other, and Minnesota's mix of special seminars and programmatic intervention in the middle.

For a small school like Sarah Lawrence, with a traditional student body, teaching the older continuing education students separately—at least initially—seemed to make sense. A later director of the center attributed the program's success to Raushenbush's selectivity in choosing the new students and the care she used in preparing them for the regular academic program.[15] Sarah Lawrence planners believed that special seminars and dedicated curricula eased the transition for both students and faculty. Students studied alongside other mature scholars in special classes taught by sympathetic faculty; those teachers worked with counselors to decide when a student was ready to move into the regular degree program. Such careful assessment assured other faculty across the institution that the center's students were ready for traditional collegiate work.

Minnesota used a range of curricular approaches for its continuing education clientele. Elizabeth Cless worked in the extension school on curricula specifically for women, offering what she called "rusty lady seminars" that targeted mature women who had been away from school but wished to renew their skills and update their knowledge. Such courses mirrored the special curriculum at Sarah Lawrence. Virginia Senders took responsibility for Minnesota's undergraduate program, offering programs in residence halls and student organizations that aimed at traditional-aged collegians still making decisions about their education and their future. A set of counselors specifically designated for Minnesota Plan students also contributed to the program, working in the Student Counseling Bureau alongside colleagues serving the traditional student body.[16]

Minnesota's program was, perhaps necessarily, more decentralized than Sarah Lawrence's. At times, such decentralization caused problems of communication and divided loyalties among staff members, but weekly staff meetings and monthly reports across the program helped strengthen cohesion and share information. Decentralization and variety were important features of the Minnesota Plan, given its "desire to see the aims of and objectives of the program accepted into the normal, on-going functions of the institution."[17]

Having students accepted into the regular functions of the university was likewise a goal at Michigan. Founders there, after observing the pioneer programs, decided not to offer a separate curriculum for their continuing education students. With a strong commitment to changing attitudes and opportunities on Michigan's large campus, director Jean Campbell favored Minnesota's approach of opening the resources of the university and moving women more flexibly into existing options, rather than creating a special program like Sarah Lawrence's. Campbell observed that traditional educators viewed special treatment of women as "coddling" that threatened "the sanctity of the academic degree"; she noted that to them "special arrangements equal an inferior performance."[18] Following recommendations from its advisory committee of deans, Michigan's center stressed that its students would always meet the regular standards of the institution. When applying such criteria, Campbell concluded that "women make a very successful transition with good supportive guidance and a cautious approach."[19]

Large universities like Michigan and Minnesota could present women with a variety of educational and programmatic options, all available within the variegated institution. Sarah Lawrence, on the other hand, offered only a traditional bachelor's degree on a small suburban campus. Its center-based curriculum could serve only a handful of students annually. To expand the college's offerings, especially in response to the large number of interested students who already held degrees, Raushenbush generated several creative academic arrangements.

Many women who initially inquired at the center were already college graduates seeking counseling about career opportunities rather than finishing a bachelor's degree. Raushenbush observed that nearly half of such clients indicated strong interest in becoming teachers. She partnered with New York University to create a part-time master's program in education, allowing women to take their initial coursework at Sarah Lawrence and then to move to NYU for advanced courses and apprentice teaching. The success of this arrangement for education students led to a similar joint program with NYU's School of Social Work and later to a master's in library science degree with New York's Pratt Institute. These cooperative ventures allowed Raushenbush to stretch beyond her small campus, utilizing the resources of New York City and its educational institutions. Such creativity particularly appealed to the Carnegie Corporation: having provided Sarah Lawrence with a start-up grant, they extended support by adding $100,000 in 1964 and $213,000 in 1966, specifically to fund the cooperative institutional ventures.[20]

Although the continuing education programs were quite different and were tailored to their settings, each experimented with how best to serve a population presenting new needs, sometimes moving in directions they had not expected. Even the Radcliffe Institute, which, with its target audience of Ph.D. holders, seemed so different from the other three, created an array of programs trying to accommodate as many women as possible. Although Radcliffe's primary focus remained on year-long fellowships for associate scholars, Mary Bunting and Constance Smith tried out a variety of directions for the Institute over its first several years, many of which were generated by Bunting's ability as a fundraiser.

Bunting had initially resisted identifying her program with the continuing education movement, but the inclusion of several efforts moved the Radcliffe Institute closer to that definition.[21] Like the other three programs, Radcliffe found itself offering guidance and career counseling to hundreds of local women who did not qualify for the associate scholar fellowship but who nonetheless turned to the Institute for advice on rejuvenating their educational plans. In 1963 a program with elements of the Minnesota Plan came to the Institute via the Radcliffe Seminars. For more than a decade the Seminars had offered part-time adult education in a small program that paralleled the much larger Harvard Extension School. Although many Radcliffe courses carried no academic credit of their own, students could petition to apply Seminar credits toward the Harvard B.A. in extension studies, but not toward the traditional Harvard degree.[22] The Seminars remained part of the Institute for more than a decade.

Several years later, although it had not intended to support advanced schooling, the Radcliffe Institute added fellowships for women seeking to complete graduate training.[23] The Institute had frequently seen applicants to the associate scholars program who did not yet hold the Ph.D. but who pleaded for time and support to finish their studies. With funding from the Charles E. Merrill Trust, the Institute created fellowships for part-time graduate study throughout New England, ultimately serving seventy-two women. A related program was funded by the Josiah Macy Foundation in 1966 to support women physicians needing part-time opportunities to complete residencies and internships.[24] Even with a different focus in mind, Radcliffe—like the other continuing education programs—tried to respond flexibly when clients were drawn to the center by its unusual commitment to women.

LIMITATIONS OF THE PROGRAMS

Intentional experimentation, rather than precision, marked the early programmatic approaches to continuing education for women. Since institutions had rarely tried to meet the needs of this population, the initial efforts found both successes and limitations. Changing approaches to counting credits and applying financial aid as well as crafting curricula that supported returning women students had proved reasonably successful. But three areas remained particularly difficult: fulfilling the programs' commitment to researching their field, expanding beyond a middle-class clientele, and understanding the effect of students' uncertain ambitions.

All four programs had expressed a commitment to researching their student populations and the results of their programmatic efforts. In their applications for Carnegie support, Minnesota, Sarah Lawrence, and Radcliffe all included research as an important element of their plans. For its part, Carnegie was eager to publicize the programs and used its October 1962 *Quarterly* to highlight continuing education efforts. Yet, recognizing the limits of its own financial support, the *Quarterly* asserted that "the programs are imaginative and valuable, but taken together they affect no more than a few hundred people. What is needed is experimentation, and action following experimentation, on a far grander scale."[25]

The programs did produce studies of their students, but this work rarely extended beyond programmatic evaluation. Minnesota published detailed results after five years of the Plan, and Sarah Lawrence surveyed its work after a decade.[26] The reports included quantitative information about the students, stressing their backgrounds, their needs, and the eventual use of their education; they also recorded the programs' early efforts and offered advice to others, based on their experience. Thus, other programs could examine budgets, curricular arrangements, financial aid provisions, and admissions criteria at programs that had succeeded. The directors disseminated information through consultations with dozens of new programs across the country, and they wrote descriptive articles and delivered speeches about the centers.[27] Staff members generally found, however, that the daily demands of serving clients prohibited them from undertaking deeper research or connecting to the newer, more theoretical scholarship beginning to build on women's issues.

At Radcliffe, psychologist Martha White spent part of her time as counselor to public clients and part as the Institute's researcher, hoping to address the center's research expectations. She conducted a study of the first two cohorts of associate scholars, using lengthy interviews and group meetings conducted over several months. Like the other program evaluations, White's examined the women's backgrounds and their own assessments of their experience.[28]

Generally, the scholars reported being very pleased with their Radcliffe experience. All but two of the more than thirty respondents to the evaluation process rated the fellowship as "excellent," dramatically describing it as "a rebirth" and "a life-preserver." Like others, they most appreciated the financial support, which not only allowed them to secure time for work, but also eliminated their feeling of draining family resources through their research efforts. Overall, fellows identified money, time to work, and recognition of themselves as scholars as the strongest positive factors from the fellowship.[29]

The scholars also discussed some of the fellowship's challenges, including tension between focusing on their own work and sharing in the Institute community. Because the Institute fostered scholarly connections—recommending, for instance, that every scholar attend the others' public colloquium presentations—some felt torn between focusing on their own work and exploring the social benefits of interpersonal connections with other female scholars. At the same time, a few noted that the promised strong connections to Harvard and its faculty seemed "unfulfilled."[30]

Psychologist White attempted to move beyond mere reporting about the scholars to theorizing about their experience, using nascent ideas from the field of women's career development. Hoping to explore their career commitment, she asked the scholars to characterize themselves as either "professionals" or "amateurs," and she expressed surprise when several rejected her dichotomy. As the scholars explained, their values did not include being recognized by others; rather, they worked for personal gratification and satisfaction, not the status that her use of "professionalism" implied. They reminded White that one of the Institute's contributions was "in the way it has selected professionals whether the achievement has been there so the world would recognize."[31] Although White recognized that many of the scholars carried such personal definitions of professional success, she nonetheless argued that they had "missed a crucial period of socialization into their profession." She regarded their futures warily, noting "they are at a point in their work when the excellence which they seek may be difficult to achieve unless they participate in the career-structure of their fields. To put it forcefully, the question is, can women such as these be committed to truly professional work without some form of career commitment?"[32]

Like White, some of the counselors at Minnesota and Michigan wrote papers on continuing education students, trying to draw wider conclusions from their experiences. Raushenbush and Senders both contributed papers about such students during their service on the education committee of the President's Commission on the Status of Women.[33] Generally, however, the research output of the centers disappointed their founders' goals. The Radcliffe Institute's mixed research record bothered Bunting, who later assessed: "I don't think we learned as much as we could have."[34] Radcliffe supported a few research projects, but, like the ACE Commission on the Education of Women, found itself more often offering a stamp of approval to sympathetic projects than having money to fund them.[35]

Jean Campbell was also ultimately dissatisfied with all the centers' research productivity, but she offered an interesting explanation of why her program at Michigan struggled. She explained that the primacy awarded research at a university like Michigan actually worked against the center. In the planning stages, members of Michigan's advisory committee had offered mixed signals about the center's research capacities. Although they encouraged the center to include research in its mission, these deans and professors simultaneously observed that it lacked the components of a traditional Michigan research center, especially faculty affiliates and a dedicated research team. Without senior faculty, outside funding, and an ongoing investigative agenda, Campbell concluded that the center was unlikely to produce work that matched its sponsors' expectations.[36] In many ways, the expectation of research productivity might have been misplaced.

Campbell also found the research contributions of the continuing education movement as a whole underdeveloped. She attended a 1967 Kellogg Foundation conference convened to discuss research understanding of the burgeoning programs. Although impressed with the enormous growth of the programs over just a few years, she concluded that "their energy and ingenuity needed a firmer base." Presentations were useful and informative, but "there were no new hypotheses; few new directions were noted."[37]

A second limitation of the programs that appeared only with time was their targeted focus on middle-class women who could afford the educational opportunities that the colleges provided. Early on, this hardly seemed a problem, given the genesis of the continuing education idea. Reclaiming women who had left college to pursue family life and who now wished to resume education or work predetermined a mostly middle-class student clientele. At Minnesota, with its land-grant mission and statewide visibility, the reach was fairly wide and drew new interest to the institution even as it remained attuned to middle-class clients. The appeal of the Minnesota Plan was noted by an assistant to the university president, who enthusiastically told Elizabeth Cless that executives from a large local bank reported that "among the questions frequently asked [by newcomers to Minneapolis] are those that relate to your program for the ladies."[38] For a land grant institution, extending its reach to new citizens represented a mark of success.

Situated in a wealthy suburban community, Sarah Lawrence's Center for the Continuing Education of Women attracted many students precisely because of its prestige. In the first years, clients overwhelmingly came from educated, even professional, households; the ten-year analysis showed that fully a third were married to husbands with doctorates. Yet after ten years, the Center's director sought ways to reach a wider clientele, noting that success with a privileged population gave planners an understanding of how they could help women from a wider range of backgrounds.[39]

At Radcliffe, alumnae challenged the Institute's focus. Many of these educated women felt that the program's attention to professionalism denigrated those who, perhaps like themselves, chose to concentrate on family, home, and community.[40] A different criticism attacked the Institute's elitism; many observers felt that by ignoring women still seeking college in favor of those already moving toward professional roles, Radcliffe neglected the most important needs. Here, the Institute relied on Mary Bunting's view of "opening up the top," explaining that they hoped to influence new professional opportunities by providing women the skills and credentials needed to succeed professionally.[41] In its early years, the Institute defended itself against such charges, rarely raising questions about expanding to a less middle-class clientele.

A third limitation facing the continuing education programs was the effect of clients' uncertain educational and career ambitions on programmatic directions and the measurement of success. Each of the programs was reluctant to demand firm career or educational goals of their clients, whether young students still finding their way or mature women hoping to reenter the professional work force. Hesitation over insisting on clients' goals was understandable, given the array of choices facing women and the obvious difficulties of managing home and career; program founders had personally confronted challenges in negotiating career, personal, and family demands. Furthermore, lack of specific goals among the continuing education population hardly seemed a problem early on; the very idea of institutions attending to neglected needs was sufficient ambition. However, by trying to accommodate both casual students and career-minded women, the programs diffused their efforts, leading them to a mix of programmatic options and ultimately making their success harder to assess.

Commitment to a future job or profession, or even to completing a degree, was not required of participants at any of the four continuing education sites. In an era that recognized women's psychological needs, personal enrichment became an acceptable goal. At Sarah Lawrence the program sought candidates who displayed "intellectual ability, discipline and curiosity, ability to do independent work, courage to be oneself, strong motivation for returning to education, and the ability to own one's time."[42] Although the program hoped to produce college graduates, it did not insist that students commit to finishing their degrees.

The Minnesota Plan also sought women with motivation, ability, and opportunity, adding that "strong intellectual curiosity and the ability to do college level work are basic requirements."[43] With its variety of resources, Minnesota could accommodate a wide array of returning women, whether or not they committed to earning degrees. From the start, Minnesota relied on its land grant mission to create new opportunities for citizens even if they did not have precise goals. It marketed the Plan as "a program to mobilize all the resources of the University in an attempt to meet flexibly and individually the diverse time-tables, interests, and questions of individual women."[44] Neither the Carnegie grantor nor the university insisted on college completion over personal fulfillment.

In some ways, the programs proved better at helping women envision educational plans than carrying them to fruition. Minnesota, for all its variety, found better success with the general counseling program than with either the undergraduate program or the "rusty ladies" seminars. The university's role as the largest educational agency in the state made the provision of counseling alongside tailored educational programs a comfortable fit. The imbalance in clientele surprised the Plan's organizers, who had expected more interest in the continuing education courses, but even they acknowledged that it seemed easier to counsel women about how to proceed than to create specific programs or classes that served them well.[45]

Likewise at Sarah Lawrence, a survey of the Center's continuing education population concluded that, although most expressed satisfaction with the program, those seeking marketable skills or counseling for graduate work were least satisfied with the center's efforts. Those with particular plans noted that the program "had less to offer than for those in search of a new direction." However, Raushenbush had intentionally organized the Sarah Lawrence efforts around women with uncertain goals, believing that "their lives up to that point had been family oriented and that they would find, with serious study, an opening up of their world and would *discover* a direction that was right for them."[46] Her interests, plus the strengths of her small center, seemed better suited to women in search of a new focus than for those with precise plans in mind.

Focused on offering a fellowship experience rather than providing degrees, the Radcliffe Institute had even more difficulty marking its success. Mary Bunting had hesitated to insist that fellows have a goal beyond reinvigorating their intellectual productivity. In early statements, she simply emphasized returning the scholar to the world of scholarship or creativity, noting that, "once she has been made visible professionally through her work at the Institute, she will be claimed for further activity—in an academic institution, in government, in business, in industry, in the arts."[47] Creating specific new opportunities was not a goal; the Institute assumed that its scholars would be welcomed into the academic world.

The focus on helping women with mixed career histories sometimes hurt perceptions of the Institute's academic strength. One director lamented that the early publicity, so helpful in drawing women clients, nonetheless created a "picture of adult drop-outs and retreads that has never been entirely erased from the public image of the Institute." She resented the view that Institute scholars were insufficient intellectuals, instead finding them noteworthy "not so much by capacity for revival as for survival in an era when the odds against professional success were no less real for being publicly ignored."[48] However, overcoming the image of "retreaded" scholars would prove to be a difficult sell in the hierarchical academic job market.

The Radcliffe Institute turned to quantifying fellows' productivity as one approach to judging its success. In her Director's Report of 1963, Constance Smith noted that several of the initial scholars had entered college teaching, including a few teaching freshman seminars at Harvard. She further reported that "during the past two years, twelve manuscripts have been completed, and a number of new studies have been undertaken," along with two new volumes of poetry and two shows by the creative artists. Fifteen scholars from the original two cohorts were "working professionally," including several professors and researchers, a lawyer, and two journalists.[49]

But, aware of the difficulties of balancing professional careers, the Institute also allowed for the unpredictability of fellows' future contributions. "It is not expected—nor would it be feasible—that all the Institute members will continue their professional work at a steady pace," director Smith explained. "Women's lives and working schedules necessarily are subordinate to family situations. It is a mistake to expect continuity in professional development when some disruption is almost inevitable."[50] Sensitive to the criticism that the "pulls and pressures which diverted them originally" would continue to affect the scholars once they left the Institute, Mary Bunting noted, "There can be no such guarantee, but there is very little worth doing whose outcome can be guaranteed."[51]

Unlike the programs at Minnesota, Michigan, and Sarah Lawrence, which focused on collegiate degrees, the Radcliffe Institute had attempted a tougher task by trying to reinsert women into the academic marketplace. Degree-oriented programs worked to effect shifts in collegiate policies by awarding credit or certifying part-time study. But in trying to alter the academic marketplace, Radcliffe faced a situation less amenable to singular experiments. All the programs aimed to influence participants' motivation, ambition, and self-confidence, even as they enhanced their academic credentials either through new degrees or intensive research opportunities. Less reliable was the chance to use the new skills in the professional or academic marketplaces. Ultimately, Bunting's "climate of unexpectation" still swirled around women, complicating their next steps after completing the continuing education experience.

ASSESSING THE CONTINUING
EDUCATION MOVEMENT

As Mary Bunting indicated, planners of the women's continuing education movement had no guarantee of success in the early 1960s. Women's educators had simply recognized a need to reclaim the educational and career potential of mature students and then searched for ways to reopen their collegiate opportunities. In doing so, they adjusted, stretched, and reorganized academic structures to allow older students to work at a slower pace or to renew neglected skills. They did not overhaul collegiate education. In following this adaptive approach, the continuing education programs helped their chances of short-term success but may have inhibited longer-term change. When the women's liberation movement reached campuses in the later 1960s and 1970s, the continuing education movement was regarded as limited and even minimal compared to the interests of a new clientele. Ultimately, the limitations of adaptive reform and the challenges of the new women's liberation movement muted the contributions of continuing education.

Through her long involvement with women's continuing education, including twenty years as director of Michigan's Center for the Education of Women, Jean Campbell became a thoughtful analyst of the contributions of continuing education. In a series of articles and speeches spanning her tenure, Campbell assessed the movement's long-term effects, relying on both the specifics of Michigan's experience and her knowledge of national continuing education efforts. She was often tough in her conclusions about continuing education, especially when using insights from new feminist perspectives.[52] Campbell was especially concerned that continuing education's approach to adaptive reform inhibited its ability to create long-term academic change. The ultimate goal of continuing education, especially at Michigan, was to create lasting change in institutional structures and responses. As she analyzed progress from the perspective of the 1970s, Campbell was, if not disheartened, at least discouraged. In 1970 a national survey showed that only 50 percent of colleges had made "any institutional adjustments to fit the special needs" of women, even though most allowed women to return to degree programs. Although Campbell appreciated the movement's very real gains, in her judgment "the institutional change brought about by these programs, impressive in an absolute sense, has been disappointing."[53] She cited researcher Carole Leland, whose 1973 study of continuing education agreed that "by no means has the early challenge of the 1960s been fulfilled. Seldom have our colleges shown any more flexibility or enlightenment with regard to women than a host of other societal institutions."[54]

Yet the type of change sought by women's leaders might also account for the difficulties in achieving it. Exploring what she called the "adaptive" nature of continuing education efforts, Campbell borrowed an analysis from women's history about differences between reform politics and radical politics. The former fosters adjustments and accommodations within existing structures, while the latter seeks widespread structural and attitudinal change. Campbell suggested that continuing education programs were "essentially adaptive, seeking wider opportunities, compensatory support, and greater access to the academic system," noting that in this way their "leaders are in the tradition of political and institutional *reform*." A reformist approach would likely, in the long run, "fall short of fundamental social change."[55]

The continuing education programs, she explained, had chosen a "compensatory" approach, repairing problems that had stymied women's ongoing participation. Although this method might have been the most logical avenue at the time, Campbell suggested that it had not significantly advanced the cause of deep institutional change: "Present programs and services for women are innovative and energetic, but in all cases somewhat marginal to the educational power structure." As she explained, "insofar as measures are compensatory, they are not central. Insofar as they are not central, they require the constant attention of the compensatory agency to ward off the effects of competing pressures."[56] By allowing themselves to operate at the margins of academe, the programs had limited the success they might achieve.

Yet Campbell and Leland may have been premature in their negative analysis of women's continuing education contributions. From a longer-range view, the movement can be seen as having introduced institutional changes that benefited later student populations. The flexible academic arrangements and recognition of varied student needs that continuing education fostered became accepted as sound educational practice in later eras.

Even during the late 1960s, when student protests challenged campus policies, scholars recognized the value of procedures piloted by continuing education. Writing about the new student insistence on academic flexibility, Jacquelyn Mattfeld cited an array of contributions sparked by continuing education: "wider acceptance of individualized programs; the abolition of compulsory courses, distribution and major requirements, and fixed residence requirements; the validation of credit toward the degree of work satisfactorily completed at other institutions; the introduction of credit for field work, the arts, and life experience; the loosening of the four-year, full-time-in-the-ivory-tower attitudes to permit both acceleration and extension of the degree program to suit [an] individual student's needs."[57] Although the women's continuing education programs had advanced these ideas on a smaller scale, they had provided opportunities for institutions to experiment with new arrangements and expectations.

Thirty years later such flexible academic arrangements assumed even greater importance as institutions increasingly served "under-prepared" students. As the adult student market burgeoned throughout the 1980s and 1990s, a successful history of managing accommodations was helpful to financially strapped institutions. Extension programs and adult education had experimented with flexible arrangements, but the continuing education for women movement constituted a coherent grouping of programs and clientele that served as a pilot for institutional change.

Some of the harsh self-assessment by Campbell and others might have resulted from viewing their work from the perspective of the changing academic and cultural environment of the 1970s and 1980s, rather than recalling actual opportunities of the early-1960s. Campbell understood that both the commitment to equity for women and its meaning had changed since the early postwar period. The original impetus for women's continuing education came when advocates realized that equity meant more than mere access: to reclaim their educational careers, women needed not only readmission to campus but a supportive environment as well. Yet Campbell recognized that equity concern for women had rarely spurred institutions to address their needs. Cold War economic and manpower worries had driven most of the attention to women; equity was a later interest and a byproduct. As Campbell explained, "It was this atmosphere of 'social need' that sold our University administrators. . . . I have always doubted that a Center would have been approved just because women have the right to develop their talents as equal human beings without the impetus of apparent economic necessity."[58] What was barely understood at the time, she noted, was how the combination of external and internal barriers inhibited women's participation.[59]

Some understandings about equity and the limits of compensatory programming came to continuing education advocates only after the late-1960s women's movement provided a new impetus and analytical tools. As the women's movement advanced in the 1970s and 1980s, women found a language and a framework for placing individual educational needs into a larger conception. At that point, continuing education leaders often seemed defensive when comparing their accomplishments to the growing work in affirmative action, women's studies, women's centers, and campus demands for more equitable treatment of women.[60] Such a comparison overlooked the fact that continuing education was, for its time, a large step forward on behalf of women.

Two factors worked against a smooth connection between continuing education and the newer, more radical women's programs: class differences between the clients and founders, and generational differences among women's educators. Because continuing education was directed at married women with children seeking to re-enter academe, its clients were older and generally middle-class women. Likewise, the movement's leaders often understood these issues because of their own similar histories; they were married women who had struggled, but ultimately succeeded, within the existing structures of colleges and universities.[61] In an environment increasingly attuned to concerns of minority and lesbian women, the narrow focus of continuing education soon seemed restrictive and limited.

The life-span approach grounding women's continuing education also quickly fell into disfavor among new feminists less patient with the assumption that women should attend to education and career only after satisfying family demands.[62] Reviewing in 1980 the origins of its early 1960s women's programming, Kathryn Clarenbach of the University of Wisconsin blasted the "life in stages doctrine" valued by continuing education programs: "The notion implied acceptance of the status quo, had a limited middle-class orientation, continued the stereotypes of woman as economic dependent and primary parent, opened no new options, and relegated women to perpetual second-class achievers." She added that "the idea had broad support precisely because it was convenient and rocked no boats."[63] Although some of Wisconsin's early work to extend its campus resources and offer fellowships for women actually matched those at Michigan and Minnesota, the spirit and language of its efforts came from the new women's liberation movement.[64]

Campbell and others understood that their early push for continuing education had remained unconnected to a larger social movement on behalf of women. Like other work for women in the early postwar era, from the American Council on Education to the President's Commission on the Status of Women, continuing education focused on helping individuals rather than creating a collective approach to solving deeper structural issues. As Campbell explained, "large numbers of women who did not necessarily relate their experience to the particulars of the movement apparently did understand a greater cultural and psychological 'permission' to think about education and work in combination with decisions about family rather than in stages or not at all."[65] In the early 1960s, family needs were always primary in women's educational planning.

Although the life-span approach rarely challenged prevailing assumptions, it did allow women to plan careers in concert with family responsibilities. Its sequential understanding of women's lives, although rejected by the 1970s, offered a solution that suited its time. Seeing women's needs in a progression allowed planners at Sarah Lawrence, Minnesota, Radcliffe, Michigan, and elsewhere to support cultural expectations of women's role in the home while still offering ways for them to widen their contributions.

When a new feminist consciousness arose on university campuses, continuing education and its life-span approach was often rejected as dated and limiting. Feminism of the 1970s grew uncomfortable with existing cultural, economic, and psychological ideologies, always framed within a set of patriotic expectations. Yet the continuing education programs had created important bases on which women's advocates could build new programs and assert new expectations. They had provided entering wedges for mature women students on campuses, and they had pushed universities to make accommodations for nontraditional students. Less insistent and more quiet than the new demands, the earlier programming had nonetheless sustained women's interests through an era of complicated decision making. They were more a product of, than a challenge to, their era.

Conclusion

The programs created to support women's continuing education proved extremely popular within a short time of their introduction. From the University of Minnesota's initial effort in 1960, hundreds of similar programs for women appeared on college campuses by 1974.[1] However, although popular, continuing education programs were not especially long-lived. Cultural changes effected by the women's movement of the late 1960s began to demand more from campuses, and they particularly challenged continuing education's life-span approach to women's work and education. Less content to put their plans on hold while raising families, middle-class women of the 1970s and 1980s soon insisted on more flexibility around their education than the continuing education programs had either advocated or envisioned, pushing those programs to either change or wither.[2]

WOMEN'S PROGRAMS IN LATER YEARS

Each of the four women's continuing education programs considered in this book adapted somewhat successfully to new ways of seeing and serving women, instituting several programmatic iterations over subsequent decades. More than forty years after their founding, all continue to function, albeit with differences in organization and mission. Two keys to the programs' long-term survival were emphasizing their roles as women's centers rather than as mere curricular entry points for mature women, and turning their attention to national issues rather than addressing purely local women's concerns.

Within a few years the Minnesota Plan sharpened its focus to two strands: one for women's counseling, always a programmatic strength; and the other a wide-reaching women's center that sponsored conferences and fostered research on gender. The Plan's focus on special curricula and programming for its returning women students gave way as it turned increasingly to national-level treatment of women's issues through efforts in research, policy, and practice. Emphasizing its role as a women's center more than a curricular program sustained the university-wide effort over time.[3]

The University of Michigan's continuing education center succeeded by repeatedly reinterpreting its flexible mission of "advocacy, research, and service" to address the changing needs of women, both on the Ann Arbor campus and nationally. The program strengthened local services for women by emphasizing counseling, creating a popular scholarship program, and fostering the university's new commission on the status of women. When that commission as well as new research centers on women's issues appeared on the Michigan campus, the continuing education center offered itself as a sturdy, experienced partner. These partnerships fostered the center's movement into national issues as Michigan increasingly conducted wide-ranging research on women's employment and educational concerns.[4]

While continuing to provide fellowships for women scholars, the Radcliffe Institute joined other Radcliffe programs to create a national group of centers for research on women. Radcliffe's Schlesinger Library on the history of women in America and its Murray Research Center for the study of human development joined the Radcliffe Institute (renamed for Mary Bunting in 1978) to create a setting of national prominence for research on women. In doing so, Radcliffe College took on the role of fostering attention to women's issues both within the Harvard University environment and on the larger national scene. But in assuming this task, the Institute gradually shifted its target clientele. Although still attending to women with Ph.D.s, Radcliffe eventually turned to boosting those who had already secured places on the academic tenure track and now needed support to advance professionally; the earlier focus on women seeking their first professional position faded in focus. The 1999 merger of Radcliffe College with Harvard University muted the female aspect of the fellowship program, aiming instead to integrate women's concerns within the Harvard environment.[5]

Situated at the smallest institution, Sarah Lawrence's Center for the Continuing Education of Women remained more locally focused on serving mature women students than the larger programs with greater resources and wider reach. Yet, the Sarah Lawrence program adapted over time by addressing women with needs different from those of the early 1960s clientele. Sarah Lawrence's center continued to offer programs and counseling to ease collegiate entry for nontraditional students but determined to expand its clientele by attracting local working- and middle-class students for whom college represented a newer venture.[6]

Not all the postwar programs survived to accommodate new approaches to women's educational concerns. The ACE's Commission on the Education of Women conducted a difficult fight from 1953 to 1962 to secure funding and attention for women's issues. When a new ACE president arrived in 1961, he closed the commission's doors, claiming that women's concerns would be integrated into other ACE educational projects. Thus, when the women's movement began to influence higher education later in the 1960s, ACE could claim little organizational presence in these discussions. Only in 1973 did ACE create a new Office for Women in Higher Education (OWHE), which three decades later remains a premier and vocal advocate for policy on collegiate women. The OWHE was opened by then-president of ACE, Roger Heyns, the same advocate who a decade earlier had helped establish Michigan's women's continuing education center.

John Kennedy's President's Commission on the Status of Women had an intentionally short organizational life from 1961 to 1963, but a longer reach in influencing policy concerns for women. Catching the tide as the first 1960s group designed to assess women's status, the President's Commission spurred the creation of state-level commissions on women, a concept that, over the next two decades, spread to universities and professional organizations.[7] At universities, such commissions frequently became organizational homes for gender-related policy concerns, while campus women's centers addressed the practical needs of women students and faculty. The President's Commission, through its original mission and its longer-term contributions, affected large issues of national policy, treating education as an important base for women's development. Esther Peterson's hope that the commission's work would be taken up by other advocacy groups found some fulfillment throughout the 1970s and beyond.

The two professional associations—the American Association for University Women and the National Association of Deans of Women—addressed different clientele with different resources in the early postwar decades. AAUW served a large base of women, including both professionals and college graduates not pursuing employment, while NADW remained attuned to women deans on college campuses. Like the women's continuing education programs, AAUW repeatedly shifted its focus over time to address women with a wide range of educational concerns. The creation of its educational foundation in 1955 invigorated AAUW's fundraising capacities, and it continues as a premier national women's organization, lobbying for legislation affecting women and annu-ally contributing more than \$3 million for fellowships and other programs on women's behalf.[8]

NADW, on the other hand, was unable to sustain itself permanently. Through-out the 1980s and 1990s the organization struggled with both finances and mis-sion, as the position of dean of women faded in prominence and new collegiate professionals increasingly turned to non-gender-based organizations that ad-dressed a wider range of issues. Over time, NADW tried to expand its reach be-yond deans and counselors, eventually changing its name to the generic National Association of Women in Education. However, unlike other women's organiza-tions that attracted support, NAWE suffered from an unclear mission and client base, finally closing its doors in 1999.[9]

COMMITMENT TO INDIVIDUAL DECISION MAKING

Three cultural changes of the 1960s affected the long-term prospects of the early postwar programs for women: the women's liberation movement, the civil rights movement, and the growth of a Great Society approach to educa-tion. Ironically, the women's movement that coalesced after publication of *The Feminine Mystique* in 1963 and the creation of the National Organization for Women in 1966 may have had the most negative impact on earlier educational efforts for women. Once a stronger awareness of women's needs and a more confident way of demanding attention developed, earlier approaches on behalf of women seemed muted and ineffectual. The adaptive nature of the continuing education programs, the self-criticism of NADW, and the halting approach to research by the ACE CEW were seen as too mild after stronger feminist goals took hold. The earlier programs provided a base for later campus developments but were frequently rejected or ignored by those new efforts as too quiet in tone, demands, and visibility.

Founders of the earlier efforts, often members of an older generation, general-ly supported reform over radicalism. As Jean Campbell explained about effecting change at the University of Michigan: "I had been here since 1946 and I knew that you couldn't walk into the men's Union, and I knew what a male place it is. . . . So it was with a strong sense of realism that we approached this."[10] Esther Raushenbush also recognized different generational approaches to educational change, noting: "I think that many of the things that women like me wanted to see brought about and tried to bring about, in our respectful way of working within the system, and had very little success with, these younger women in the feminist movement have brought about by their more militant, more aggressive, less compromising attitudes."[11] The realism and adaptation that marked postwar advocacy seemed ill-suited to new feminist approaches.

The civil rights movement, building throughout the mid-twentieth century, grew louder and more forceful in the 1960s. Its main effect on postwar women's programs was spotlighting their narrow appeal to middle-class, white, college-going women. While such women constituted an important element of collegiate populations, national efforts to foster more equitable treatment for people of color revealed how limited postwar college planners had been in extending their programs to new audiences. AAUW and NADW eventually faced challenges to organizational integration, and the continuing education programs committed themselves to expanded clientele, but these efforts seemed slow and even meager as new groups began to claim a firmer place on collegiate campuses. The enormous growth of community colleges throughout the 1960s and 1970s promised a new avenue for collegiate attendance, growing into an important entry point for both women and students of color.

The growth of the civil rights movement, combined with opportunities generated by the affluence of the 1960s, prompted Lyndon Johnson's Great Society efforts on behalf of poor and minority citizens. As research by scholars like Michael Harrington, Daniel Patrick Moynihan, and James Coleman suggested, education could become an important lever for effecting social change, especially for improving the life chances of poorer Americans.[12] The President's Commission on the Status of Women had recognized the beginnings of such thinking, calling on education to provide the stimulus and the means for women to expand their opportunities. But, as the commission's final report shows, its early 1960s educators backed away from the ramifications of using education as a social lever, relying instead on older approaches like continuing education and personal choices by individual women.

Commitment to individual choice, whereby each woman arrived at a personal calculus for dealing with the surrounding patriotic, economic, cultural, and psychological ideologies, characterized advocacy for women in the early postwar period. Americans of the 1950s and early 1960s—especially the middle-class population that enjoyed expanded choices—lived in a complicated era, surrounded by Cold War concerns over America's safety, mixed economic messages about women's value to the work force, cultural hopes that women's commitment to family would stabilize a buffeted nation, and psychological challenges that pushed for self-fulfillment within a limited purview. The array of messages women received turned their decisions about education, career, and family into difficult balancing acts among personal preference, family demands, and national need. In the face of such variety, many students and educators took a short-term view, recommending education that supported the family role and hoping that women would stay in college long enough to build a base for subsequent interests. Advocates addressed such choices with programs to ensure that later, when family needs had been satisfied, colleges would welcome these older, "rusty" students back to the classroom.

Although some advocates began to see larger structural issues involved and sought collective approaches to supporting women, the preference for individual decision making over collective action marked the first twenty years of the postwar period. Research on women, as fostered by the ACE Commission on the Education of Women, was only beginning to see explanations for women's issues that went beyond differences in their individual motivation. Professional groups like AAUW and NADW lamented the diminution of the dean's role but often blamed their own lack of preparation rather than any notion of widespread discriminatory practice. The President's Commission on the Status of Women, with the widest-ranging agenda and expertise, advanced only scattered recommendations for collective challenges on behalf of women.

Although the individually focused postwar programs, from the ACE CEW, to the women's professional groups, to continuing education centers, seem mild when compared to more radical efforts that appeared later in the 1960s and 1970s, their unique brand of activism holds value in women's educational history. First, by fostering research on women, they created a knowledge base that supported later work in women's studies, women's research centers, and support programs for women's needs.[13] Without expanding research knowledge beyond the narrow limits of the 1950s, subsequent programs would have had a weaker foundation on which to build their arguments for women. Second, the programs provided a network for women's advocates. Rosters of commission members, organizational leaders, scholars, and program planners show colleagues connecting across varied roles that allowed them to share information, build programs, and provide mutual support. American women's educational advancement has rarely succeeded without the support of female networks.[14] Third, the programs offered a generational bridge from the energetic women of World War II to the activists of the late 1960s. Although scholarly and popular attention more frequently examines wartime women and 1960s feminists, the activism of 1950s and early 1960s female leaders deserves recognition on its own terms.

Postwar women are often stereotyped as unwitting participants in a cultural ideology that muted ambition and hindered experimentation, yet advocates for their higher education sustained interest in women's issues during the era. By fostering networks, supporting research, and creating programs, these postwar advocates enacted their own sort of activism during a time of mixed expectations for women. Their valuable work in educational research, practice, and policy provided a base on which later efforts built, even as it helped clarify women's varied approaches to complicated demands.

Notes

INTRODUCTION

1. One year before her death, Raushenbush collated and edited her papers into a volume entitled *Occasional Papers on Education* (Bronxville, N.Y.: Sarah Lawrence College, 1979). The quote is from page 407.

2. Claudia Goldin, *Understanding the Gender Gap: An Economic History of American Women* (New York: Oxford University Press, 1990); see also Alice Kessler-Harris, *Out to Work: A History of Wage-Earning Women in the United States* (New York: Oxford University Press, 1982).

3. National Center for Education Statistics, *120 Years of American Education: A Statistical Portrait* (Washington, D.C.: Office of Educational Research and Improvement, 1993). See also Table 2.1.

4. See Maggie Finnegan, "From Spurs to Silk Stockings: Women in Prime-Time Television, 1950–1965," *UCLA Historical Journal* 11 (1991): 1–30.

5. William Chafe, *The Paradox of Change: American Women in the Twentieth Century* (New York: Oxford Press, 1991); Eugenia Kaledin, *Mothers and More: American Women in the 1950s* (Boston: Twayne Publishers, 1984); see also Sara M. Evans, *Born for Liberty: A History of Women in America*, 2d ed. (New York: Free Press, 1997); Amy Scher, "Cold War on the Home Front: Middle Class Women's Politics in the 1950s" (Ph.D. diss., New School for Social Research, 1995); Susan Ware, "American Women in the 1950s: Nonpartisan Politics and Women's Politicization," in *Women, Politics, and Change*, ed. Louise Tilly and Patricia Gurin (New York: Russell Sage Foundation, 1990): 281–99.

6. Elaine Tyler May, *Homeward Bound: American Families in the Cold War Era* (New York: Basic Books, 1988); Stephanie Coontz, *The Way We Never Were: American Families and the Nostalgia Trap* (New York: Basic Books, 1992); Karen Zarlengo, "Civilian Threat, the Suburban Citadel, and Atomic Age American Women," *Signs: Journal of Women in Culture and Society* 24, no. 4 (1999): 925–58; Wini Breines, *Young, White, and Miserable: Growing up Female in the Fifties* (Boston: Beacon Press, 1992).

7. See, generally, Susan M. Hartmann, *The Other Feminists: Activists in the Liberal Establishment* (New Haven: Yale University Press, 1998); Susan Lynn, *Progressive Women in Conservative Times: Racial Justice, Peace, and Feminism, 1945–the 1960s* (New Brunswick, N.J.: Rutgers University Press, 1992); Joanne Meyerowitz, ed., *Not June Cleaver: Women and Gender in Postwar America, 1945–1960* (Philadelphia: Temple University Press, 1994).

8. Dorothy Sue Cobble, "Recapturing Working-Class Feminism: Union Women in the Postwar Era," in *Not June Cleaver*, ed. Meyerowitz, 57–83; Nancy Gabin, *Feminism in the Labor Movement: Women and the United Auto Workers, 1935–1975* (Ithaca, N.Y.: Cornell University Press, 1990); Hartmann, *The Other Feminists*.

9. Harriet Hyman Alonso, "Mayhem and Moderation: Women Peace Activists During the McCarthy Era," in *Not June Cleaver*, 128–50; Susan Dion, "Challenges to Cold War Orthodoxy: Women and Peace, 1945–64" (Ph.D. diss., Marquette University, 1991); Amy Swerdlow, "The Congress of American Women: Left-Feminist Peace Politics in the Cold War," in *U.S. History as Women's History: New Feminist Essays*, ed. Linda Kerber, Alice Kessler-Harris, and Kathryn Sklar (Chapel Hill: University of North Carolina Press, 1995), 296–312.

10. Leila J. Rupp and Verta Taylor, *Survival in the Doldrums: The American Women's Rights Movement, 1945 to the 1960s* (New York: Oxford University Press, 1987), esp. chap. 3.

11. Allen Berube, *Coming Out Under Fire: The History of Gay Men and Women in World War II* (New York: Free Press, 1990); John D'Emilio, *Making Trouble: Essays on Gay History, Politics, and the University* (New York: Routledge, 1992); Donna Penn, "The Sexualized Woman: The Lesbian, the Prostitute, and the Containment of Female Sexuality in Postwar America," in *Not June Cleaver*, 358–81.

12. Bernice McNair Barnett, "Black Women's Collectivist Organizations: Their Struggles during the Doldrums," in *Feminist Organizations: Harvest of the New Women's Movement* ed. Myra Marx Ferree and Patricia Yancey Martin (Philadelphia: Temple University Press, 1955), 181–99; Darlene Clark Hine, "Black Professionals and Race Consciousness: Origins of the Civil Rights Movement, 1890–1950," *Journal of American History* 89, no. 4 (2003): 1279–94; Hartmann, *The Other Feminists*, chap. 6.

13. Ruth Feldstein, *Motherhood in Black and White: Race and Sex in American Liberalism, 1930–1965* (Ithaca, N.Y.: Cornell University Press, 2000); Susan Lynn, *Progressive Women in Conservative Times: Racial Justice, Peace, and Feminism, 1945–the 1960s* (New Brunswick, N.J.: Rutgers University Press, 1992).

14. Goldin, *Understanding the Gender Gap;* Kessler-Harris, *Out to Work.*

15. Three notable exceptions are Barbara Miller Solomon, *In the Company of Educated Women: A History of Women and Higher Education in America* (New Haven, Conn.: Yale University Press, 1985), as a general study; Paula Fass, *Outside In: Minorities and the Transformation of American Education* (New York: Oxford University Press, 1989), especially chapter 5, which examines the "female paradox" around curriculum planning in 1950s higher education; and Claudia Goldin, "The Meaning of College in the Lives of American Women: The Past One Hundred Years," National Bureau of Economic Research, Working Paper No. 4099, 1992, which applies an economic analysis to women's use of college.

16. Mabel Newcomer, A *Century of Higher Education for American Women* (New York: Harper & Brothers, 1959), table 2, p. 46.

17. By the late 1990s, one-third of community college students were non-white and 58 percent were female. Forty percent of all African American students and 55 percent of all Hispanic students began their higher education in the two-year institutions (National Center for Educational Statistics, *Digest of Education Statistics* [Washington, D.C.: Office

of Educational Research and Improvement, 1999]; National Center for Educational Statistics, *Digest of Education Statistics* [Washington, D.C.: Office of Educational Research and Improvement, 2000]). In 1957 women constituted less than 36 percent of community college students.

18. Dissatisfactions with the client base of programs at Sarah Lawrence College, the University of Minnesota, and Radcliffe College are discussed in chapter 7.

19. Raushenbush, 1974 Addendum to "Reminiscences of Esther Raushenbush," in the Columbia University Oral History Research Office Collection, 27.

CHAPTER I: POSTWAR GENDER EXPECTATIONS AND REALITIES

1. Greeley story described in Eli Ginzberg and Alice Yohalem, *Educated American Women: Self-Portraits* (New York: Columbia University Press, 1966), 41–50.

2. Ibid., 47, 49–50.

3. For discussions of women's postwar experience, see William Chafe, *The Paradox of Change: American Women in the Twentieth Century* (New York: Oxford University Press, 1991); Susan M. Hartmann, "Women's Employment and the Domestic Ideal in the Early Cold War Years," in *Not June Cleaver: Women and Gender in Postwar America, 1945–1960*, ed. Joanne Meyerowitz (Philadelphia: Temple University Press, 1994); and Joanne Meyerowitz, "Beyond the Feminine Mystique: A Reassessment of Postwar Mass Culture, 1946–1958," in *Not June Cleaver*, 229–62.

4. See Chafe, *The Paradox of Change;* Kenneth Jackson, *Crabgrass Frontier: The Suburbanization of the United States* (New York: Oxford University Press, 1985); Eugenia Kaledin, *Mothers and More: American Women in the 1950s* (Boston: Twayne Publishers, 1984); and Alice Kessler-Harris, *Out to Work: A History of Wage-Earning Women in the United States* (New York: Oxford University Press, 1982).

5. Claudia Goldin, *Understanding the Gender Gap: An Economic History of American Women* (New York: Oxford University Press, 1990); Hartmann, "Women's Employment and the Domestic Ideal."

6. Raymond F. Howes, ed., *Women in the Defense Decade* (Washington, D.C.: American Council on Education, 1952).

7. For a general discussion of the Cold War era, see Chafe, *Paradox of Change.*

8. Over two centuries, American understandings of women's citizenship shifted. In the Revolution, women played both public and private roles in the new political culture. Later, when citizenship became defined through voting and property rights, their role shifted to more private political decision making, where the family shared a single view. After winning suffrage in 1920, women assumed a different stance as citizens, but a long-standing view of women as "republican mothers" supporting the nation through their homes remained in the public consciousness. By the Cold War era, women citizens defending the nation by sustaining familial values prevailed. See Sara Evans, *Born for Liberty: A History of Women in America*, 2d ed. (New York: Free Press, 1997); Linda Kerber, *No Constitutional Right to be Ladies: Women and the Obligations of Citizenship* (New York: Hill & Wang, 1998).

9. Chafe, *The Paradox of Change;* Evans, *Born for Liberty;* Kaledin, *Mothers and More;*

Elaine Tyler May, *Homeward Bound: American Families in the Cold War Era* (New York: Basic Books, 1988).

10. May, *Homeward Bound.*

11. Kristina Zarlengo, "Civilian Threat, the Suburban Citadel, and Atomic Age American Women," *Signs: Journal of Women in Culture and Society* 24, no. 4 (1999): 925-58.

12. Howes, *Women in the Defense Decade,* 16-17.

13. Ibid., 67-68.

14. "When Nixon Took on Khrushchev," *U.S. News and World Report,* 3 August 1959, 36-9; Nixon and Khrushchev Argue in Public as U.S. Exhibit Opens," *New York Times,* 25 July 1959, 1, 3; May, *Homeward Bound.*

15. "Municipal housekeeping," "social housekeeping," and "social feminism" all refer to a Progressive Era movement in which middle-class women used the idea of their maternal strengths to attack problems in the public domain. It allowed women like Jane Addams and numerous clubwomen to assume public leadership on social issues. See "social housekeeping" in Linda Eisenmann, ed., *Historical Dictionary of Women's Education in the United States* (Westport, Conn.: Greenwood Press, 1998), 390-92.

16. Meyerowitz, "Beyond the Feminine Mystique," 240, 241.

17. Harriet Hyman Alonso, "Mayhem and Moderation: Women Peace Activists During the McCarthy Era," in *Not June Cleaver,* 131.

18. Margaret Rossiter, *Women Scientists in America: Before Affirmative Action, 1940-1972* (Baltimore: Johns Hopkins University Press, 1995), 51-52.

19. Quoted in ibid., 53.

20. Dael Wolfle, *America's Resources of Specialized Talent: A Current Appraisal and a Look Ahead* (New York: Harper & Brothers, 1954).

21. Susan Rimby Leighow, "An 'Obligation to Participate': Married Nurses' Labor Force Participation in the 1950s," in *Not June Cleaver,* 42.

22. Ibid., 47.

23. Ibid., 50.

24. National Manpower Council, *Womanpower: A Statement by the National Manpower Council with Chapters by the Council Staff* (New York: Columbia University Press, 1957), 9.

25. Ibid., 262.

26. Barbara Clowse, *Brainpower for the Cold War: The Sputnik Crisis and the National Defense Education Act of 1958* (Westport, Conn.: Greenwood Press, 1981); Roger Geiger, *Research and Relevant Knowledge: American Research Universities Since World War II* (New York: Oxford University Press, 1993).

27. Thomas N. Bonner, "Sputnik and the Educational Crisis in America," *Journal of Higher Education* 29, no. 4 (April 1958): 177-84; Clarence B. Hilberry, "Sputnik and the Universities," *Journal of Higher Education* 29, no. 7 (October 1958): 375-80.

28. James L. Sundquist, *Politics and Policy: The Eisenhower, Kennedy, and Johnson Years* (Washington, D.C.: Brookings Institution, 1968); Lawrence E. Gladieux and Thomas Wolanin, *Congress and the Colleges: The National Politics of Education* (Lexington, Mass.: D.C. Heath, 1976). I thank Nancy Diamond for her insights into these developments.

29. U.S. Department of Health, Education, and Welfare, *The National Defense Student Loan Program: Basic Facts* (1971), 1.

30. Clowse, *Brainpower*, 159.

31. Rossiter, *Women Scientists in America*, 78.

32. Goldin, *Understanding the Gender Gap*, 10.

33. National Manpower Council, *Womanpower*, 162.

34. Chafe, *The Paradox of Change*; Kessler-Harris, *Out to Work*.

35. Goldin's *Understanding the Gender Gap* considers women in the workforce across the range of economic and age backgrounds. For a more specific analysis of the behavior of female college graduates in the labor force, see Goldin, *The Long Road to the Fast Track: Career and Family*, Working Paper 10331 (Cambridge, Mass.: National Bureau of Economic Research, 2004).

36. Chafe, *The Paradox of Change*, 10.

37. Ibid., 78.

38. Ibid., 153.

39. Kessler-Harris, *Out to Work*, 276.

40. Goldin, *Understanding the Gender Gap*.

41. National Manpower Council, *Work in the Lives of Married Women* (New York: Columbia University Press, 1958). The volume evolved from discussions at a six-day conference of 82 participants from academe, industry, government, labor, and nongovernmental organizations.

42. Ginzberg used the findings from *Womanpower* to spark the deeper discussions in *Work in the Lives of Married Women*; however, the quotation used here appears in *Womanpower*, p. 92.

43. Eli Ginzberg, *Lifestyles of Educated Women* (New York: Columbia University Press, 1966, 88–98.

44. NMC, *Womanpower*, 29.

45. Ibid., 237.

46. Kessler-Harris, *Out to Work*; and Ruth Milkman, *Gender at Work: The Dynamics of Job Segregation by Sex During World War II* (Urbana: University of Illinois Press, 1987).

47. "Compensatory work" gradually took over as a term recognizing that while women might not perform all jobs equal to men's, many of their tasks were comparable and deserved comparable wages. See Dorothy Sue Cobble, "Recapturing Working-Class Feminism: Union Women in the Postwar Era," in *Not June Cleaver*, 57–83; Nancy Gabin, *Feminism in the Labor Movement: Women and the United Auto Workers, 1935–1975* (Ithaca, N.Y.: Cornell University Press, 1990); and Susan Hartmann, *The Other Feminists: Activists in the Liberal Establishment* (New Haven, Conn.: Yale University Press, 1998).

48. Goldin, *Understanding the Gender Gap*.

49. Ibid., 181.

50. Ibid.; NMC, *Womanpower*.

51. Kessler-Harris, *Out to Work*, 302.

52. The idea of "separate spheres" for men and women developed in the early nineteenth century, arguing that women had superior skills in the home and with families, while men prospered in the public arena. Over time, some women stretched their "sphere" to embrace public efforts like teaching and nursing by emphasizing how these fields benefited from women's special touch. After 1900, the notion of "municipal housekeeping"

was emphasized by clubwomen who took special responsibility for public health and welfare concerns. See Linda Eisenmann, "Creating a Framework for Interpreting U.S. Women's Educational History: Lessons from Historical Lexicography," *History of Education* 31 (2001): 5.

53. Evans, *Born for Liberty;* U.S. Department of Commerce, Bureau of the Census, *Historical Statistics of the United States: Colonial Times to 1970* (White Plains, N.Y.: Kraus International Publications, 1989).

54. Bureau of the Census, *Historical Statistics,* 49.

55. Ibid., 385; see also chapter 2 of this book.

56. Jackson, *Crabgrass Frontier.*

57. NMC, *Womanpower,* 136–37.

58. Ibid.

59. William Chafe, *The American Woman: Her Changing Social, Economic, and Political Roles, 1920–1970* (New York: Oxford University Press, 1972), 217.

60. David Halberstam, *The Fifties* (New York: Fawcett Columbine, 1993), 195.

61. Maggie Finnegan, "From Spurs to Silk Stockings: Women in Prime-Time Television, 1950–1965," *UCLA Historical Journal* 11 (1991): 1–30.

62. Kaledin, *Mothers and More,* 27.

63. William Whyte, *The Organization Man* (New York: Simon & Schuster, 1956); Sloan Wilson, *The Man in the Gray Flannel Suit* (New York: Simon & Schuster, 1955); David Riesman, *The Lonely Crowd: A Study of the Changing American Character* (Garden City, N.Y.: Doubleday, 1953); Vance Packard, *The Status Seekers* (New York: D. McKay Co., 1959).

64. Talcott Parsons, *Essays in Sociological Theory* (Glencoe, Ill.: Free Press, 1949); and *The Social System* (Glencoe, Ill.: Free Press, 1951).

65. Betty Friedan, for example, accused functionalist thinkers of consigning women to "a kind of deep freeze–like Sleeping Beauties, waiting for a Prince Charming to waken them, while all around the magic circle the world moved on" (*The Feminine Mystique* [New York: Dell Publishing, 1963/1983], 127).

66. Chafe, *The Paradox of Change.*

67. Mamie Till-Mobley and Christopher Benson, *Death of Innocence: The Story of the Hate Crime That Changed America* (New York: Random House, 2003); and Christopher Metress, ed., *The Lynching of Emmett Till: A Documentary Narrative* (Charlottesville, Va.: University of Virginia Press, 2003).

68. Ruth Feldstein, "'I Wanted the Whole World to See': Race, Gender, and Constructions of Motherhood in the Death of Emmett Till," in *Not June Cleaver,* 265; and Feldstein, *Motherhood in Black and White: Race and Sex in American Liberalism, 1930–1965* (Ithaca, N.Y.: Cornell University Press, 2000).

69. Feldstein, "I Wanted the Whole World to See."

70. Ibid.

71. Margaret Mead, *Male and Female: A Study of the Sexes in a Changing World* (New York: William Morrow & Co, 1949).

72. Alva Myrdal and Viola Klein, *Women's Two Roles: Home and Work* (London: Routledge & Kegan Paul, 1956), 145.

73. Melody Miller, Phyllis Moen, and Donna Dempster-McClain, "Motherhood,

Multiple Roles, and Maternal Well-Being: Women of the 1950s," *Gender and Society* 5, no. 4 (1991): 565–82.

74. NMC, *Work in the Lives of Married Women*, 12, 13.

75. Abby Scher, "Cold War on the Home Front: Middle Class Women's Politics in the 1950s" (Ph.D. diss., New School for Social Research, 1995).

76. Quoted in Susan Lynn, *Progressive Women in Conservative Times: Racial Justice, Peace, and Feminism, 1945–the 1960s* (New Brunswick, N.J.: Rutgers University Press, 1992), 117–19.

77. Susan Ware, "American Women in the 1950s: Nonpartisan Politics and Women's Politicization," in *Women, Politics, and Change*, ed. Louise Tilly and Patricia Gurin (New York: Russell Sage Foundation, 1990), 281–99.

78. Ibid., 288.

79. Lynn, *Progressive Women in Conservative Times*, especially chapter 2.

80. Ellen Carol Dubois, "Eleanor Flexner and the History of American Feminism," *Gender and History* 3 (1991): 1.

81. Harriet Hyman Alonso, "Mayhem and Moderation: Women Peace Activists During the McCarthy Era," in *Not June Cleaver*, 128–150; Susan Dion, "Challenges to Cold War Orthodoxy: Women and Peace, 1945–1964" (Ph.D. diss., Marquette University, 1991); and Amy Swerdlow, "The Congress of American Women: Left-Feminist Peace Politics in the Cold War," in *U.S. History as Women's History: New Feminist Essays*, ed. Linda Kerber, Alice Kessler-Harris, and Kathryn Sklar (Chapel Hill: University of North Carolina Press, 1995), 296–312.

82. Daniel Horowitz, *Betty Friedan and the Making of The Feminine Mystique: The American Left, the Cold War, and Modern Feminism* (Amherst: University of Massachusetts Press, 1998), 224.

83. Joanne Meyerowitz, "Beyond the Feminine Mystique" in *Not June Cleaver;* and Eva Moskowitz, "'It's Good to Blow Your Top': Women's Magazines and a Discourse of Discontent, 1945–1965," *Journal of Women's History* 8, no. 3 (1996): 66–98.

84. Claudia Zanardi, Introduction, in Claudia Zanardi, ed., *Essential Papers on the Psychology of Women* (New York: New York University Press, 1990), 1–38; Ellen Herman, *The Romance of American Psychology: Political Culture in the Age of Expert* (Berkeley: University of California Press, 1995).

85. Simone de Beauvoir, *The Second Sex*, trans. H. M. Parshley (New York: Knopf, 1953; orig. 1952).

86. Horowitz, *Betty Friedan*.

87. Friedan spent only a year at Berkeley before relinquishing a prestigious fellowship and leaving graduate school. In *The Feminine Mystique*, she attributes this decision to a romantic relationship, saying that her then-boyfriend resented her success and that she worried about choosing a lonely career over love. Later scholarship suggests that Friedan's thinking at the time was more complicated, involving her uncertainty over psychology as a focus and academe as a career. Moreover, her political activism was growing, stoking her interests beyond an academic life (see Horowitz, *Betty Friedan*).

88. Quoted in Friedan, *The Feminine Mystique*, 108, 116.

89. Florence Denmark and Michele Paludi, eds., *Psychology of Women: A Handbook*

of Issues and Theories (Westport, Conn.: Greenwood Press, 1993); and Samuel Slipp, *The Freudian Mystique: Freud, Women, and Feminism* (New York: New York University Press, 1993).

90. Herman, *The Romance of American Psychology.*

91. Philip Wylie, *A Generation of Vipers* (New York: Rinehart, 1942).

92. Herman, *The Romance of American Psychology.*

93. Marynia Farnham and Ferdinand Lundberg, *Modern Woman: The Lost Sex* (New York: Harper & Brothers, 1947).

94. Quoted in *The Feminine Mystique*, 119, 120.

95. Meyerowitz, "Beyond the Feminine Mystique," 229–62.

96. Moskowitz, "It's Good to Blow Your Top," 67.

97. Ibid., 85.

98. Wini Breines, "The 'Other Fifties': Beats and Bad Girls," in *Not June Cleaver,* 397; see also Breines, *Young, White, and Miserable: Growing Up Female in the Fifties* (Boston: Beacon Press, 1992).

99. Alfred C. Kinsey, Walter Pomeroy, and C. E. Martin, *Sexual Behavior in the Human Male* (Philadelphia: Saunders, 1948); Kinsey, and Staff of the Institute for Sex Research, *Sexual Behavior in the Human Female* (Philadelphia: Saunders, 1953).

100. Kinsey, *Sexual Behavior in the Human Female.*

101. Allen Berube, *Coming Out Under Fire: The History of Gay Men and Women in World War II* (New York: Free Press, 1990).

102. John D'Emilio, *Making Trouble: Essays on Gay History, Politics, and the University* (New York: Routledge, 1992).

103. Donna Penn, "The Sexualized Woman: The Lesbian, the Prostitute, and the Containment of Female Sexuality in Postwar America," in *Not June Cleaver,* 358–81.

104. Cited in ibid., 372.

105. Michael Sedlak, "Attitudes, Choices, and Behavior: School Delivery of Health and Social Services," in *Learning from the Past: What History Teaches Us About School Reform,* ed. Diane Ravitch and Maris Vinovskis (Baltimore: Johns Hopkins University Press, 1995), 57–94.

106. Regina Kunzel, "White Neurosis, Black Pathology: Constructing Out-of-Wedlock Pregnancy in the Wartime and Postwar United States," in *Not June Cleaver,* 306.

107. E. Franklin Frazier, *The Negro Family in the United States* (Chicago: University of Chicago Press, 1939).

108. Ginzberg and Yohalem, *Educated American Women,* 49.

CHAPTER 2: EDUCATORS CONSIDER THE POSTWAR COLLEGE WOMAN

1. Eli Ginzberg and Alice Yohalem, *Educated American Women: Self-Portraits* (New York: Columbia University Press, 1966), 129.

2. Ibid., 130

3. Mabel Newcomer, *A Century of Higher Education for American Women* (New York: Harper & Brothers, 1959), table 2, p. 46.

4. Ibid.

NOTES TO PAGES 44–50   243

5. Quoted in Richard Freeland, *Academia's Golden Age: Universities in Massachusetts, 1945–1970* (New York: Oxford University Press, 1992), 75.

6. Carol S. Gruber, *Mars and Minerva: World War I and the Use of Higher Learning in America* (Baton Rouge: Louisiana State University Press, 1975); Freeland, *Academia's Golden Age*.

7. The nationally prominent Institute for Social Research at the University of Michigan and the Jet Propulsion Laboratory at the California Institute of Technology exemplify such postwar creations. See Roger Geiger, *Research and Relevant Knowledge: American Research Universities Since World War II* (New York: Oxford University Press, 1993), and Hugh Davis Graham and Nancy Diamond, *The Rise of American Research Universities: Elites and Challengers in the Postwar Era* (Baltimore: Johns Hopkins University Press, 1997).

8. David Riesman, *Constraint and Variety in American Education* (Lincoln: University of Nebraska Press, 1956).

9. Graham and Diamond, *The Rise of American Research Universities*, 38.

10. Michael Bennett, *When Dreams Came True: The GI Bill and the Making of Modern America* (Washington, D.C.: Brassey's, 1996), 243.

11. Ibid.; Keith Olson, *The G.I. Bill, the Veterans, and the Colleges* (Lexington: University Press of Kentucky, 1974).

12. Olson, *The G.I. Bill*.

13. National Center for Educational Statistics, *120 Years of American Education: A Statistical Portrait* (Washington, D.C.: Office of Educational Research and Improvement, 1993), 76. The figure was over 14 percent of just the 18–21 age cohort. See *Digest of Education Statistics* (Washington, D.C.: National Center for Education Statistics, 1978), 103.

14. Olson, *The G.I. Bill*, 45.

15. In fact, some all-female teachers colleges became coeducational after the male veterans influx. Hunter College in New York City offers one example.

16. Bennett, *When Dreams Came True;* Daniel Clark, "The Two Joes Meet—Joe College, Joe Veteran: The G.I. Bill, College Education, and Postwar American Culture," *History of Education Quarterly* 38 (1998) 2: 165–89; Hilary Herbold, "Never a Level Playing Field: Blacks and the GI Bill," *Journal of Blacks in Higher Education* 6 (Winter 1994/95): 104–8; Reginald Wilson, "GI Bill Expands Access for African Americans," *Educational Record* 75, no. 4 (1994): 32–39.

17. Herbold, "Never a Level Playing Field," 106.

18. Ibid.

19. June Willenz, "Invisible Veterans," *Educational Record* 75, no. 4 (1994): 41.

20. Ibid., 46.

21. Clark, "The Two Joes Meet," 198.

22. Susan M. Hartmann, *The Home Front and Beyond: American Women in the 1940s* (Boston: Twayne Publishers, 1982), 106.

23. Dorothy Gies McGuigan, *A Dangerous Experiment: One Hundred Years of Women at the University of Michigan* (Ann Arbor, Mich.: Center for the Education of Women, 1970), 112.

24. National Center for Educational Statistics, *120 Years of American Education*, 76.

25. U.S. Department of Commerce, Bureau of the Census, *Historical Statistics of the*

United States: Colonial Times to 1970 (White Plains, N.Y.: Kraus International Publications, 1989), 383.

26. Olson, *The G.I. Bill*, 103.

27. Freeland, *Academia's Golden Age*, 88.

28. Ibid., 93.

29. Patricia Albjerg Graham, *Progressive Education: From Arcady to Academe: A History of the Progressive Education Association, 1919–1955* (New York: Teachers College Press, 1967); Diane Ravitch, *The Troubled Crusade: American Education, 1945–1980* (New York: Basic Books, 1983).

30. Harvard University Committee on the Objectives of a General Education in a Free Society, *General Education in a Free Society: Report of the Harvard Committee* (Cambridge, Mass.: Harvard University, 1945).

31. Barbara Clowse, *Brainpower for the Cold War: The Sputnik Crisis and the National Defense Education Act of 1958* (Westport, Conn.: Greenwood Press, 1981).

32. President's Commission on Higher Education, *Higher Education for American Democracy: A Report of the President's Commission on Higher Education* (New York: Harper & Brothers, 1947).

33. Geiger, *Research and Relevant Knowledge*, 186; see also Margaret Rossiter, *Women Scientists in America: Before Affirmative Action, 1940–1972* (Baltimore: Johns Hopkins University Press, 1995).

34. President's Commission, *Higher Education for American Democracy*, 1:8.

35. Ibid., 1:42, chap. 2

36. Ibid., 2:30.

37. U.S. Department of Commerce, Bureau of the Census, *Historical Statistics of the United States: Colonial Times to 1970* (White Plains, N.Y.: Kraus International Publications, 1989), 380. Please note that statistics can vary, depending on the age group used as the base.

38. President's Commission, *Higher Education for American Democracy*, 2:42–43. Subsequent page references are in the text.

39. Clark, "The Two Joes Meet."

40. National Center for Educational Statistics, *120 Years of American Education.*

41. National Manpower Council, *Womanpower: A Statement by the National Manpower Council with Chapters by the Council Staff* (New York: Columbia University Press, 1957), 201.

42. George Baker, ed., *A Handbook on the Community College in America: Its History, Mission and Management* (Westport, Conn.: Greenwood Press, 1994).

43. Allen Witt, James Wattenbarger, James Gollattscheck, and Joseph Suppiger, *America's Community Colleges: The First Century* (Washington, D.C.: American Association of Community Colleges, 1994), 185.

44. National Center for Educational Statistics, *Digest of Education Statistics* (Washington, D.C.: Office of Educational Research and Improvement, 1999); National Center for Educational Statistics, *Digest of Education Statistics* (Washington, D.C.: Office of Educational Research and Improvement, 2000).

45. National Education Association, Research Division, *Teacher Supply and Demand in Universities, Colleges, and Junior Colleges, 1957–58 and 1958–59* (Higher Education Services Research Report 1959), R10, 33.

46. Jeanne Noble, *The Negro Woman's College Education* (New York: Teachers College, Columbia University, 1956), Appendix D.

47. Ibid.; see also Amy Thompson McCandless, *The Past in the Present: Women's Higher Education in the Twentieth-Century South* (Tuscaloosa: University of Alabama Press, 1999).

48. Patricia Albjerg Graham, "Expansion and Exclusion: A History of Women in American Higher Education," *Signs: Journal of Women in Culture and Society,* 3(4), (1978) 771.

49. National Education Association, "Teacher Supply and Demand in Degree-Granting Institutions, 1954–55," *Research Bulletin of the National Education Association* 33, no. 4 (1955): 133 (entire issue).

50. Barbara Solomon, *In the Company of Educated Women: A History of Women and Higher Education in America* (New Haven, Conn.: Yale University Press, 1985), table 6.

51. National Education Association, "Teacher Supply and Demand," 133.

52. Ibid., table 6, p. 133.

53. Ibid., table 7, p. 134.

54. Ibid., 162.

55. National Education Association, Research Division, *Teacher Supply and Demand in Universities, Colleges, and Junior Colleges, 1957–58 and 1958–59,* Higher Education Series Research Report 1959–R10, 25.

56. Ibid., tables 14 and 15, 22 and 23.

57. U.S. Department of Health, Education, and Welfare, Office of Education, *College and University Faculties: Recent Personnel and Instructional Practices,* Bulletin 1959 (7) (Washington, D.C.: U.S. Government Printing Office, 1959), 38–39.

58. Ibid., 38.

59. Theodore Caplow and Reese McGee, *The Academic Marketplace* (New York: Basic Books, 1958), 111–12.

60. Ibid., 226.

61. Theodore Caplow and Reese McGee, *The Academic Marketplace* (Revised) (New Brunswick, N.J.: Transaction Publishers, 2001), xii.

62. Alan Bayer, "College and University Faculty: A Statistical Description," *ACE Research Reports* 5, no. 5 (June 1970); Helen Astin and Alan Bayer, "Sex Discrimination in Academe," *Educational Record* 53 (1972): 101–18.

63. Helen Horowitz names these subcultures "college women," "outsiders," and "rebels," in *Campus Life: Undergraduate Cultures From the End of the Eighteenth Century to the Present* (New York: Knopf, 1987).

64. Betty Friedan, *The Feminine Mystique* (New York: Dell Publishing, 1963/1983), 151, 153, 155.

65. Carolyn Bashaw, *"Stalwart Women": A Historical Analysis of Deans of Women in the South* (New York: Teachers College Press, 1999).

66. Beth Bailey, *Sex in the Heartland* (Cambridge, Mass.: Harvard University Press, 1999).

67. Ernest Havemann and Patricia West, *They Went to College: The College Graduate in America Today* (New York: Harcourt, Brace and Company, 1952).

68. Pepper Schwartz. "Research on Relationships," in *Authors of Their Own Lives:*

Intellectual Autobiographies by Twenty American Sociologists, ed. Bennett Berger (Berkeley: University of California Press, 1990), 367. For overall discussion of Jewish students on campus, see Paul Ritterband and Harold Wechsler, *Jewish Learning in American Universities: The First Century* (Bloomington: Indiana University Press, 1994).

69. Wini Breines, "The 'Other Fifties:' Beats and Bad Girls," in *Not June Cleaver: Women and Gender in Postwar America, 1945–1960,* ed. Joanne Meyerowitz (Philadelphia: Temple University Press, 1994), 391.

70. Peter Wallenstein, "Black Southerners and Non-Black Universities: Desegregating Higher Education, 1935–1967," *History of Higher Education Annual* 19 (1999): 121–48.

71. McCandless, *The Past in the Present,* 225–27.

72. Schwartz, "Research on Relationships," 368.

73. Carolyn Heilbrun, "Men Were the Only Models I Had," *Chronicle of Higher Education* (12 October 2001), B8. See Heilbrun's subsequent book, *When Men Were the Only Models We Had: My Teachers Barzun, Fadiman, Trilling* (Philadelphia: University of Pennsylvania Press, 2002).

74. Graham, "Expansion and Exclusion."

75. Jessie Bernard, *Academic Women* (University Park: Pennsylvania State University Press, 1964) 198.

76. Rossiter, *Women Scientists in America,* 85.

77. Radcliffe College Faculty-Trustee Committee, *Graduate Education for Women: The Radcliffe Ph.D.* (Cambridge, Mass.: Harvard University Press, 1956), 36.

78. Ibid., 27.

79. National Education Association, "Teacher Supply and Demand in Degree-Granting Institutions, 1954–55"; National Education Association, Research Division, *Teacher Supply and Demand in Universities, Colleges, and Junior Colleges;* Dael Wolfle, *America's Resources of Specialized Talent: A Current Appraisal and a Look Ahead* (New York: Harper and Bros., 1954); Marguerite Zapoleon, *The Outlook for Women in the Medical and Health Services,* U.S. Department of Labor, Women's Bureau, Bulletin 203, nos. 1–12 (Washington, D.C.: Government Printing Office, 1945–1946); Zapoleon, *The Outlook for Women in the Biological Sciences,* U.S. Department of Labor, Women's Bureau, Bulletin 223, no. 3 (Washington, D.C.: Government Printing Office, 1948); Zapoleon, *The Outlook for Women in Chemistry,* U.S. Department of Labor, Women's Bureau, Bulletin 223, no. 2 (Washington, D.C.: Government Printing Office, 1948); Zapoleon, *The Outlook for Women in Science,* U.S. Department of Labor, Women's Bureau, Bulletin 223, no. 1 (Washington, D.C.: Government Printing Office, 1948); and Zapoleon, *The Outlook for Women in Social Work,* U.S. Department of Labor, Women's Bureau, Bulletin 235, no. 1 (Washington, D.C.: Government Printing Office, n.d.); Zapoleon, "The Myth of the Marriage-Career Conflict," in *New Horizons for College Women,* ed. Leo Muller and Ouida Muller (Washington, D.C.: Public Affairs Press, 1960), 79–87; National Manpower Council, *Womanpower* (New York: Columbia University Press, 1957).

80. Wolfle, *America's Resources of Specialized Talent,* 137. Subsequent page references are cited in the text.

81. See note 79 above.

82. Zapoleon, "The Myth of the Marriage-Career Conflict," 87.

83. National Manpower Council, *Womanpower*, 207–8.

84. Ibid., 191–2. For a discussion of the range of this curricular debate, see Paula Fass, *Outside In: Minorities and the Transformation of American Education* (New York: Oxford University Press, 1989).

85. Friedan, *The Feminine Mystique*, 150, 161.

86. Wolfle, *America's Resources of Specialized Talent*.

87. John Summerskill, "Dropouts From College," in *The American College: A Psychological and Social Interpretation of the Higher Learning*, ed. Nevitt Sanford (New York: John Wiley & Sons, 1962), 631.

88. Ibid., 631, 632.

89. Lynn White Jr., *Educating Our Daughters: A Challenge to the Colleges* (New York: Harper & Brothers, 1950), 18.

90. Cited in Ibid., 26.

91. The term "coed" was used widely during the postwar era to refer to women students. The lack of recognition of how the term defined women solely as adjuncts to men—the presumed "real" students—indicates the depth of treatment of women as "incidental."

92. Havemann and West, *They Went to College*, 54.

93. Ibid., 130, 104.

94. Marynia Farnham and Ferdinand Lundberg, *Modern Woman: The Lost Sex* (New York: Harper & Bros, 1947).

95. National Education Association, Commission on the Reorganization of Secondary Education, *The Cardinal Principles of Secondary Education* (Washington, D.C.: Government Printing Office, 1918).

96. National Center for Educational Statistics, *120 Years of American Education*.

97. David Angus and Jeffery Mirel, *The Failed Promise of the American High School, 1890–1995* (New York: Teachers College Press, 1999); Graham, "Expansion and Exclusion," 759–73.

98. White, *Educating Our Daughters*.

99. Radcliffe College Faculty-Trustee Committee, *Graduate Education for Women*.

100. Bernard, *Academic Women*.

101. Radcliffe College, *Graduate Education for Women*, Table F, 22. Subsequent references to this study are cited in the text.

102. Rossiter, *Women Scientists in America*.

103. Robert Bannister, *Jessie Bernard: The Making of a Feminist* (New Brunswick, N.J.: Rutgers University Press, 1991).

104. Biographer Bannister emphasized Bernard's tendency to rewrite her personal history and to ignore personal slights out of self-protection.

105. Rossiter, *Women Scientists in America*.

106. Bernard, *Academic Women*, 62. Subsequent page references are cited in the text.

107. David Riesman, *Some Continuities and Discontinuities in the Education of Women* (Bennington, Vt.: Bennington College, 1956), 21.

108. Harold Taylor, "The Demands of Modern Society," in *New Horizons for College Women*, ed. Leo Muller and Ouida Muller (Washington, D.C.: Public Affairs Press, 1960), 88–100; David Riesman, *Constraint and Variety in American Education*; Riesman, *Some*

Continuities and Discontinuities; Riesman, "Two Generations," in *The Woman in America,* ed. Robert Lifton (Boston: Beacon Press, 1964), 72–97.

109. Mabel Newcomer, *A Century of Higher Education for American Women* (New York: Harper & Brothers, 1959).

110. Kate Mueller, *Educating Women for a Changing World* (Minneapolis: University of Minnesota Press, 1954).

111. Noble, *The Negro Woman's College Education.*

112. Mirra Komarovsky, *Women in the Modern World: Their Education and Their Dilemmas* (Boston: Little, Brown, 1953).

113. Friedan, *The Feminine Mystique.*

114. Taylor, "The Demands of Modern Society," 93, 92.

115. Riesman, *Some Continuities and Discontinuities.*

116. Newcomer, *A Century of Higher Education.* Subsequent page references are in the text.

117. Mueller, *Educating Women,* 18. Subsequent page references are in the text.

118. Noble, *The Negro Woman's College Education,* 101. Subsequent page references are in the text.

119. Komarovsky, *Women in the Modern World,* 48. Subsequent page references are in the text.

120. Friedan, *The Feminine Mystique,* 357. Subsequent page references are in the text.

121. Heilbrun, "Men Were the Only Models I Had," B10.

CHAPTER 3: RESEARCH

1. Lloyd-Jones, Report on the CEW for the Philips Foundation, 26 March 1955, ACE records, collection B-22, box 2, folder 14, Schlesinger Library, Radcliffe Institute for Advanced Study, Harvard University (hereafter Schlesinger).

2. Notes on the NADW committee meeting 16 May 1952, ACE records, box 1, folder 2, Schlesinger.

3. Lynn Gangone, "Navigating Turbulence: A Case Study of a Voluntary Higher Education Association" (Ph.D. diss., Teachers College, Columbia University, 1999), 174.

4. Ellis L. Phillips Sr. was founder and head of the E. L. Phillips Company, a lighting manufacturer.

5. The record is incomplete on how NADW reached its decision. Naomi Brown interviewed the five NADW presidents of 1951–61, finding different opinions about the decision, about the wisdom of NADW ceding the money to ACE, and about whether ACE's perceived prestige was the primary factor in their assuming the work. See Brown, "The National Association of Women Deans and Counselors, 1951–1961" (Ph.D. diss., University of Denver, 1963); especially 88–117 and appendices.

6. For a discussion of ACE in relationship to other higher education groups, see Hugh Hawkins, *Banding Together: The Rise of National Associations in American Higher Education, 1887–1950* (Baltimore: Johns Hopkins University Press, 1982).

7. Althea Hottel in *Women in the Defense Decade,* ed. Raymond Howes (Washington, D.C.: American Council on Education, 1952), 72.

8. Notes on the NADW committee meeting, 16 May 1952, ACE records, box 1, folder 2, Schlesinger.

9. Lucile Allen to the members of the committee, 26 May 1952, ACE records, box 1, folder 2, Schlesinger.

10. Frederick Hochwalt to Adams, 31 July 1952, ACE records, box 1, folder 2, Schlesinger.

11. For instance, the American Association of University Professors sponsored "Committee W" on the status of women in 1918. The committee worked for about a decade, was disbanded, and reappeared only in the 1970s. See Mariam K. Chamberlain, ed., *Women in Academe: Progress and Prospects* (New York: Russell Sage, 1988), 277.

12. Minutes of the 23 March 1953 meeting, ACE records, box 1, folder 3, Schlesinger.

13. Ibid., p. 12.

14. Hottel to Lloyd-Jones, 24 February 1953, ACE records, box 1, folder 3, Schlesinger.

15. NADW—the original instigator for the commission—saw its involvement diminish over time, although eight of its members served on CEW across the decade. See Brown, "National Association of Women Deans," esp. p. 131.

16. Agenda for 17–19 June 1953 meeting, ACE records, box 1, folder 5, Schlesinger.

17. Minutes of the 23 March 1953 meeting.

18. Although ACE had formally disbanded the Committee on the Defense Decade, it kept a smaller panel called the Continuing Committee of the Women's Conference as a way to maintain their work on women's democratic role.

19. Minutes of the 5 January 1953 meeting with the Continuing Committee, ACE records, box 1, folder 3, Schlesinger.

20. Minutes of the 23 March 2964 meeting, p. 8.

21. Agenda for the 17–19 June 1953 meeting. The seven researchers were: Robert Blake, a psychologist from the University of Texas; Marie Jahoda, a psychologist at New York University and associate director of its Research Center for Human Relations; Mary Jones, from the education department at University of California, Berkeley; Florence Kluckhohn, sociologist at Harvard's Social Science Research Center; Theodore Newcomb, of the University of Michigan sociology and psychology departments; W. Lloyd Warner, a University of Chicago anthropologist and sociologist; and Robin M. Williams, Jr., director of the Social Science Research Center at Cornell. Each submitted a paper in advance, then discussed the findings at the meeting.

22. For a summary of these papers, see ACE records, box 8, folder 114; for original papers, see carton 12, Schlesinger.

23. Hottel to Arthur Adams, 14 July 1953, ACE records, box 1, folder 5, Schlesinger.

24. Progress Report, September 1953, ACE records, box 1, folder 5, Schlesinger.

25. Hottel and Lloyd-Jones, "Proposal for a Study of Women as Individuals, Their Contributions to Society and of the Implications for Education," July 1953, ACE records, folder 5, Schlesinger, p. 2.

26. Eurich to Adams, 15 February 1954, ACE records, box 1, folder 9, Schlesinger.

27. Minutes of the 23 November 1953 meeting, box 1, folder 6, Schlesinger.

28. Lloyd-Jones to Hottel, citing Dr. Sibley, the SSRC official, 10 November 1953, ACE records, box 1, folder 8, Schlesinger; Gunnar Myrdal, *An American Dilemma: The Negro Problem and Modern Democracy* (New York: Harper & Brothers, 1944).

29. Lloyd-Jones to Anderson, 19 October 1954, ACE records, box 2, folder 11, Schlesinger.

30. Minutes of the 30–31 March 1954 meeting, ACE records, box 1, folder 9, Schlesinger.

31. Althea Hottel, *How Fare American Women?* (Washington D.C.: American Council on Education, 1955).

32. Ibid., 14–15.

33. "Interim Report [on *How Fare American Women?*]," ACE records, box 1, folder 10, Schlesinger.

34. Louis Benezet to Esther Lloyd-Jones, 11 February 1955, ACE records, box 4, folder 39, Schlesinger.

35. Ibid.

36. Althea Hottel, paper delivered at the 6 March 1953 meeting of the Eighth National Conference on Higher Education in Chicago, ACE records, box 1, folder 6, Schlesinger, p. 4.

37. Ibid., p. 54.

38. February 1956 Newsletter, ACE records, box 2, folder 19, Schlesinger, p. 4.

39. Undated proposal, ACE records, box 2, folder 16, Schlesinger; see also February 1956 newsletter, box 2, folder 19, p. 4.

40. Regarding the grants, see the minutes of the 15 January 1957 ACE Executive Committee meeting, ACE records, Schlesinger.

41. In addition to scholars of women's education, representatives attended from foundations, including the Carnegie Corporation, the Fund for the Advancement of Education, and the Lilly Endowment, and from organizations including the AAUW and the Women's Bureau.

42. See chapter 2 above for a discussion of the scholarly viewpoints represented by these speakers.

43. *The Education of Women: Signs for the Future,* ed. Opal David (Washington, D.C.: American Council on Education, 1958).

44. Ibid., 10.

45. Ibid., see Part Two: "Motivation of Women for Higher Education," 23–47.

46. See Tiedeman, "Career Development of Women: Some Propositions," in ibid., 64–74; see Nevitt Sanford, "Motivation of High Achievers," in ibid., 34–39.

47. Ibid., see Part Four: "Current Trends in the Education of Women," 83–121.

48. Kate Mueller, *Educating Women for a Changing World* (Minneapolis: University of Minnesota Press, 1954)

49. *Signs for the Future,* 75–81.

50. Dael Wolfle, *America's Resources of Specialized Talent: A Current Appraisal and a Look Ahead* (New York: Harper & Brothers, 1954).

51. Ibid.; National Manpower Council, *Womanpower: A Statement by the National Manpower Council with Chapters by the Council Staff* (New York: Columbia University Press, 1957); Minutes of the 14 February 1958 meeting, ACE records, box 2, folder 21, Schlesinger.

52. Mary Bunting, draft of a proposal on evaluation of college-level work outside the regular pattern, 20–21 November 1958 meeting, folder 21, Schlesinger.

53. *The Span of a Woman's Life and Learning* (Washington D.C.: Commission on the Education of Women of the American Council on Education, 1960).

54. Arthur Adams to Manning Pattillo, 16 December 1959, entry 14, box 127, folder 14, Records of the Office of President Adams, American Council on Education Collection at the Hoover Institution Library and Archives, Stanford University (hereafter Hoover).

55. Logan Wilson was not known as a particular supporter of women. His 1942 book, *Academic Man: A Study in the Sociology of the Profession* (New York: Oxford University Press) contained only one reference to women—one that found them responsible for depressing academic wages. I thank Nancy Diamond of Temple University for calling my attention to Wilson's scholarship.

56. David to Robert Sutherland, April 1961, Records of President Adams, entry 14, box 155, folder 6, Hoover.

57. David to Logan Wilson, report, Records of President Wilson, entry 17, box 1, folder 11, Hoover.

58. Florence Anderson was influential in bringing Carnegie Corporation attention and funding to women's programming in the early 1960s. A graduate of Mount Holyoke College, she joined Carnegie as a clerical secretary and rose to the position of corporation secretary—an officer's role—in 1954. Anderson and the Carnegie-funded programs will be discussed in Part Three.

59. *Education and a Woman's Life*, ed. Lawrence Dennis (Washington D.C.: American Council on Education, 1962).

60. Ibid., 75.

61. Ibid., 125–40.

62. Wilson explained to a commission meeting that, in his general ACE reorganization, a number of committees had been discontinued. Yet he affirmed ACE interest in women's education and explained the intention to incorporate that issue into a new commission on academic affairs. Ultimately, that commission consolidated the Commission on the College Student, the Committee on College Teaching, and the Commission on Instruction and Evaluation, but the Commission on the Education of Women was not mentioned, nor were any of its members invited onto the new group. Only one woman served on the initial Commission on Academic Affairs. Minutes of the Committee for the Conference on the Continuing Education of Women, 8 February 1962, Records of President Wilson, box 4, folder 7, entry 17, Hoover.

63. In 1973, ACE created a new Office of Women in Higher Education (OWHE), which continues today. The OWHE provides "information and counsel to constituencies within the higher education community regarding policies, issues, education, and research that influence women's equity, diversity, and advancement." For a historical view of OWHE, see Helen S. Astin, "Appendix B: Some Historical Notes on the American Council on Education's Involvement with the Concerns of Women in Higher Education," in *Some Action of Her Own: The Adult Woman and Higher Education* (Lexington, Mass.: Lexington Books, 1976), 139–45; and Carol S. Pearson, Donna L. Shavlik, and Judith G. Touchton, eds., *Educating the Majority: Women Challenge Tradition in Higher Education* (New York: American Council on Education/Macmillan Publishing Company, 1989).

64. Minutes of the 12–13 May 1960 meeting, ACE records, box 3, folder 23, Schlesinger, p. 23.

CHAPTER 4: PRACTICE

1. McCarn was called Counselor to Women at the time of her dismissal. My discussion of McCarn's story is based on Kathryn Tuttle, "What Became of the Dean of Women? Changing Roles for Women Administrators in American Higher Education, 1940–1980" (Ph.D. diss., University of Kansas, 1996).

2. Quoted in Tuttle, "What Became of the Dean of Women?" 152.

3. Anne Firor Scott, *Natural Allies: Women's Associations in American History* (Urbana: University of Illinois Press, 1991), 177–80.

4. Although NADW changed its name to add "Counselors" in 1956, as discussed below, this chapter will use "NADW" throughout.

5. For AAUW membership figures, see Susan Levine, *Degrees of Equality: The American Association of University Women and the Challenge of Twentieth-Century Feminism* (Philadelphia: Temple University Press, 1995) 104; for NADW membership figures, see Naomi Brown, "The National Association of Women Deans and Counselors, 1951–1961" (Ph.D. diss., University of Denver, 1963) 73.

6. Tuttle, "What Became of the Dean of Women?" 196.

7. For a general discussion of women's efforts in these areas, see Barbara Solomon, *In the Company of Educated Women* (New Haven, Conn.: Yale University Press, 1985); for a more specific focus on women's networking, see Linda Eisenmann, "Creating a Framework for Interpreting U.S. Women's Educational History: Lessons from Historical Lexicography," *History of Education* 30, no. 5 (2001): 453–70.

8. Brown, "The National Association," 92.

9. For discussions regarding NADW's decision to give the Phillips gift to ACE, see Brown, "The National Association"; JoAnn Fley, "A Celebration and Recognition of the Thirty-four past Presidents of the National Association for Women Deans, Administrators, and Counselors" (paper presented at the National Association for Women Deans, Administrators, and Counselors, Detroit, Michigan, March 1978); and Lynn Gangone, "Navigating Turbulence: A Case Study of a Voluntary Higher Education Association" (Ph.D. diss., Teachers College, Columbia University, 1999).

10. Esther Lloyd-Jones and Margaret Smith, *A Personnel Program for Higher Education* (New York: McGraw-Hill, 1938); Lloyd-Jones and Smith, *Student Personnel Work as Deeper Teaching* (New York: Harpers, 1954).

11. Gangone, "Navigating Turbulence," 154–55.

12. Minutes, 1959–60 Round-up, 8 August 1960, American Association of University Women Archives, 1881–1976, reel 99 (Microfilming Corporation of America, 1980) (hereafter AAUW Archives); for a good discussion of AAUW's beginnings, see Levine, *Degrees of Equality*.

13. The Carnegie Foundation's offer of a collegiate pension system in the 1910s was the first real pressure for colleges and universities to meet outside standards. Only schools meeting certain curricular, financial, and faculty standards were eligible for the pension. Within two decades, regional accrediting bodies such as the North Central Association began to assert standards. In a period increasingly dominated by research institutions, little attention was paid to the women's colleges. For a general discussion of accreditation,

see Hugh Hawkins, *Banding Together: The Rise of National Associations in American Higher Education, 1887–1950* (Baltimore: Johns Hopkins University Press, 1992).

14. The challenge in studying a membership organization is understanding that actions and dictates of the national office do not necessarily match the preferences or experience of local members. As Scott notes, the variance between local and national approaches in such groups can resemble "different worlds" (Scott, *Natural Allies*, 179). Here, I generally take the perspective of the national headquarters, while recognizing the disadvantages of doing so. Levine, in her official history of AAUW, *Degrees of Equality*, primarily examined headquarters, although she occasionally tested the national approach against local experience, primarily using the Durham, North Carolina, branch.

15. Gangone, "Navigating Turbulence," 154; for NADW's beginnings, see also Jana Nidiffer, *Pioneering Deans of Women: More than Wise and Pious Matrons* (New York: Teachers College Press, Columbia University, 2000).

16. Chambers' story is told in Levine, *Degrees of Equality*, 168–70.

17. Ibid.

18. Margaret Habein, "Should Women be Educated Differently from Men?" *Journal of the National Association of Deans of Women* 13 (March 1950): 121.

19. Mirra Komarovsky, "Measuring the Yardsticks," *Journal of the American Association of University Women* 41, no. 4 (Summer 1948): 211.

20. President's Commission on Higher Education, *Higher Education for American Democracy: A Report of the President's Commission on Higher Education* (New York: Harper & Brothers, 1947); National Manpower Council, *Womanpower: A Statement by the National Manpower Council with Chapters by the Council Staff* (New York: Columbia University Press, 1957).

21. Resolutions on Education, 1957, reel 114, no. 114, AAUW Archives.

22. Ibid.

23. Dolan and Lilia Buday, "Higher Education Roundup for 1959–60," reel 99, no. 245, AAUW Archives.

24. Levine, *Degrees of Equality*, 84.

25. Discussions of the fellowship program can be found in Levine, *Degrees of Equality*, and in Ruth Tryon, *Investment in Creative Scholarship: A History of the Fellowship Program of the American Association of University Women, 1890–1956* (Washington, D.C.: AAUW, 1957).

26. Levine, *Degrees of Equality*, 32.

27. Ibid., 96.

28. Anne Firor Scott suggests that women's organizations commonly raise money in labor-intensive ways, without accounting for their own labor, and target spending to very specific purposes (*Natural Allies*, 179).

29. Tryon, *Investment in Creative Scholarship*, x.

30. Ibid., chap 1.

31. Ibid., chaps. 4–5.

32. Levine, *Degrees of Equality*, 148.

33. National Education Association, "Teacher Supply and Demand in Degree-granting Institutions, 1954–55," *Research Bulletin of the National Education Association* 33, no. 4 (1955): 127–62; for a discussion of women faculty, see chapter 2. See also Susan B. Carter,

"Academic Women Revisited: An Empirical Study of Changing Patterns of Women's Employment as College and University Faculty, 1890–1963," *Journal of Social History* 14 (Summer 1981), 675–99.

34. Eleanor Dolan, "Present AAUW Special Services and Research Projects in the Field of Women's Higher Education," 15 February 1959, reel 99, AAUW Archives. See also Margaret Rossiter, *Women Scientists in America: Before Affirmative Action, 1940–72* (Baltimore: Johns Hopkins University Press, 1995), especially chapter 9.

35. Ibid.

36. For a general discussion of the early College Faculty Program, see Ann Kelsall, "The Continuing Education of Women: New Programs, Old Problems, Fresh Hopes," in *Women in College and University Teaching*, ed. Joseph V. Totaro (Madison: University of Wisconsin, 1963).

37. Sites included Alabama, Florida, Georgia, Kentucky, Louisiana, Mississippi, North Carolina, South Carolina, Tennessee, Texas, and Virginia.

38. "The College Faculty Program: A Three-year Experiment and its Results," n.d. [c. 1966]; for the College Faculty Program [CFP] see reel 100, nos. 253–72, AAUW Archives.

39. "The AAUW Educational Foundation College Faculty Program: Final Report," June 1968, reel 100, no. 256, AAUW Archives.

40. "The AAUW Crusade Information Sheet," 29 July 1960, reel 100, no. 272, AAUW Archives.

41. "Report to the Research-Projects Committee," 30 October 1964, reel 100, no. 254, AAUW Archives.

42. Levine, *Degrees of Equality*, 140. In fact, AAUW opened membership to graduates of such professional programs only in 1963.

43. Dolan, "Present AAUW Special Services," reel 99, AAUW Archives.

44. Linda M. Perkins, "The African American Female Elite: The Early History of African American Women in the Seven Sister Colleges, 1880–1960," *Harvard Educational Review* 67, no. 4 (1997): 722; see also James D. Anderson, *The Education of Blacks in the South, 1860–1935* (Chapel Hill: University of North Carolina Press, 1988), especially chapter 7.

45. Levine, *Degrees of Equality*, 30.

46. Ibid., 33.

47. See Susan Lynn, *Progressive Women in Conservative Times: Racial Justice, Peace, and Feminism, 1945–the 1960s* (New Brunswick, N.J.: Rutgers University Press, 1992), especially chapter 2.

48. For AAUW's racial struggles, Hottel's leadership, and the DC branch's reaction, see Levine, *Degrees of Equality*, chap. 6, pp. 104–35.

49. Beverly Jones, "Mary Eliza Church Terrell," in *Black Women in America: An Historical Encyclopedia*, ed. Darlene Clark Hine (Brooklyn, N.Y.: Carlson Publishing, 1993), 1157–59.

50. In addition to integrating the AAUW dining room, Terrell and her colleagues pushed the issue in various DC establishments. Her challenge to Thompson's Restaurant produced a court case, *District of Columbia* v. *John Thompson*, that in 1953 resulted in a ruling that DC's code allowing segregated eateries was unconstitutional (ibid., 1159).

51. Levine, *Degrees of Equality*, 117–18.

52. *Washington Branch of American Association of University Women* v. *American*

Association of University Women et al, 79 F. Supp. 88, 16 July 1948; *American Association of University Women et al v. Washington Branch of American Association of University Women,* 85 U.S. App. D.C. 163, 175 F.2d 368, 1949.

53. The courts had ruled that only the national AAUW convention could change by-laws, including membership requirements relating to race.

54. Mary Carter, "The Educational Activities of the National Association of College Women, 1923–1960" (masters thesis, Howard University, 1962), 65.

55. Levine, *Degrees of Equality,* 120.

56. The story of the NACW, especially to 1954, is in Carter, " Educational Activities of the NACW"; Linda Perkins, "The National Association of College Women: Vanguard of Black Women's Leadership and Education, 1923–1954," *Journal of Education* 172, no. 3 (1990); and Hilda Davis and Patricia Bell-Scott, "The Association of Deans of Women and Advisers to Girls in Negro Schools, 1929–1954: A Brief Oral History," *Sage* 6, no. 1 (Summer 1989).

57. Perkins, "The National Association of College Women," 67.

58. Carter, "Educational Activities of the NACW," 47–50.

59. As the NACW journal shows, even decades after Slowe's death, leaders continued to cite her as their model and to use her goals as yardsticks for the organization's success. See also Carter, "Educational Activities of the NACW."

60. Ibid., 106.

61. Ibid., 101–2; see chapter 9 for a discussion of post-1954 changes.

62. Report of the Fellowship Committee, *Journal of the National Association of College Women* (1948): 21.

63. For general background on Slowe, see Karen Anderson, "Brickbats and Roses: Lucy Diggs Slowe, 1883–1937," in *Lone Voyagers: Academic Women in Coeducational Institutions, 1870–1937,* ed. Geraldine Clifford (New York: Feminist Press, 1989), 281–307.

64. For discussions of the Association, see Davis and Bell-Scott, "Association"; see also, "Association of Deans of Women and Advisers to Girls in Negro Schools," in *Black Women in America,* ed. Hine, 49–51.

65. "Colored Deans of Women" is Ruth Brett's term for the group; see Ruth Brett [Quarles], Edna Calhoun, Lucille Piggot, Hilda Davis, and Patricia Bell-Scott, "A Symposium: Our Living History: Reminiscences of Black Participation in NAWDAC," *Journal of the National Association of Women Deans, Administrators, and Counselors* 33, no. 2 (Winter 1979): 3. For many years the women deans met jointly with a group of black men deans and advisers. In 1954 the two groups merged into the National Association of Personnel Workers, to the consternation of some female members who felt that the women's group was the stronger entity; see Davis and Bell-Scott, "Association." The quotation about their mission is from Hine, "Association," 50.

66. In fact, many years passed before NADW changed its policy to prohibit segregated settings. See Brett, Calhoun, Piggott, Davis, and Bell-Scott, "A Symposium," 4.

67. Ibid., 7, 5.

68. Ibid., 3–4.

69. Jeanne Noble, *The Negro Woman's College Education* (New York: Teachers College Press, Columbia University, 1956).

70. For a discussion of the President's Commission's approach to race, see chapter 5.

71. Regarding the AAUW, see Levine, *Degrees of Equality*, 131–35.

72. Ibid., 142.

73. *Journal of the National Association of Women Deans and Counselors* 25, no. 2 (Winter 1961).

74. The figure dropped to 10 percent by 1971; Dorothy Truex, "Education of Women, the Student Personnel Profession, and the New Feminism," *Journal of the National Association of Women Deans and Counselors* 35, no. 1 (Fall 1971): 3.

75. For a good discussion of Scott and his impact on the field, see Robert Schwartz, "Reconceptualizing the Leadership Roles of Women in Higher Education: A Brief Note on the Importance of the Dean of Women," *Journal of Higher Education* 68, no. 5 (1997): 502–22.

76. Tuttle, "What Became of the Dean of Women?" connects the changes in the 1948 ACE revision to the influence of the Truman Commission.

77. Kate Hevner Mueller, *Educating Women for a Changing World* (Minneapolis: University of Minnesota Press, 1954).

78. Mueller's story is told in Tuttle, "What Became of the Dean of Women?" chap. 4.

79. See Tuttle, "What Became of the Dean of Women?" esp. 167–95.

80. Ibid., 189.

81. Gangone, "Navigating Turbulence," 163.

82. Tuttle, "What Became of the Dean of Women?" 190.

83. Helen Hosp, Committee Report, *Journal of the American Association of University Women* 39, no. 4 (Summer 1946): 231.

84. Alice Lloyd, "Women in the Postwar College," *Journal of the American Association of University Women* 39, no 3 (Spring 1946): 131–34.

85. Ibid., 191–94.

86. Tuttle characterizes this relationship as tense, especially at 189ff.

87. For discussions of the early deans, see Nidiffer, *Pioneering Deans of Women;* also see Geraldine Clifford, ed., *Lone Voyagers: Academic Women in Coeducational Universities, 1870–1937* (New York: Feminist Press, 1989).

88. Katharine McBride, "The Dean and the Universe," *Journal of the National Association of Deans of Women* 17, no. 4 (Summer 1954): 170.

89. Arthur Adams, "The Role of the Dean of Women on the College Campus," *Journal of the National Association of Women Deans and Counselors* 26, no. 1 (Fall 1962): 23.

90. See *Journal of the National Association of Deans of Women* 18, no. 2 (Winter 1955).

91. The decision on joining the new federation is discussed in Gangone, "Navigating Turbulence," 166–74 and Brown, "The National Association," especially chapters 1 and 2.

92. Tuttle, "What Became of the Dean of Women?" 294ff.

93. Brown, "The National Association," 459–60.

94. Ibid., 443.

95. Gangone, "Navigating Turbulence," 173–80.

96. Membership figures computed from Brown, "The National Association," 74; and Gangone, "Navigating Turbulence," 178.

97. Brown, "The National Association," 73.

98. Ibid., 105.

99. Eunice Hilton, "President's Report," *Journal of the National Association of Women Deans and Counselors* 19, no. 4 (Summer 1956): 161; Barbara Catton, "Our Association in Review," *Journal of the National Association of Women Deans and Counselors* 20, no. 1 (Fall 1956): 9.

100. This name shift was only the first of several, none of which ultimately proved successful in sustaining the group. In 1973, NADW added "Administrators" to its title, reaching out to all women working on campuses; by 1991, in a fight for organizational survival, it adopted the generic name "National Association of Women in Education." As Gangone, "Navigating Turbulence," details, this shift signaled a confused sense of the group's audience and mission.

101. Ruth Barry and Beverly Wolf, *Modern Issues in Guidance Personnel Work* (New York: Teachers College, Columbia University, 1963). For discussions of NADW's response to the Barry and Wolf critique, see Brown, "The National Association," especially 247–53; and Gangone, "Navigating Turbulence," especially 181–93.

102. Brown, "The National Association," 248–49.

103. Estelle Freedman, "Separatism as Strategy: Female Institution Building and American Feminism, 1870-1930," *Feminist Studies* 5 (Fall, 1979): 512–29.

104. Gangone, "Navigating Turbulence," 189.

105. Katherine Blyley, "Report on the National Meeting," *Journal of the National Association of Deans of Women* 12, no. 4 (Summer 1948): 164.

106. Gangone, "Navigating Turbulence," 190.

107. Sarah Blanding, "The Dean's Contribution to the Life of Our Times," *Journal of the National Association of Deans of Women* 9, no. 4 (Summer 1946): 148.

108. Eunice Roberts, "Keynote Speech," *Journal of the National Association of Women Deans and Counselors* 22, no. 4 (Summer 1959): 152–53.

109. Jessie Bernard, *Academic Women* (University Park: Pennsylvania State University Press, 1964); also, see above, chapter 2.

110. Helen Schleman, "The Committee S Report of the AAUP as Viewed by the Dean of Women," *Journal of the National Association of Women Deans and Counselors* 27, no. 4 (Summer 1965): 147–48.

111. Eunice Hilton, "'The Feminine Mystique': A Special Message to Counselors of Women," *Journal of the National Association of Women Deans and Counselors* 27, no. 2 (Winter 1964): 61–62.

112. Dorothy Truex, "Education of Women, the Student Personnel Profession, and the New Feminism," *Journal of the National Association of Women Deans and Counselors* 35, no. 1 (Fall 1971): 13.

CHAPTER 5: POLICY

1. Agnes Meyer, PCSW member biography, collection B-26, box 6, folder 37, Schlesinger.

2. Information about Meyer's life is drawn from Barbara Sicherman and Carol Hurd Green, eds., *Notable American Women: The Modern Period: A Biographical Dictionary*

(Cambridge, Mass.: Belknap Press of Harvard University Press, 1980), 471–73; and Katharine Graham, *Personal History* (New York: Alfred A. Knopf, 1997).

3. Graham, *Personal History*, 252, 27.

4. Ibid., 173.

5. From Executive Order 10980 Establishing the President's Commission on the Status of Women, in *American Women: The Report of the President's Commission on the Status of Women and Other Publications of the Commission*, ed. Margaret Mead and Frances Kaplan (New York: Charles Scribner's Sons, 1965), 208.

6. Useful discussions of Peterson's work in the Women's Bureau and on the PCSW appear in Cynthia Harrison, *On Account of Sex: The Politics of Women's Issues, 1945–1968* (Berkeley: University of California Press, 1988); and Kathleen Laughlin, *Women's Work and Public Policy: A History of the Women's Bureau, U.S. Department of Labor, 1945–1970*, (Boston: Northeastern University Press, 2000).

7. Harrison, "Specific Bills for Specific Ills," in *On Account of Sex*, chap. 3.

8. For a good discussion of the history of protective labor legislation, see Alice Kessler-Harris, *Out to Work: A History of Wage-Earning Women in the United States* (Oxford University Press, 1982).

9. Debra Stewart, *The Women's Movement in Community Politics in the U.S.: The Role of Local Commissions on the Status of Women* (New York: Pergamon Press, 1980); Harrison, *On Account of Sex*.

10. Executive Order 10980, in *American Women*, 207.

11. Esther Peterson, interview by Ann Campbell, 20 January 1970, John F. Kennedy Library Oral History Program, 57.

12. Minutes of the President's Commission on the Status of Women, 12–13 February 1962 meeting, box 1, executive letter 3, John F. Kennedy Library (21 February 1962).

13. Harrison, *On Account of Sex*, 125.

14. *American Women*, 66.

15. Dael Wolfle, *America's Resources of Specialized Talent: A Current Appraisal and a Look Ahead* (New York: Harper & Brothers, 1954); National Manpower Council, *Womanpower: A Statement by the National Manpower Council with Chapters by the Council Staff* (New York: Columbia University Press, 1957).

16. Harrison, *On Account of Sex*, 144–45.

17. Ibid.

18. *American Women*, 45–54, 118–27. Subsequent page citations to this report are given in the text.

19. "When Nixon Took on Khrushchev," *U.S. News and World Report*, 3 August 1959, 36–9; Nixon and Khrushchev Argue in Public as U.S. Exhibit Opens, " *New York Times*, 25 July 1959, 1, 3; see also chapter 1 above.

20. Esther Peterson, interview by Ann Campbell, 63; *American Women*, see Appendix III, 219–28 regarding a summary of the consultation on "Problems of Negro Women."

21. Esther Peterson, interview by Ann Campbell, 63.

22. Transcript of the 1 April 1963 Commission, p. 281, box 5, John F. Kennedy Library.

23. Regarding the Education Committee, see *American Women* 25–34, 101–10; regarding the Home and Community Committee, see 35–44, 111–17.

24. Minutes of the President's Commission on the Status of Women 1–2 April 1963 meeting, box 3, folder 1, John F. Kennedy Library; the Education Committee report begins on 15.

25. Information on committee members is in folder 37, Schlesinger Library.

26. Richard Altenbaugh, *Education for Struggle: The American Labor Colleges of the 1920s and 1930s* (Philadelphia: Temple University Press, 1990).

27. Susan Levine, *Degrees of Equality: The American Association of University Women and the Challenge of Twentieth-Century Feminism* (Philadelphia: Temple University Press, 1995), 216.

28. Bunting, Transcript of the 2 May 1962 meeting of the Education Committee, box 7, folder 42, Schlesinger 5.

29. Only seven committee members attended the first meeting: Bunting, Harvey, Meyer, Raushenbush, Schleman, Tompkins, and Ware (who participated unofficially, as a member of the PCSW). Meyer attended only the May meeting. The questions appear throughout the May 1962 transcript.

30. Minutes of the Education Committee, 2 May 1962, box 7, folder 42, Schlesinger, p. 2.

31. Evelyn Perloff, *Education for Women: A Bibliography of What Has Been Said, 1950–1961*, box 6, folder 38, Schlesinger.

32. Edna Amidon, "The Education of Women for their Role in the Home" (Background paper for the Education Committee of the PCSW, 1962), box 6, folder 38, Schlesinger, p. 46.

33. Elizabeth Drews, "The Second Sex and the Third Force," box 6, folder 38, p. 19, Schlesinger.

34. Virginia Senders, "The Place of Counseling in the Education of Women," box 6, folder 38, p. 19, Schlesinger.

35. United States Employment Service, "Counseling in the Public Employment Service," box 6, folder 39 (For the Subcommittee on Counseling, of the Committees on Government Contracts, Education, and New and Expanded Services, January 1963); Esther Westervelt, "The Recruitment and Training of Educational/Vocational Counselors of Girls and Women," folder 39 (For the Subcommittee on Counseling, n.d.), Schlesinger.

36. Ruth Prokop, "The Community College," folder 39; see also chapter 2 above.

37. Antonia Chayes to Members of the Committee on Education in progress report memorandum, 24 August 1962, box 7, folder 42, Schlesinger, p. 3.

38. Although a small meeting of the education committee was held on October 29–30, 1962, committee chair Bunting was unable to attend and no transcript was made. It is unclear who attended and how the meeting progressed. Based on the December transcript, it appears that those present discussed the initial worksheets. In addition, in November Chayes prepared an "impressionistic" report based on her attendance at that meeting; this report covers the first pages of the worksheets and, in Chayes' words, "runs out of steam" at the college years (see note 40 below).

39. It is useful to remember that not all members attended all meetings; in fact, the collegiate educators often predominated in the gatherings. Although other members provided input between meetings, the committee's focus leaned toward collegiate and continuing education issues.

40. Chayes, Memorandum to the Committee on Education regarding the 29–30 October meeting, 29 November 1962, box 6, folder 41, Schlesinger, p. 2.

41. For a discussion of the postwar disagreements over federal school aid, see Diane Ravitch, *The Troubled Crusade: American Education, 1945–1980* (New York: Basic Books, 1984).

42. Transcript of the 4–5 December 1962 meeting, box 6, folder 41, Schlesinger.

43. "Statement on Family Planning" (Background paper for the October 1962 meeting), box 6, folder 39, Schlesinger.

44. Transcript of the 27 May 1963 meeting of the PCSW, box 2, folder 13, Schlesinger, 198.

45. Transcript of the 7 February 1963 meeting of the Education Committee, box 7, folder 44, Schlesinger, pp. 23–24.

46. Ibid., 56.

47. Ibid., 90.

48. Ibid., 30ff.

49. Although Bunting did not respond in the committee session to the discussion of Friedan, she had, in fact, for a short time considered co-authorship with Friedan. Mary I. Bunting, oral memoir with Jeanette Bailey Cheek, pp. 87–88, Schlesinger.

50. Transcript of the 7 February 1963 meeting of the Education Committee, p. 53.

51. Ibid., 115.

52. Gunnar Myrdal, *An American Dilemma: The Negro Problem and American Democracy* (New York: Harper Brothers, 1944); Michael Harrington, *The Other America: Poverty in the United States* (New York: Macmillan, 1962); U.S. Department of Labor, Office of Policy Planning and Research [Daniel Patrick Moynihan], *The Negro Family: The Case for National Action* (Washington, D.C.: Government Printing Office, 1965); James S. Coleman et al., *Equality of Educational Opportunity* (Washington, D.C.: Government Printing Office, 1966). For a discussion of the relationship of social science, education, and federal policy in the 1960s, see Ravitch, *The Troubled Crusade*, especially chapter 5. See also Lee Rainwater, *The Moynihan Report and the Politics of Controversy* (Cambridge, Mass.: MIT Press, 1967); and Cynthia E. Harrison, *On Account of Sex: The Politics of Women's Issues, 1945–1968* (Berkeley: University of California Press, 1988).

53. Committee on Education, "Summary of Report of Committee on Education," 27 March 1963, box 6, folder 41, Schlesinger, p. 1.

54. Ibid., p. i.

55. *Summary of the Final Report of the Committee on Education*, 12 February 1963, folder 41, Schlesinger. This "summary" report was secretary Chayes' review of what the committee's final report would include. It differs from the final report in many ways but is useful for revealing the committee's thinking. The committee's final report was submitted to the PCSW on March 27, 1963.

56. Minutes of the President's Commission on the Status of Women 1–2 April 1963 meeting, box 3, folder 1, John F. Kennedy Library; the education committee report begins on 15.

57. Page references to this report in the text are to the edition published by Scribner's in 1965.

58. The sections dealing with Education and Counseling are at 25–34 and 101–10.

59. Edward Eddy, "On Being Female," review of *American Women, New York Times*, 1 August 1965, BR 6.

60. *American Women*, 160–77.

61. Esther Peterson, interview by Ann Campbell, 62.

62. Ibid., 77–78.

63. Harrison, *On Account of Sex*, 174; for evaluations of the PCSW, see Laughlin, *Women's Work and Public Policy*.

64. For an analysis of the contributions of these state commissions, see Harrison, Laughlin, and Stewart, *The Women's Movement in Community Politics*.

65. *Oral History of Kathryn F. Clarenbach*, Schlesinger Library, copied from the State Historical Society of Wisconsin, part of the Midwestern Origins of the Women's Movement Project, Gerda Lerner (September 1987, 1989).

CHAPTER 6: WOMEN'S CONTINUING EDUCATION AS AN INSTITUTIONAL RESPONSE

1. This review of Bunting's life relies on Mary Bunting, interview by Jeanette Cheek, "Oral History Interview with Mary I. Bunting," September 1978, Radcliffe College Archives, Schlesinger; and "One Woman, Two Lives," *Time*, 3 November 1961, 109–12.

2. An excellent history of adult education, focusing primarily on nonformal education, is Joseph F. Kett, *The Pursuit of Knowledge Under Difficulties: From Self-Improvement to Adult Education in America, 1750–1990* (Stanford, Calif.: Stanford University Press, 1994). Kett emphasizes that the years before World War II saw adult education beginning to move into the colleges; the real collegiate growth, he asserts, came after World War II. See especially chapter 12, "The Learning Society," 403–54.

3. Land grant institutions—often named state universities—grew out of two pieces of federal legislation, the 1862 and 1890 Morrill Land Grant Acts. The acts gave each state the proceeds of sales of land to be used for agricultural and mechanical needs of their populace, generally focusing on the practical aspects of higher education. For general discussion of these institutions, see Frederick Rudolph, *The American College and University: A History* (New York: Vintage Books, 1962; reprint, University of Georgia Press, 1990).

4. For a good discussion of how these continuing education issues affected women, see Helen S. Astin, ed., *Some Action of Her Own: The Adult Woman and Higher Education* (Lexington, Mass.: Lexington Books, 1976).

5. Elizabeth Cless, "The Birth of an Idea: An Account of the Genesis of Women's Continuing Education," in Astin, *Some Action of Her Own*, 7. Cless terms the women's continuing education effort "a radical but undervalued movement for educational reform," p. 3.

6. Virginia Senders, interview by Donald Opitz, 8 January 2000, Minnesota Women's Center Collection, University of Minnesota Archives (hereafter MN Archives).

7. Senders describes the plane crash in a variety of places. Most accessible are Donald L. Opitz, *Three Generations in the Life of the Minnesota Women's Center: A History, 1960–2000* (University of Minnesota: 1999); and Senders, interview by Opitz.

8. Senders' early ideas are explained in "A Program for the Continuation of Productive Intellectual Activity by Women College Graduates," 1953, ACE records, Series B-22, folder

9, Schlesinger; and "Let's Stop Wasting Our Women" [undated but c. 1957], in Minnesota Women's Center Collection, MN Archives.

9. ACE CEW collection, folder 9, Schlesinger.

10. Senders, interview by Opitz.

11. Senders, "The Minnesota Plan for Continuing Education: A Progress Report," *Educational Record* (October 1961): 261–69.

12. "The Minnesota Plan for the Continuing Education of Women," proposal to Carnegie Corporation, box 2, Minnesota Women's Center Collection, MN Archives, p. 1.

13. Ibid., 1.

14. "The Minnesota Plan," *Educational Record*, 271.

15. Although language about the program is the same in the original proposal, a more accessible version appears in Senders' "The Minnesota Plan" article, especially p. 278.

16. Douvan, "Adolescent Girls: Their Attitude Toward Education," in *The Education of Women: Signs for the Future*, ed. Opal David (Washington, D.C.: American Council on Education, 1959), 23–29.

17. Douvan quoted in *A Five-Year Report 1960–65 of the Minnesota Plan for the Continuing Education of Women*, ed. Vera M. Schletzer et al. (Minneapolis: University of Minnesota, 1967), 7.

18. Viola Klein and Alva Myrdal, *Women's Two Roles: Home and Work* (London: Routledge and Kegan Paul, 1956).

19. National Manpower Council, *Womanpower: A Statement by the National Manpower Council* (New York: Columbia University Press, 1957); and *Work in the Lives of Married Women* (New York: Columbia University Press, 1958).

20. Draft script of television program, "To Be Continued," Publicity folder, box 1, Minnesota Women's Center Collection, MN Archives. The program was part 6 of the series *Freedom to Learn*, prepared for public television and broadcast to forty markets in 1962.

21. Kett describes the origins of Ford's Fund for Adult Education as an outgrowth of Robert Maynard Hutchins' commitment to a "Great Books" curriculum. With Hutchins' encouragement, the Ford Fund focused on humanistic education throughout the 1950s; it ceased operations in 1961. See Kett, *The Pursuit of Knowledge*, 424–25.

22. Carnegie Corporation of New York, *Annual Report 1960*, 42.

23. *Who's Who in America*, Vol. 30 (Chicago: A. N. Marquis, 1958–59); oral history interview of Florence Anderson, 1966, in the Columbia University Research Office Collection.

24. Cless, "The Birth of an Idea," 7–8; see also a discussion of Anderson and her influence in Barry Dean Karl, "Going for Broke: The Historian's Commitment to Philanthropy," in *Philanthropic Foundations*, ed. Ellen C. Lagemann (Bloomington: Indiana University Press, 1999), 288–89.

25. Anderson to Vera Schletzer, 24 October 1963, Collection 951, General Extension Division, box 16, Women's Continuing Education, 1960–66, MN Archives.

26. *The Planner* (newsletter of the Minnesota Plan), November 1960, Box 1, Minnesota Women's Center Collection, MN Archives.

27. Senders, "The Minnesota Plan," *Educational Record*, 271–72.

28. 1963 form letter in box 1, Minnesota Women's Center Collection, MN Archives.

29. Senders, "The Minnesota Plan," *Educational Record*, 271–72.

30. Raushenbush, "Unfinished Business: Continuing Education for Women," *Educational Record* (October 1961): 263.

31. See Ruth Lyon, "The Center for Continuing Education at Sarah Lawrence College (1962–1976)" (master's thesis, Sarah Lawrence College, 1976) for a discussion of Raushenbush's approach to her faculty.

32. For a good discussion of the pedagogical approach, see chapter 4 in Bert Loewenberg, "Education for Women in Mid Span: The Center for Continuing Education at Sarah Lawrence College," unpublished manuscript, Sarah Lawrence College Archives.

33. Raushenbush, "What Now?" *Sarah Lawrence Alumnae Magazine* (February 1960): 8–9, 14–16.

34. Opal David to Esther Raushenbush, 2 June 1960, box 1, Raushenbush folder, Center for Continuing Education collection, Sarah Lawrence College Archives (hereafter Sarah Lawrence Archives).

35. "A Proposal for the Continuing Education of Women," 13 February 1961, Raushenbush folder, Sarah Lawrence Archives.

36. Clarence Faust to Paul Ward, 15 May 1961, Raushenbush folder, Sarah Lawrence Archives.

37. Raushenbush to Elizabeth Pascal, 31 May 1961, Carnegie Corporation folder, box 10, Sarah Lawrence Archives.

38. Anderson to Ward, 18 April 1961, ibid.

39. Anderson to Raushenbush, 9 November 1961, ibid.

40. "The Present State of Affairs with Regard to the Center for Continuing Education," 1 April 1962 statement, ibid.

41. "The Center for Continuing Education, 1962–63," annual report, Sarah Lawrence Archives.

42. Ibid., 8.

43. Ibid., 19.

44. 1974 Addendum to "Reminiscences of Esther Raushenbush" 1973, p. 15, in the Columbia University Oral History Research Office Collection.

45. Bunting discusses her work at Douglass College in her oral history; the Douglas College programs emphasized here are well described in Kimberley Dolphin Wheaton, "Challenging the 'Climate of Unexpectation:' Mary Ingraham Bunting and American Women's Higher Education in the 1950s and 1960s" (Ph.D. diss., Harvard University, 2001).

46. Douglass College was the coordinate women's college at Rutgers University, just as Radcliffe College was the women's coordinate of Harvard University. Although Bunting was called "dean" at Douglass and "president" at Radcliffe, she often claimed that she had more autonomy in the Douglass/Rutgers setting.

47. Wheaton, "Challenging the 'Climate of Unexpectation,'" 47–54.

48. Mary Bunting, "From *Serratia* to Women's Lib and a Bit Beyond," *American Society for Microbiology News* 37, no. 3 (August 1971): 48.

49. The "climate of unexpectation," discussed further below, was a term first used by Bunting in "One Woman, Two Lives."

50. Mary Bunting, "From *Serratia*," 49.

51. The "garden" metaphor comes from Bunting, "Interview," 120.

52. Mary Bunting, "The Radcliffe Institute," 279–86.

53. The idea of "hidden dissuaders" mirrors the "hidden persuaders" of Vance Packard's influential book on advertising. See Packard, *The Hidden Persuaders* (New York: McKay, 1957); also, Bunting, "A Huge Waste: Educated Womanpower," *New York Times Magazine*, 7 May 1961, 109.

54. Mary Bunting, "The Radcliffe Institute," 281.

55. Theodore Caplow and Reese McGee, *The Academic Marketplace* (New York: Basic Books, 1958); Radcliffe College Faculty-Trustee Committee [Cronkhite], *Graduate Education for Women: The Radcliffe Ph.D.* (Cambridge, Mass.: Harvard University Press, 1956); see also chapter 2.

56. Mary Bunting, "The Radcliffe Institute for Independent Study," *Educational Record* (October 1961): 283.

57. Bunting, "Interview," 93.

58. Cless, "The Birth of an Idea," 7.

59. The story of Bunting's work with the trustees is told in Minutes of the Radcliffe Council, the Board of Trustees, and the Institute Executive Committee, as well as in Bunting's "Interview"; see also Wheaton, "Challenging the 'Climate of Unexpectation,'" chap. 3.

60. The story of individual and foundation contributions to the continuing education movement constitutes an interesting case study in philanthropy. Further discussed in chapter 7, it is explored within the wider context of women's philanthropy in Linda Eisenmann, "Brokering Old and New Philanthropic Traditions: Women's Continuing Education in the Cold War Era," in *Women and Philanthropy in Education*, ed. Andrea Walton, 148–66 (Bloomington: Indiana University Press, 2005).

61. Bunting, "Interview," 97–98.

62. Ibid.

63. Rockefeller Brothers Fund, *The Pursuit of Excellence: Education and the Future of America* (New York: Doubleday, 1958); *Excellence: Can We Be Equal and Excellent Too?* (New York: Harpers, 1961).

64. Bunting to John Gardner, 11 October 1960, Records of the Bunting Institute, Series 6-1.

65. Bunting tells the story of Rockefeller approaching her when he heard about the Institute in Bunting, "Interview," 99–100; Wheaton, however, emphasizes the previous connection with Blanchette, who introduced Bunting to her brother-in-law ("Challenging the 'Climate of Unexpectation,'" 121). Bunting had a tendency to stress serendipity in her published materials.

66. White, *The Next Step: A Guide to Part-time Opportunities in the Greater Boston Area for the Educated Woman* (Cambridge: Radcliffe Institute, 1964).

67. Mary Bunting, "The Radcliffe Institute," 282–83, 293.

68. Bunting, "Interview," 101.

69. Constance E. Smith was a professor of political science who had worked with Bunting at Douglass College. Her dual appointment as director of research for Rutgers'

Eagleton Institute attracted Bunting, who hoped to use the Radcliffe Institute to extend research on women. Bunting believed that an experienced academic like Smith could both support the Institute fellows and advocate for Institute issues in the Harvard community. See Bunting, Statement at Memorial Service for Constance E. Smith, Harvard University, December 10, 1970, author's collection.

70. Smith, "Institute Appoints First 22 Scholars," *Radcliffe: News from the College*, Summer 1961, 1, 3.

71. Ibid.

72. Interviews with the scholars appear in the June 1986 *Radcliffe Quarterly*, issue devoted primarily to the Institute's 25th anniversary; Randall, 15.

73. Ibid., 14.

74. Ibid., 18.

75. The *Times* coverage of Sarah Lawrence is noted in "The Present State of Affairs with Regard to the Center for Continuing Education," 1 April 1962 statement, Sarah Lawrence Archives.

76. Hechinger, "Radcliffe Plans Institute to Aid the Gifted Woman," *New York Times*, 20 November 1960; headlines noted in memo to Bunting and the Trustees from Deane Lord, Director of News Office, n.d. [c. December 1960], Records of the Bunting Institute, Series 6–1.

77. Bunting, "Our Greatest Waste of Talent is Women," *Life*, 13 January 1961; "A Huge Waste: Educated Womanpower," *New York Times Magazine*, 7 May 1961; "One Woman, Two Lives," *Time*, 3 November 1961, 109–12.

78. Bunting, "A Huge Waste," 112.

79. Minnesota's discussions with ACE around the Itasca conference are in President J. L. Morrill's papers, Box 254, folder "Women, 1957, 1960–61," MN Archives.

80. Throughout the 1960s, Carnegie support to women's programming never exceeded 3 percent of its total U.S. grants (data gathered from Annual Reports of the Carnegie Corporation, 1959 to 1969). For further discussion of the foundations' later support of women's issues, see Rosa Proietto, "The Ford Foundation and Women's Studies in American Higher Education," in *Philanthropic Foundations*, ed. Ellen Condliffe Lagemann (Bloomington: Indiana University Press, 1999), 282; Mariam Chamberlain and Alison Bernstein, "Philanthropy and the Emergence of Women's Studies," *Teachers College Record* 93 (Spring 1992): 556–68; and, generally, Andrea Walton, ed., *Women and Philanthropy in Education* (Bloomington: Indiana University Press, 2005).

81. The University of Michigan was chosen here as a representative of the "second-phase" programs because of its strong archival sources. Extant today as a thriving center for women's education, Michigan has clear roots in the continuing education movement.

82. For one important case, see Polly Welts Kaufman, ed., *The Search for Equity: Women at Brown University, 1891–1991* (Hanover, N.H.: Brown University Press, 1991). For other examples of female support, see Lynn D. Gordon, *Gender and Higher Education in the Progressive Era* (New Haven, Conn.: Yale University Press, 1990).

83. Ruth Bordin, *Women at Michigan: The 'Dangerous Experiment,' 1870s to the Present* (Ann Arbor: University of Michigan Press, 1999).

84. For references and background on Cain and the other founders, see Jean Campbell,

oral history interview with Linda Eisenmann and Jeanne Miller, 2 October 2000, Ann Arbor, Michigan; and Bordin, *Women at Michigan*, 72–74.

85. The story of Cain's approach to Heyns is commonly told at Michigan's Center for the Education of Women. For a reflection, see Campbell, oral history interview.

86. Cain, "A Memo and Suggestion for the University of Michigan: The Continuing Education of Women," August 1962, box 1, folder 1, Center for the Education of Women Collection, Bentley Historical Library, University of Michigan (hereafter Bentley).

87. [Cain and Clover Flanders] "The Continuing Education of Women-Selected References," bibliography found in unprocessed papers of the Continuing Education Committee (CEC), Center for the Education of Women, University of Michigan, Ann Arbor, Michigan.

88. Cain, "Summary of Activities (February 1–July 13, 1963) in Connection with The University of Michigan Project on the Continuing Education of Women," box 6, folder "Proposal for CEW," Bentley. Regent Murphy was also a consultant in education to the Governor's Commission on the Status of Women, an offshoot of Kennedy's President's Commission on the Status of Women.

89. The September 1962 meeting is summarized in Alison T. Myers, Memo to Continuing Education for Women Committee, March 12, 1964, box 6 [1986 accession], Bentley.

90. Cain, "Report to the Alumnae Committee on the Continuing Education of Women," 16 April 1963, unprocessed papers of CEC.

91. The September 1963 protocol, the survey, and summaries of the results are all available in the unprocessed papers of CEC, CEW.

92. Myers, Memo to Continuing Education for Women Committee, 12 March 1964, box 6, Bentley.

93. Cain, "Recommendations for a Center for the Continuing Education of Women," 19 June 1963, box 1, folder 1, CEW collection, Bentley.

94. Cain, "Proposal for a Center for the Continuing Education of Women, The University of Michigan," 27 May 1964, box 1 and box 6, Bentley.

95. Ibid., 5, 10.

96. See minutes and correspondence of Executive Advisory Committee, box 1, folder 1, CEW collection, Bentley.

97. See chapter 7 for discussion of these programs and their support from Carnegie.

98. Minutes, Executive Advisory Committee, 3 February 1964, box 1, folder 1, CEW collection, Bentley.

99. Cain, oral history interview with Jean Campbell and Jane Likert, by Ruth Bordin, CEW, 1989.

100. In 1924, professor George Herbert Palmer had contributed funds to create a professorship at Michigan to be held by a woman in honor of his wife, Alice Freeman Palmer, an early Michigan graduate who became President of Wellesley and dean of women at University of Chicago. That professorship languished, however, when the history department proposed filling it with a man. In the 1950s the alumnae had rejuvenated this fund-raising project as the Alice Freeman Palmer Professorship and were still contributing to it in 1964 (Bordin, *Women at Michigan*).

101. Cobb's work is detailed in the unprocessed papers of CEC, CEW.

102. Minutes of Alumnae Council Committee on Continuing Education of Women, unprocessed papers of CEC, CEW, 12 June 1964, 2.

103. A plaque that hangs outside Michigan's center lists the original major donors, including 24 individuals, 3 alumnae clubs, and 7 honorary gifts.

104. Michigan's founders remembered both men as helpful, especially Heyns. After leaving Michigan in 1965, Heyns built a distinguished national career, first as chancellor of the University of California at Berkeley, and then as president of ACE. In fact, Heyns was presiding over ACE when it opened its Office for Women in Higher Education in 1973.

105. A summary of the Center's first-year activities can be found in box 1 and box 6, CEW Collection, Bentley.

106. Jean Campbell, "Women Drop Back In: Educational Innovations in the 60s," in *Academic Women on the Move*, ed. Alice S. Rossi and Ann Calderwood (New York: Russell Sage Foundation, 1973), 104–5.

CHAPTER 7: THE CONTRIBUTIONS AND LIMITATIONS OF WOMEN'S
CONTINUING EDUCATION

1. Virginia Senders curriculum vitae, box 14; press release on Senders' leaving, box 1, Minnesota Women's Center Collection, MN Archives. From 1963 to 1966, Senders worked as associate director of the New England Board of Higher Education.

2. Louise Cain, Jean Campbell, and Jane Likert, oral history interview with Ruth Bordin, University of Michigan Center for the Education of Women, 1989; Jean Campbell, oral history interview with Linda Eisenmann and Jeanne Miller, 2 October 2000, Ann Arbor, Michigan.

3. Cain, Campbell, and Likert oral history interview, 1989; for Heyns' encouragement around the sabbaticals, see Ruth Bordin, *Women at Michigan: The "Dangerous Experiment," 1870s to the Present* (Ann Arbor: University of Michigan Press, 1999).

4. Jean Campbell, oral history interview, 2000; and Bordin, *Women at Michigan*, 72–74.

5. Cain, Campbell, and Likert oral history interview, 1989.

6. For a general discussion of women's continuing education of the early 1960s, see Helen S. Astin, ed., *Some Action of Her Own: The Adult Woman and Higher Education* (Lexington, Mass.: Lexington Books, 1976), generally; and particularly therein, Elizabeth Cless, "The Birth of an Idea: An Account of the Genesis of Women's Continuing Education."

7. Melissa Lewis Richter and Jane Banks Whipple, *A Revolution in the Education of Women: Ten Years of Continuing Education at Sarah Lawrence College* (Bronxville, N.Y.: Sarah Lawrence College, 1972), 22, 75.

8. Campbell, Report to the Executive Committee, folder Executive Committee Minutes and Correspondence, box 6, CEW collection, Bentley Historical Library, 16 May 1967, 3.

9. In fact, the scholarship effort became one of CEW's notable projects throughout its history. By 1970 (celebrating the centennial of women's admission to Michigan), the Michigan center offered its first scholarship.

10. Esther Raushenbush, "Unfinished Business: Continuing Education for Women," *Educational Record* (October 1961): 269.

11. Concerned about liability issues, the university only reluctantly supported the child care center. Student activism around this issue was rare in the early 1960s.

12. Senders discussed the situation for part-time students in "Opportunities for Adult Education at the University of Minnesota," memorandum, undated [1960?], box 1, Minnesota Women's Center Collection, MN Archives.

13. Marjorie Downing to Raushenbush, 11 June 1962, Center for Continuing Education collection, Sarah Lawrence Archives.

14. Reminiscences of Esther Raushenbush, Addendum, 1974, in the Columbia University Oral History Research Office Collection, 20.

15. Alice Olson, interview by author, Bronxville, New York, 14 February 2000.

16. Virginia Senders, "The Minnesota Plan for Continuing Education: A Progress Report," *Educational Record* (October 1961): 261–69.

17. Vera M. Schletzer et al., *A Five-Year Report 1960–65 of the Minnesota Plan for the Continuing Education of Women* (Minneapolis: University of Minnesota, 1967), 20.

18. Campbell to Rosalind Loring, folder "Adult Education Association," CEW Collection, Bentley Historical Library, 12 October 1967.

19. Ibid.

20. Richter and Whipple, *A Revolution*, 58.

21. Mary Bunting, interview by Jeanette Cheek, "Oral History Interview with Mary I. Bunting," September 1978, Radcliffe College Archives, Schlesinger Library, Harvard University, 93.

22. Alice Smith, *History of the Radcliffe Institute, 1960–1971* (Cambridge, Mass.: Radcliffe College, 1971). The Seminars program always struggled to differentiate itself from Harvard's Extension School. It remained as part of the Institute until a major Radcliffe reorganization in 1977.

23. The graduate fellowships resembled those of AAUW's College Faculty Program discussed in chapter 4, and the new E. B. Fred Fellowships for graduate study at the University of Wisconsin (a program also supported by the Carnegie Corporation). See Marian L. Thompson and Lawrence Sager, *Report on the E. B. Fred Fellowship for Mature Women, 1963–68: A Program in Continuing Education* (Madison: University of Wisconsin, 1970).

24. See Smith, *History of the Radcliffe Institute*.

25. "Back to School," *Carnegie Corporation of New York Quarterly*, October 1962, box 4, Minnesota Women's Center collection, MN Archives.

26. Schletzer, *A Five-Year Report*; Richter and Whipple, *A Revolution*.

27. See, for example, the trio of articles about the continuing education programs at Radcliffe, Minnesota, and Sarah Lawrence in the October 1961 *Educational Record*, as well as reports about these three in Lawrence E. Dennis, ed., *Education and a Woman's Life* (Washington, D.C.: ACE, 1963).

28. Martha White, "Conversations with the Scholars, 1961–63," series 5–4, carton 3, Radcliffe College Archives.

29. White did personal interviews with 12 scholars from the original cohort, and con-

ducted group interviews with the members of the second cohort. In all, 37 women participated in the first two cohorts. The quotations are from chapter 2, pp. 10–15.

30. Ibid., chapter 3.

31. Ibid., chapter 5, p. 9.

32. Ibid., chapter 6, pp. 3, 14.

33. See papers in Schletzer et al., *A Five-Year Report;* Richter and Whipple, *A Revolution;* see also Schletzer, "Project Women: A Problem in Motivation," *Minnesota Counselor,* 1965, box 1, Minnesota Women's Center collection, MN Archives; Virginia Senders, "The Place of Counseling in the Education of Women," 12 October 1962, collection B-26, box 6, folder 39, Schlesinger; Raushenbush, "Some Brief Life Histories Illustrating the Problems and Possibilities in the Professional Life of Women," 15 October 1962, box 6, folder 40, Schlesinger.

34. Bunting, interview by Jeanette Cheek, 118.

35. See, for example, Charlotte Davis McGee, *The Radcliffe Institute Fellows 1961–74: A Profile,* 1975, Records of the Bunting Institute, series 1, box 6, Schlesinger; Jean Pool, *Life Styles of Radcliffe Institute Scholars,* 1964, series 5-4, box 1, Schlesinger; Alice Ryerson, *Report on Study of Scholars at the Radcliffe Institute, 1961–62,* series 5-4, box 1, Schlesinger.

36. Campbell, 2000 oral history interview, 18.

37. Jean Campbell, "Women Drop Back In: Educational Innovations in the 60s," in *Academic Women on the Move,* ed. Alice S. Rossi and Ann Calderwood (New York: Russell Sage Foundation, 1973), 114.

38. Willard Thompson to Elizabeth Cless, 6 February 1963, Collection 951, General Extension Division, Dean's folder, MN Archives.

39. Richter and Whipple, *A Revolution,* 13, 33.

40. Alice Smith, *History,* 26.

41. Ibid., 35.

42. Richter and Whipple, *A Revolution,* 22.

43. 1961 program brochure, box 1, Minnesota Women's Center Collection, MN Archives.

44. Schletzer et al., *A Five-Year Report,* 19.

45. "Annual Report of the Minnesota Plan for the Continuing Education of Women for the Carnegie Foundation," 1961, Collection 951, General Extension, Women's Continuing Education, 1960–1966, MN Archives.

46. Ruth Lyon, "The Center for Continuing Education at Sarah Lawrence College (1962–1976)" (master's thesis, Sarah Lawrence College, 1976), 20.

47. Mary Bunting, "The Radcliffe Institute for Independent Study," *Educational Record* (October 1961): 283.

48. Alice Smith, *History,* 25. Alice Smith was not related to first Institute director Constance Smith (1960 to 1970).

49. Constance Smith, *The Radcliffe Institute for Independent Study: Report of the Director, 1963* (Cambridge, Mass.: Radcliffe College, 1963) unpaginated [7].

50. Ibid., unpaginated [7–8].

51. Bunting, "The Radcliffe Institute for Independent Study, November 1960" ["Blue Book"], 7.

52. Campbell, "Why Have a Continuing Education Program?" keynote speech, Towson State College, Baltimore, Maryland, 26 October 1973, CEW Library; "The University of Michigan, Center for Continuing Education of Women, 1964–1984: A Report," CEW Library; "The Integration of Service, Advocacy and Research in a University Women's Center," Speech at the International Interdisciplinary Congress on Women, Haifa, Israel, 26 December 1981, CEW Library; "Alternative Patterns for Recurrent Education: The Nontraditional Student in Academe," in *Women in Higher Education*, ed. W. Todd Furniss and Patricia Albjerg Graham, (Washington, D.C.: American Council on Education, 1974); "Women Drop Back In."

53. Campbell, "Women Drop Back In," 114.

54. Leland quoted ibid., 116.

55. Campbell, "Women Drop Back In," 117.

56. Ibid., 118.

57. Mattfeld quoted in Campbell, "Women Drop Back In," 111. Jacquelyn A. Mattfeld's piece ("A Decade of Continuing Education-Dead End or Open Door?" unpublished manuscript, Brown University, 1971) is liberally cited here and in other articles by continuing education pioneers. However, it is not readily available in academic libraries, nor is it extant in any continuing education archives. .

58. Campbell, memorandum "To Staff: Re: The Job(s) Ahead," undated [1974/1975], box 3, folder, McGuigan: Intra-Office Correspondence, 1970–78, CEW Collection, Bentley Library.

59. Campbell, "The University of Michigan, 1964–1984," esp. 1–3.

60. Campbell, 2000 interview; Raushenbush, Reminiscences Addendum, 1974,

61. Campbell, "Alternative Patterns for Recurrent Education," 198.

62. See, for example, Joy K. Rice, "Continuing Education for Women, 1960–75: A Critical Appraisal," *Educational Record* (Fall 1975): 240–49.

63. Kathryn F. Clarenbach, "Continuing Education: A Personal View," in Marian J. Swoboda and Audrey J. Roberts, eds., *Women Emerge in the Seventies: University Women: A Series of Essays* (Madison: University of Wisconsin Press, 1980), 123.

64. In addition to Clarenbach, "Continuing Education," see Thompson and Sager, *Report on the E. B. Fred Fellowship for Mature Women, 1963–68*, 1970.

65. Campbell, "The Integration of Service, Advocacy and Research," 5.

CONCLUSION

1. U.S. Department of Labor, Employment Standards Administration, Women's Bureau, *Continuing Education for Women: Current Developments* (Washington, D.C.: Government Printing Office, 1974); see also Jessie Bernard's critique that these figures do not sufficiently distinguish among the types of services provided to women in "Women's Continuing Education: Whither Bound?" in *Some Action of Her Own: The Adult Woman and Higher Education*, ed. Helen S. Astin (Lexington, Mass.: Lexington Books, 1976), 109–24.

2. For a discussion of these later changes, see Alice S. Rossi and Ann Calderwood, eds., *Academic Women on the Move* (New York: Russell Sage, 1973), especially Jo Freeman, "Women on the Move: The Roots of Revolt," 1–32.

3. Donald L. Opitz, *Three Generations in the Life of the Minnesota Women's Center: A History, 1960–2000* (Minneapolis: University of Minnesota, 1999); Linda Eisenmann, "'Our Respectful Way of Working Within the System': 1950s Origins of Continuing Education for Women at the University of Minnesota and Sarah Lawrence College," paper presented at the annual meeting of the American Educational Research Association, New Orleans, 2000.

4. Linda Eisenmann," Advocacy, Research, and Service: The Pioneering Origins of the University of Michigan's Center for the Education of Women," University of Michigan, Center for the Education of Women Research Paper Series, Winter 2001; Jean Campbell, interview with Linda Eisenmann and Jeanne Miller, 2 October 2000, Ann Arbor, Michigan.

5. Linda Eisenmann, "Weathering 'A Climate of Unexpectation': Gender Equity and the Radcliffe Institute, 1960–1995," *Academe* (July/August 1995): 21–25; Eisenmann, "Befuddling the 'Feminine Mystique': Academic Women and the Creation of the Radcliffe Institute, 1950–1965," *Educational Foundations* 10, no. 3 (Summer 1996): 5–26.

6. Alice Olson [director of Sarah Lawrence center], interview by author, Bronxville, New York, 14 February 2000; Eisenmann, "'Our Respectful Way of Working Within the System.'"

7. Debra Stewart, *The Women's Movement in Community Politics in the U.S.: The Role of Local Commissions on the Status of Women* (New York: Pergamon Press, 1980).

8. Susan Levine, *Degrees of Equality: The American Association of University Women and the Challenge of Twentieth-Century Feminism* (Philadelphia: Temple University Press, 1995).

9. For an exploration of why NADW did not survive, see Lynn Gangone, "Navigating Turbulence: A Case Study of a Voluntary Higher Education Association" (Ph.D. diss., Teachers College, Columbia University, 1999). Gangone suggests that NADW was too small and too specialized to compete with women's interests in other, more prominent, educational organizations.

10. Campbell, oral history interview with Linda Eisenmann and Jeanne Miller (CEW, University of Michigan, 2000), 26.

11. 1974 Addendum to "Reminiscences of Esther Raushenbush," in the Columbia University Oral History Research Office Collection, 26–27.

12. Michael Harrington, *The Other America: Poverty in the United States* (New York: Macmillan, 1962); U.S. Department of Labor, Office of Policy Planning and Research [Daniel Patrick Moynihan], *The Negro Family: The Case for National Action* (Washington, D.C.: Government Printing Office, 1965); James S. Coleman et al., *Equality of Educational Opportunity* (Washington, D.C.: Government Printing Office, 1966).

13. For discussion of these programs, see Mariam K. Chamberlain, ed., *Women in Academe: Progress and Prospects* (New York: Russell Sage Foundation, 1988), and Carol S. Pearson, Donna L. Shavlik, and Judith G. Touchton, eds., *Educating the Majority: Women Challenge Tradition in Higher Education* (New York: American Council on Education/ Macmillan Publishing, 1989).

14. For a discussion of women's use of networking across generations, see Linda Eisenmann, "Creating a Framework for Interpreting U.S. Women's Educational History: Lessons from Historical Lexicography," *History of Education [U.K.]* 30, no. 5 (2001): 453–70.

Index

National Research Council, 122
National Science Foundation, 51, 194
National Women's Party (NWP), 4, 111, 144
networking, by women, 7, 252n7, 271n14
networks, of women's organizations, 115
Newcomb, Theodore, 95
Newcomer, Mabel, 76, 77–78
New Deal, 144
New Frontier, 144
New York University, 215
Nicholson, Norman, 146
Niebuhr, Reinhold, 199
Niebuhr, Ursula, 199
Nixon, Richard, 14–15, 19, 152
Noble, Jeanne, 56–57, 76, 79–80, 130, 136, 152
Noether, Emiliana, 200
nontraditional students, 181–82, 211–17, 230
Northwestern University, 112–13, 132
Nurse Training Act, 174
nursing, 16–17, 19, 103

Oberholtzer, Kenneth, 156
Oberlin College, 124
O'Byrne, Mother Eleanor, 92
Office for Women in Higher Education (ACE), 230, 251n63
Organization Man, The (Whyte), 29
Ozzie and Harriet, The Adventures of, 29

Packard, Vance, 30, 264n53
Palmer, Alice Freeman, 266n100
Parent Teacher Association, 32
Parsons, Talcott, 30
part-time students, 212–13, 223
patriotic ideology, 13–19, 41, 44–45; and ACE CEW, 91, 93; and continuing education, 208; definition of, 12, impact of, 180, 232
peace movement, 4
Penn, Donna, 5
Perloff, Evelyn, 159
Peterson, Esther, 144–47, 155, 167, 174, 230
philanthropy, and women's education, 96–97, 264n60, 265n80
Phillips, Kathryn, 87, 89–90, 91, 97, 115, 153
Planned Parenthood, 163
postwar period, historiography of, 4–5
Pratt Institute, 216

President's Commission on Equal Employment Opportunity, 145
President's Commission on Higher Education (Truman Commission), 51–54, 55, 118, 132, 138
President's Commission on the Status of Women (PCSW), 7, 141–76, 197, 227, 230–32; committee on education, 154–68; and continuing education, 180, 204, 219; and day care, 153; and ERA, 147–49; and racial issues, 151–53
professions, women's participation in, 59, 67
Prokop, Ruth, 160
protective labor legislation, 145, 164, 169, 174, 258n8
psychoanalysis, 35, 103
psychological ideology, 8, 35–41, 42, 44–45; and continuing education, 208, 210; definition of, 12; impact of, 180, 232
psychology of women, 185–86

Quarles, Ruth Brett, 92, 115, 129

Rabinowitch, Eugene, 16
racial differences, and motherhood, 40
racial discrimination, and AAUW, 124–27
Radcliffe College, 179, 193–201, 212–27, 229, 263n46
Radcliffe Institute for Independent Study, 193–201
Radcliffe Seminars, 216
Randall, Lillian, 200
Raushenbush, Esther: as continuing education expert, 201, 203, 208; on PCSW, 155, 159, 162; and Sarah Lawrence Center, 189–93, 213–21 passim; on women, 1, 231
Rawalt, Marguerite, 148, 149
research, growth of in universities, 47
Reserve Officer Training Corps (ROTC), 133
residency requirements, 212
Richardson, Elliot, 18
Riesman, David, 30, 47, 76, 77, 173
Roberts, Eunice, 138
Roberts, Owen J., 127
Rockefeller, Laurance, 198, 264n65
Rockefeller Brothers Fund, 122, 198, 206
Rockefeller Foundation, 16, 66, 97, 183, 206

Washington, Booker T., 77
Wellesley College, 200
Wells, Harry, 112
Wells, Herman B., 132
West, Patricia Salter, 70
Westervelt, Esther, 159–60
White, Lynn, Jr., 70, 71, 72, 77, 118
White, Martha, 198, 218–19
Whyte, William H., 29
Williams, Robin, 94
Wilson, Logan, 108, 251nn55&62
Wilson, Sloan, 29–30
Wirtz, Willard, 174
Wolf, Beverly, 137–38
Wolfle, Dael, 16, 66, 69, 105, 149
Womanpower, 17–19, 20–29 passim, 118; on college students, 55, 68, 105
"womanpower," 17–19, 59; and ACE CEW, 88–111 passim; and black women, 79; and continuing education, 185, 197; and PCSW, 142–46 passim; and women's organizations, 140
women: and class issues, 12, 228; collegiate participation of, 3; as deans, 113–40; and demographic changes, 98; and differential treatment, 157–58; and discrimination, 60–61, 74–76, 92, 103; as faculty, 73–76, 121–23, 249n11; family expectations for, 99, 107; as graduate students, 57–65, 73; as homemak-

ers, 153–54, 164, 204; ideologies about, 12; as "incidental students," 5, 28, 45–46, 54–57, 75, 83; labor force participation of, 19–27; nature of advocacy for, 5; and networking, 233–34; political involvement of, 15; professional work, 28; and professions, 20, 218, 22–23; research about, 88–89; and scientific careers, 19; and volunteerism, 32–34
Women's Bureau (Department of Labor), 26, 144–45, 174, 204
women's colleges, 65
women's continuing education. *See* continuing education for women
Women's International League for Peace and Freedom, 4, 15, 34
women's magazines, 37
women's movement, 228, 230, 231–32. *See also* feminism
World War I, labor market effects, 21
World War II, labor market effects, 21
Wylie, Philip, 37

Yale University, 179–80
Young Women's Christian Association (YWCA), 32–33, 114, 137, 144; and racial policies of, 33, 125, 179

Zapoleon, Marguerite, 67–68, 102

CPSIA information can be obtained at www.ICGtesting.com
Printed in the USA
266931BV00001BB/1/A